My Life In Peru

My Life In Peru

Cecil C. Peck

To order additional copies of this book, contact:
Xlibris Corporation
1-888-795-4274
www.Xlibris.com
Orders@Xlibris.com
99488

ACKNOWLEDGMENT

Here is a few people who inspired me:

First is my cousin
Robert Mooney.
He started me on writing. He created for me my first Yahoo Group and told me to keep a log of what I do. That someday I might create something out of it.

Linda Flynn.
My Aunt, she was always asking me when I was going to write a book

John Dunnick.
He kept telling me that all those stories were so good, that I should write a book, he was real encouraging.

My Best Friend.
Duane Isgrigg.
He was encouraging me to go adventures.

My mother.
Charlene Leininger.
She was always telling me how good my stories were, and also liked the idea of sending them to Xlibris.

My Aunt
Mary Steigleder

She was telling me how good my stories were, and was asking me when I would write a book.

My Xlibris Team
They were there to help me completely publish my book

Mostly my wife.
Fabiola Peck.
She is the love of my Life. She makes me happy when I am sad, and I just hope I do the same for her.
She was the one who was with me. She is Peruvian, and that is where the story happened . . . My life in Peru.

I, Cecil Peck, am going to try to write a book, of my Life in Peru, South America.

I first met Faby in the summer of 2000. On line. I was having a very bad day, just taking a break, checking my e-mail, and this little window popped up, saying "hello" My first response was, "who are you and what do you want?" She said her name was Fabiola, but her friends call her Ann, and she just wants a friend. It took us five years of talking on line before I went down there to see her. We talked on yahoo quick chat for the longest time. After spending one week with her, I could not stand being with out her. I returned to Lima, Peru, South America in Jan. of 2006. I love my wife very much. This is my story, some of the things I did, and seen while I was there.

We married by church in June 5, 2005. That is the date we celebrate. I spent one week there in June of 2005, then returned home and six or seven months later, I came back. We married in Peru, Lima Peru, South America. I have a lot of short stories that I wrote through out the years I lived there.

Sat. Feb. 25, 2006

Well, this one was a little too much. Faby really got me. she asked me if I like oat meal, no, I do not like oat meal-be quiet mom—any way, she said she was going to fix the oat meal, and if I still did not like it, she would fix some thing else. half way through the fixing, I noticed it looked a lot like hot chocolate, and Faby tells me to stay back. and when it was done, she says, I thought you said you don't like the oat meal. she fixed it on

Wednesday, I made her fix it again on Thursday and Friday. she said she only fixes it once a month. now why did I say (be quiet) because when I was growing up, every time mother fixed oat meal, I really did not like it one bit. until she fixed the no bake chocolate drop cookies. how many did I go through before you told me what they were made of, I for get. that's it for now

Tue. Feb. 28, 2006

A couple days ago, there was a baby dove in the park that we go through, it was having a problem. An adult dove was tearing it apart, pulling feathers out of it. The left wing had no feathers on it at all. Faby is always telling me that I can not touch the animals here. When she seen what was happening, she asked me if I was going to do any thing, I said, you don't want me touching any thing here. that did not set well with her. She then told me to help the poor little dove. as I approached, the bigger one took off, circled around, then dove bombed me, almost hitting my leg. when I reached for the little bird, it ran, I caught it, and when it realized I was not going to hurt it, it just sat in my hand and did not even try to get up, just looked up from time to time. There is a place I seen in the market where I seen different birds, like pigeons and doves and Ginny pigs. the place is actually a chicken butcher shop. Faby asked the lady there if she would help the little bird, and she said she would, I handed the bird to her, and the first thing it did was jump out of her hand, ran over the dead chickens right to me. I gave it back to her. Come noon, I went back to see the little bird, and it was playing with the Ginny pig and the pigeon that was in the cage. it looked happy. The pigeon couldn't care less, and the Ginny pig looked like it could do very well with out being jumped on, but it didn't try to hurt the bird, just kept looking at it funny. some thing like that.

Friday March 10, 2006

The oat meal was too much like mother, the way she did it, but first came the spaghetti. She asked me if I like spaghetti, of course, I like a lot. Then she asked if I like spinach-that green leafy stuff. I said smothered in miracle whip salad dressing and ketchup. She looked at me, and I said no, don't like it one bit. then one day, long before the oat meal, she gave me some green spaghetti. after I finished my first plate, she asked me if I liked it, I said more please, half way through my third plate, Faby says, I thought you don't like spinach. well, I don't, but, the two didn't click right away, I was enjoying my meal, until she asked what I thought the green sauce was made of, and that was the first time I told her not to tell me the ingredients, just feed me, I'll let her know if I don't like it. Green spaghetti is really good, until I think of what goes in to it.

Sat. March 18, 2006

Faby keeps telling me we live in the high society area, because they think they are rich, like million airs. this morning, I seen a nanny taking a rabbit for a walk. Just a couple houses down from where we live. We know she was a nanny because we have met the owners of the house.

What's worse, a couple weeks ago, Faby was taking me for a walk around the really rich part of town, where I seen a girl washing a tree-with soap and water and a scratch pad. She like the one today was wearing a nannies apron. when I seen the one washing the tree, I could not believe it, I was staring, I said to Faby, did you see that, at first she looked at me, and I said again, is she washing the tree. Yes with soap and water, the people here do that, get the poor people and have them do some of the craziest things. Faby says if we ever have the money to do these things, she would burn the tree and cook the rabbit.

Tues. April 4, 2006

Well, its been a long while, but things are slowing down a little. With the trip we took, the sandwich cart, and a dog bite, we were going crazy. Not enough time to do any thing and not enough money to get meds. Not only that, the second floor lady was really getting on our nerves. Yesterday while I was getting our stuff to sell, Faby was waiting for me at the bottom of the stairs, the power company people came knocking looking for the second floor lady. She could not answer the door, so the first floor man went to get her, Faby told me she answered her door naked, no clothes on screaming at the man that if he wants to touch her door, he has to touch her breasts. he said, the power company is here to see you and left. Then Faby got the news on why they were there. The land lord wants her out. He can not move her do to the fact he has a contract with the bank, not her. She has a three year rent free contract with the bank for crushing her house. The bank was building a building right beside her straw house and one of the walls fell over crushing her house and she made such a problem with them that they promised to pay her rent any where she wants to live for 3 years. Where we live, is considered a rich neighborhood. She does not want to move. At first the land lord loved the idea and let her in. He is getting more money than the apt. is worth. But after what she did, he wants her out and he can not do any thing, but he did cut the power. She got it turned on again. now for the ¡¡OUCH!! what she did. Apparently she has a little problem, and some of you know she is a prostitute. But she is spreading the wealth. One guy she was with called the law on her, because of what she did. The doctors say the only thing that can be done was to cut the whole thing off. When Faby told me that, I just started to cry!!!!!!! OUCH!!!!!!!!!!!!!!!!!! what she has, does not bother her at all, she did not even know she had a problem. As for the guy, it gave him a lot of sores, deep draining ones all over his manhood, and the doctors say the only thing that can be done is to cut it off before the infection goes in to the body cavity. That woman has accused me of chasing her, and harassing her. She has tried to get the land lord to kick me out, and the land lord went to Faby's aunt, next door, with her, to try to get me moved. well, Faby's aunt is some what like mommy. It was a good show, but when the police came to look for her, she went to Faby's aunt to try to hide, and the aunt was not happy, can you imagine, mommy???? just what was being said. Faby is high class, but she is very low maintenance. As for chasing her, SHE KILLED MY POTATOE!!!!!!!!!!! I was eating dinner one night, and had to go to the store for some thing, and when I got back, her underwear was hanging over my potato with a stream of water running from the underwear to my potato . . . . I was screaming, I was not happy, she went running out and told the land lord I was chasing her, I wanted her, and stuff like that.

Tuesday, April 11, 2006

about Sunday night. Faby was not pissed off at any one. the internet cafe closes at ten thirty. if fact, they all close at the same time all over Peru. Faby is not problematic. she does not go around being pissed at the world all the time. she does not think she is better than any one. she has taken me to one of the natives communities here where she spent several years living. she fought with the government to bring in power and water. as well as food for the hungry and a few other things. every time we go there, its hard to leave. they all keep saying to stay a little longer. not only that, but she is a professional actress. one e-mail sent to get a phone number, one phone call to personally invite the top two Peruvian actors over for tea, and the next day they were knocking on our door. I mean they are the best actors-T.V. stars. and they stayed for several hours, to the point they lost out on a couple other meetings and did not care about them. one other thing, and this one has me wondering what is a Duke? just before coming on line, we were walking through a very rich part of lima and she said her friend the Duke lives here. we went over she rang the intercom system a man answered, it was all in Spanish. she turned to me and said he is busy then turned back and I heard her say her full name- all four names—then I heard the voice saying no a dozen times and more talking and laughing. and Faby told me, he said to give him a minute to open the door, he is never too busy to visit with her. and we almost made him late for his meeting. we were there for about a half an hour, he had only a few minutes to get to his own meeting. as we were leaving, he said to come by again soon, but to call first so he can have his servants prepare every thing for us. by the way, the actors and actress here don't get paid much at all if they get paid any thing at all. I am wondering, if Faby is problematic-being pissed off all the time- how could she have so many friends that fall over them selves to make time for her????????????????????????????????? so, lets try to understand her a little better, PLEASE? she is really a wonderful woman I do LOVE her

Tuesday April 18, 2006

Star!!!

I think so any way. last night, well, yesterday, Faby went right in to a T.V. show, no casting, no screen test. her actor friend is the head director of the show, not the owner or producer, but the head director! the story I heard was they were having problems with the other actresses playing the wife, to the point to where one of the actresses cut the throat and arm with her finger nails! and this guy, the one Faby had invited over for tea, called her almost begging her to come. she had to do 2 takes to get her Sean in, the re-take was not even her fault. it was the fault of the other actresses. and the directors were screaming at them, I was watching, the head director, Faby's friend was talking so soft, I could not hear him, but I could hear the other directors and him as well yelling at the other actresses. when they finally got ready for Faby to come out again, she got it right, on que, perfect with out one mistake. they all loved her!!!!!!!!! they wanted her to go on the road with them for three weeks going to different countries to try to promote the show. it will be on a Spanish channel in U.S. before it is shown here in Peru. the name is Monica. they did say when they get back, they really want her to continue with the show.

Saturday May 6, 2006

Unreal . . .

is the U.S. the only country that's up side down, turned around, and backwards? I mean some of the things that go on here. its un real! Rob guy laws? is one, now the public schools . . . . what's next????? ok, what's going on is this, not only did I have to buy a test book for girls to take test in, which of course is not being used, now for them to take tests, they have to pay the teacher-one sole. Faby gave fifty cents. and we have to pay the teacher to fix and paint the chairs and tables in the class room. there is a fixer upper that works in the school, but teacher that is demanding the money says that guy is no good and she has a better one. oh, ya, she wants twenty soles per kid for paint. plus, mothers day, that is another five soles per kid plus a mothers day gift and a gift for the mothers day gift basket. and if the kids don't to that, they get a very hard time. every holiday is different except for the fact the teacher gets money-different amounts, and a gift. oh, and if the kid don't pay for the test, the kid don't take a test, a big fat ZERO!!!! now the president of the fathers association is the one who collected the money at the first of school from every one. he had got several thousand soles for repairs for the school. and he is thinking of quitting because of one of the teachers. the main one I am talking about, she has taken most of that money to her self and when he tried to stop her, she fought back with the sexual harassment thing. one of the fathers of a kid in her class tried to find out why he had to buy two books when the school has those books there, and he got put in the hospital. her husband is a publisher—get the picture. Faby and I have not confronted her personally, just making small problems, like writing notes, and telling the other mothers not to buy the books, things like that. government books are not good enough if she can make some money. and she is. she screams that she is trying to give the kids the best education possible, and most of her class is terrified to go to school. this is the second grade teacher. now there is another one, that is torching the kids, saying they have to be catholic and that all other beliefs are wrong, not only that but most of the kids do not have fathers and she is talking about family life asking how the fathers are treating them. natalia is in the second grade, Carola is in the third grade. they say I am their father, and the teachers are telling them that it is not possible, at the most I just feel sorry for them and as soon as possible I would leave them. now for the most of the belief is this, to have a north American is like winning the jack pot the lottery, be it father, husband, mother, wife—you name it. and of course all north Americans are million airs!!!!!!!!!!!! so why in the world would those two girls be in a public school if they really have a north American father??????????????? CAN YOU BELIEVE WHAT IS GOING ON HERE?????????????????????????????? the kids are envy as well as teachers, kids can be cruel. The teachers here make a minimum of nine hundred soles a month. the average Peruvian makes around two hundred soles a month. for a teacher to buy a house, it would cost him or her one hundred soles a month for around twenty or so years—a perk for being a teacher—which leaves eight hundred soles a month for food, power, water, cable, internet, phone, you name it. and it only costs about fifty soles a month to to feed a family of four. the teachers not only make four times more than the average Peruvian, but they also want to get the paycheck of the parents of their students to boot!!! like they don't make enough to start with. the rob guy law—the rob guy can rob you, beat you, and kill you and nothing will happen to the rob guy. the police would just say, you should have paid him . . . . how ever, if you are a Peruvian woman and the rob guy is a man, and he tries to rape you, the police will put him in jail for rest of his life. the only good thing I have seen so far, but if you are a north American, there is no law to protect you. its all for the Peruvians, mostly the criminals.

Thursday May 11, 2006

Ain't Right

this just ain't right at all . . . . Natalia is a strait A student. her over all grade is one hundred percent! she is number one in her class! the next kid, the number two kid has sixty percent. and the teacher wants to put natty out of the school and the director is agreeing with her!!!! WHY? because Faby is so problematic . . . . because I do not believe in paying the teacher . . . . I don't believe in what the teacher is doing . . . . the teacher has given Faby an order, to clean her class room or natty gets her one hundred percent changed to zero!!!!!!!! I mean she makes at least nine hundred soles a month if not more, plus she is trying to get all the money from her kids parents, and now she is saying that Faby is causing problems do to the fact she has a north American husband—rich—million air . . . . she should be paying for every thing first!!!!!! and she is turning all the other parents against us, there is a couple of other mothers that still talk with Faby, but not for long, they make it quick . . . . Faby has to clean the class room tomorrow. and the reason we are even putting up with this stuff is because of me. the kids need to be in school for the marriage, getting passports, adoption, visa's, and who knows what else . . . . I am wondering, how many parents there would put up with a teacher like THIS??????? having to buy books that cost more than you make in a month, paying for a test book then also having to pay for the tests and not even using the test book, having to donate food for the baskets give a gift to the teacher plus giving the teacher money to top it off with for the holladays!!!!!!!!!!!!!!!!!!!!well, how many would put up with a teacher like this???? I had to voice this one, this is from Peru . . . . this is the way Peru is . . .

P.S. some of the mothers are trying to collect money for this teachers birthday party and give her a gift basket and a dinner in a fine restraint.. one of them actually had the nerve to ask Faby to donate(((&&&%%$#$#""""!!"#%&/()=?=?)=(&%#$""#%/&((&%#%$&(/() get the picture?

Wednesday May 17, 2006

Back to the Fun Stuff

last week, Faby asked me if I like apple pie . . . . well, need I say any more??????????? remember the cake? any way, it was real good. and last week, we were in lima-near the capital—getting stuff done, and Faby seen three rob guys coming right at us! she told me to be quiet! then we seen a police officer. we went right to him, trying to hide behind him, well almost in front of him, and he looked at us, then turned around and seen the rob guys coming, he blew his whistle and stopped traffic and left, Faby and I were right on his heals!! we got across the road, the girls were with us, so Faby was trying to make sure they were still there, I looked back those guys, they did look at us, but the cars were moving by then, and we turned back around—that blasted cop was across another road and half way down the block!!! he was not letting any grass grow under his feet..faby was getting nervous, we looked up at the building we were beside, and it said "museum" Faby started talking with the guard at the door, and we went in. Faby was telling me she could not believe how fast that cop ran!!!!!!!!!! I said to her, "you told me the cops protect the rob guys here" she said, "they do, but they also protect the citizens too, and I am a citizen!" oh, Faby was not happy about that at all.. to sum it all up, its been interesting. and the museum, well, Faby knew more about the artifacts than the tour guide . . . Faby did more talking than our tour guide. that in it self was amusing. we spent about two or three hours in there. that day was some thing else, first the rob guys scared Faby, then the police man upset her, then the tour guide was giving the wrong histories about some of the pieces. we were so happy to get back home that day . . . .

Thursday May 18, 2006

Miss Leading

well, Faby thinks I am miss leading every one . . . when I was in high school, I did do a lot of baking and some cooking. when I struck out on my own, I did lots of cooking and baking, even after my first marriage, I did half the cooking and baking, well I really did not like deep fried eggs . . . . quiet papa. once I joined the army, I slacked off a bit. and I got to where I was just buying what I wanted from the store already made or pre mix boxes . . . its been years sense I even tried making any thing from scratch . . . . lots of years. about the cakes, Faby adds the ingredients and I beat the ever living "you know" out of it. the apple pie, well, I cut eight of ten apples that we used, helped her flip the doe—base a couple times and punched it a few times when she told me to, I found out that the egg white is used to seal the base to the top crust, and the yolk is used to paint the top of the pie to get the golden brown color—half what through the baking . . . I am finding out lots of things I never knew and finding out how to do things differently than I am/was use to doing. I hope that clears that up, I do help.

ps . . . I still don't like DEEP FRIED EGGS!!!!!!!!!!!!!

Wednesday May 24, 2006

Spur of the Moment

Well, I am in Chile now . . . it was something . . . . Faby is spur of the moment . . . . LIKE I USE TO BE!!!!!!!! I mean we were planning on going to Chile at the end of the month, you know, last minute rushing and things like that . . . . like I am usually doing. and a couple days ago, Faby's cousin came to visit his mother. he invited us to his place in moquagaw-the spelling is close, not sure if it is correct, but the ¨q¨ sounds like a ¨k¨ and the ¨g¨ sounds like a ¨w¨. any way, while there, her cousin is friends with the principle of the munisepaladad, like the Mayer. he works as the boss of some other place-town government type stuff. any way . . . we had one hour to pack, find a place for the girls to go. I mean, we were running!!!!!!!!! no time to call any one, no time to stop, lots of running!!!!!!!!!! we got to moquagaw looked around, nice place, very quiet, oh, if I could stay here, that is the place I want to live . . . . oh it was nice. and her cousin wants us to live there, all we have to pay is water and power, no rent,the thing is, he does not want to lose his land, the laws here are so different. if you are not living on your place, you can lose it to some one who needs it more . . . . even if you rent out your place, some times you can lose it that way as well, the renters can say you abandoned the place . . . . and they take ownership!!!!!!!!!!YA JUST GOT TO LOVE PERU!!!!!!!!!!!!!!!!!!!! !!!!!!!!!!!!!!!! any way, he wants us to live in his home because he is buying another house, he is transferring to another city and he does not want to lose his land and the home he is building. he told Faby that he would send us money every month to keep building on his house there. sounds good to me. plus I can have animals there tooooooo . . . . which I do like. any way, we went there on Sunday, sorry I missed the family chat again, but the trip was worth it. Monday, not real sure what happened there just a lot of running around, mostly Faby and her cousin, while I watched TV. Tuesday, is when it happened. Married by Law! and yesterday, we went to Tacna, had to stay the night there, and today we are in Chile!!!!!!! now about the girls they are not getting the first class treatment like they are use to. the pastor David guy we could not get a hold of in time..we tried. they went with Faby's other cousin, a woman living right behind us with her daughter.. she said she would take care of the girls, not a problem. ya, we get here and her cousin says she gave the girls to some one else. some one that Faby don't really care too much for. oh, boy, is this turning in to a story or what?????? her actor friend, the one I told you about..she told him about that. the story on that, well, he was wanting to know the address, he—Monolo—just loves the girls as do a lot of other actors. he would not go peacefully and asking politely for the girls. He would go with a lot of his friends demanding to take the girls with him!!!!!!!!!! and if they don't move fast enough, him and his friends would destroy the place looking for the girls!!!!! Faby is like nooooo don't do that,,,please don't do that, wait for me and he finally said when you get back, call me and I will meet you at the buss station and we will all go to get the girls!!!!!!!!!! Faby is so scared of what might happen to the girls . . . we told mama about that. I am asking for all to pray for them mostly . . . I do know, Carola is not happy, she is use to the first class living, or so she thinks, and we are in middle class, she just went to the bottom, and is not happy,,you should have seen the look, it was enough to make you laugh, or cry, depending on how well you know her.

Thursday May 25, 2006

Trip to Chile

well, as we were packing to go to moquagaw, we also packed the girls bags, thinking we were going to take them with us. and Faby's cousin said the 20 hour buss ride would be too much for the girls and she would take care of them. we found out that the girls were not with her cousin the day we were to be married by law. Faby was not happy at all, almost canceled the wedding, but that would not have been very smart. every were else was asking at least three times as much for the cost of the wedding. and of course, I had to leave Peru for a while, so I can get an extension on my visitation visa. Peru is really some thing. what scares Faby the most is the fact that the people that have the girls now are real close to another couple that would kill you for your purse, if you resisted. they will steal kids and sell them into slavery or other things, of course depending on the age. and the police will not do any thing to those people. YA JUST GOT TO LOVE PERU!!!!!!!!!!! and the police know all about them but will not stop them or even get in their way. which brings me to another thought . . . . I would love to start a chain mail to send to Washington dc stating feelings about how north Americans are treated in foreign countries and why we have to treat these foreigners better then our own people? any more you go into a convince store you are going in to sawdi Arabia . . . . for instance. WHATS WITH THAT??????? I have heard stories about Kuwait . . . on how a lot of north American business got stolen from the north Americans. even in Peru, in order for a north American to have any thing, they have to be married with a Peruvian, even then, the north American can not own any thing, all the marriage does is let him or her stay in Peru.. what does it take for a foreigner to stay in north America? own business, home? all they have to do is cry about how bad they are being treated and the U.S. bends over backwards for them and screws the hell out of its own citizens . . . so, what do you think of that?

Tuesday May 30, 2006

Beer

Some thing different this time. I have tasted beer from Alaska to Texas to Florida, many different kinds of beer. this may upset some people, because I always say that beer taste the same. it smells the same it taste the same. I have had some real expensive beers, and some real cheep beers, you can not get much cheaper than key stone. from Washington Rainer to Texas lone star, I for get what the Florida beer was, but it all taste the same to me. I have had Korean beer as well, several kinds, same taste. Mexican beer, sorry no different. I have had Peruvian beer, and now just last week, I had Chile beer. I'm telling you this. beer is beer, no matter where you are beer is beer, it taste the same and smells the same, the only difference is, the alcohol content, and how fast you get drunk. any way, Faby is not real worried about me and beer. now, just how did I get to drink Chile beer, the owner of the hotel wanted to go bar hopping, and his wife told him no, so she went to get some, and some of the guests and their friends showed up, plus Faby and I were honeymooning, and it turned in to a party in no time, then we were invited to join the party. we did not even have to pitch in for any thing. it was fun.

Tuesday May 30, 2006

Options

Well, after we found out the girls were ok, we went for a walk to see sights. and walked right by the main government house in Arica, Faby was telling me that they would probably not let her in because she is Peruvian. we went to a museum looked around,—this was last Sunday- and walking back we were looking at a small mountain. I kept saying that I wanted to go up it. that is another story. we went by that government building again, and we were invited in, there was some one out side saying they are giving tours. ok, so we went in. during the tour, the president of Arica was in. to my understanding, he would be like the governor. Arica is not a country, it is part of Chile, like a state. what I am getting at is this, when the tour was over, the one they called presidenta, some thing like that, let us take pictures with him, and he and Faby talked for a long time. my feet were getting numb, I don't like standing still, but I also could not leave and they just seemed to be going on forever. after the talk, we started walking back to the hotel, and Faby told me a number of times sconce we got here the only why she was going up that rock was in a taxi. but we kept getting closer and closer, and she was telling me what she and the—whom I would call the governor- was talking about. (By—the—way, Peru wants Arica back, Peru lost it in their last war with Chile. Peru has declared war with Chile six times so far, and lost every one and Chile keeps taking a little peace of Peru each time, the last war Chile took Arica. the communist guy, humala wants Arica back and says he will take it by force if he has to.) so, of course Faby was a little nerves at first. but the governor said he always has time to talk with people. so, Faby was telling him about what she does, did, and likes to do—which is help people—and of course doing this in Peru, and the problems we are having, and the problem that Peru is facing, and do you have any idea what he said??????? he said this, when Peru gets too bad, and you have not left like you want, you come here. we could use more people like you. this is stuff she was telling me as we got closer to the Arica rock. the rock is another story. we did get pictures of it. what gets me is this, how most of the people there treated us the first time we went there, and how some of them treated us this time. they do not like the Peruvians at all. but the governor told Faby if he has to, he will make her a citizen to help her out. what is the problem, why would we need the option? because by the time we get all the paper work ready, the U.S. Embassy may not be open for business. and Faby is worried. and that governor type person is very much aware of the problems that Peru is facing right now. he said he would help us as much as he could, of course, he would like us to stay there. which would not bother me at all, the ocean is clean there, Faby told me that I could not get in because its too cold, but I got slapped by it a couple times, the waves of course.

Wednesday May 31, 2006

I Don't know

I think I wrote before, I'm not real sure, about the girls, the fact that Faby and I were planning on taking them with us. we had their bags packed and they were in the buss station with us. Faby's cousin by marriage, told Faby that the buss ride would be too hard on the girls, and to leave the girls with her. her name is solidot, some thing like that. any way, apparently she did not have the girls one full night. she gave the girls away to some one else, but told Faby that the girls were close to die and they need lots of medicine. now when Faby tried to get a hold of her daughters, she was accused of over re-acting, causing scandals. things like that. that was when she was trying to find the girls. when found, the phone calls, and visits from the (what they call the gringos) was too much. as in other words, solidot and aunt maruhaw are saying that Faby had no right to do what she did. plus she had no right to just leave the girls there. Faby is still upset over that and has asked me over and over if I think she over re-acted. WELL, MOM, what do you think? we were ready to take them with us. and now, solidot and the aunt are saying that Faby and I owe one hundred soles for the medicine that they gave the girls. natilia and carola may be young, but they are not stupid. they told Faby the medicine was old and they did not get very much. plus the fact they were only with solidot for a few hours. this sure does add up, don't it? solidot still owes Faby five soles. for about four months now, and now solidot wants one hundred soles from Faby for watching the girls for a few hours and giving them some expired medicine. now for the good part. solidot gave the girls away with out their clothes. the girls have real good north American clothes that Faby's adopted father sent them. solidot was trying to keep the clothes, telling the other woman that Faby married a north American, and all north Americans are very rich. saying that she should just go and buy some new clothes to the girls and Faby's husband will pay you back. I sure am glad she did not buy in to that. from what Faby told me, after two days of waiting, she finally went to solidot house and was ringing the door bell, driving solidot and the aunt up the wall until the girls clothes were produced. the cousin lives on the aunts roof, she built a house on the aunts roof. that woman made sure the girls were satisfied, then took them back home. oh, ya, that is another problem that Faby coursed. so, I am wondering who all would say Faby was over re-acting in the fact she was calling every one she knows-remember, no one was telling her who had the girls at first, then was refusing to give her the phone number-to try to find her daughters? who would say that it was uncalled for to have so many visits and phone calls coming in? and the biggest actor, Monolo, came to visit . . . that was some thing, at first the girls were about to jump out the window-third floor. when the woman come to answer the door, she said, "I know you, you are always on TV. come in to my home any time." she was telling Faby that she just loved having the biggest TV star in her home. oh, ya, and it was one hundred and twenty soles for watching the girls for nine days. that is about forty dollars. can you imagine what was going through that woman's mind? having two little girls dumped on her, then having to fight for the clothes, then having her phone ringing off the hook, more visits than she was ever use to, but to top it off, to have the biggest TV. star in the country come over and say, "I want to see my nieces"? and you know, that woman was not causing any problems, just said, one hundred and twenty soles should be enough to take care of the food they ate and soap they used. well, for nine days, that's not bad at all. but the ones that are making the problems are solidot-the cousin, and the aunt. they are trying to make Faby feel like she is a bad mother. I keep telling her she has not come close to over re-acting. and she keeps the girls clean and fed. plus they go most places with us. once in a while, they prefer to stay home and watch TV, or a movie, but most of the time, the girls are with us every where we go.

Wednesday May 31, 2006

Peru and Chile or should that be the other way around. the walk up the Arica rock was some thing else. we stopped twice, not because we were dead tired, but to look around. that sucker was tall. there was a side walk put there so walking it was ok, not just walking on loose dirt. at the top, there was a museum. it had the history of Chile and Peru. Six times Peru declared war on Chile, and lost. the last one, they lost Arica. I am guessing that humala may have been in the military at that time, or was close to it, he is a retired army officer, well not retired, he was kicked out of the country for trying to start a revolution. he is called retired army officer. any way, can you imagine, six times declaring war/or starting a fight, and loosing? wouldn't that get a little depressing? well, being in chilled, I seen the average size of the military people there. I was starring them in the throat. and they were very polite, not like the Peruvian military, or the Peruvian police. well, the Peruvians are short, I keep looking right over their heads. them chilled people are giants. I think the biggest problem Peru has is little doggie syndrome. what else would you call it? six times picking a fight. six times loosing, and loosing city after city. now they want to pick a fight again? Faby says she really don't want to be here if Peru goes to war with Chile again, because Chile may not be as nice as they were the last time. she says Peru is her home, her country but Chile is richer, has more guns, and ammo,, and Chile may do a real number to Peru, Chile don't like Peru, and Peru of course, don't like Chile. and starting in June, Chile is putting a new restriction on Peruvians, three days no more, it has been seven days, now to three. probably because of the other guy as well, he is a socialist, but he has been Peruvian president before. he changed the Peruvian money three times while in office. each time, if you did not have your money in a bank, you lost. there was no changing it. I mean to say, the banks would not change it, you were broke. plus, he took all the food and shipped it to other countries, mainly north America, the biggest buyer. and left the people to starve. he didn't care, he was lining his pockets. Faby says his bank account must be getting low, that is why he is running for president again. Chile sees what's going on, and that's probably why they are putting the three day in place of the seven day visit. it sure was nice of that Arica president-I still think he is a governor—to invite us back.

Friday June 2, 2006

Just a note of Thanks

I don't know if any one realizes just how much danger Natalia and carola were in. the people that had them for the nine days were friends with a couple that the police would do nothing to stop them from doing any thing they wanted. the other couple, would kill you for your coat, shoes, or for what ever you had if you tried to resist them. that couple has family in the police force, in various parts of the Peruvian government, and in congress. so they are untouchable. plus they tend to steal children to sell them. and it really depends on what the buyer wants. are you getting the picture of just how much danger the kids were in? any way, the woman was very scared when she seen the U.S. code on her cell phone. that in it self made her very protective. she asked the kids just how many north Americans they knew, they said a lot. apparently there were 8 different phone numbers coming in from the U.S., there may have been more, she said she only counted 8 and was very scared to answer because she could not speak any English. but it also made her very protective of the kids. that is why I am saying THANK YOU to all who cared enough to call her. you kept Natalia and carola safe. in the Peruvians eyes, north Americans in their country have a lot of power. north Americans tend to make the world move while in their own country. those poor people were afraid of having run through with the U.S. Army! Faby told them she was about to have the army go looking. this is when we first got back. we went to see them last night to see if they were upset at us, Faby's aunt seems to think they were very upset. and do you know what they said? no, they would have done the same of not more to try to find their kids. and not only that, they do believe that they have stepped up a notch in life. they just love having a new friend—Monolo, the TV star. he has invited them to the studios three times now! they said they are not a bit upset. in fact, they said if we ever need some one to watch the kids again, to come over, morning noon or night, just any time, doesn't matter the hour. that was said last night. once again, thank you all who cared enough to call, you kept the kids safe.

Sunday June 4, 2006

Vote

well, Faby just voted, and she is not saying any thing except we have to wait until four pm. like there, voting here is very private. you do not have to tell any one who you voted for. and for the past month, on T.V. a couple of news casters, which Faby said was her friends along time ago, have been attacking the communist guy-ollanta humala. and while they were making fun of him, they were laughing. I did notice they were acting strange, and Faby told me they were making fun of humala, and the reason why? is this, they also stated that when they vote, they will catch a plane out of Peru! they have their plane tickets bought and will wait the results in some other country. but they never said where they are going. I guess they don't care if they get fired. after all, one canadate wants to kill every one, and the other one wants to starve every one. the last time Alan Garcia was president of Peru, he shipped almost all the food to the States! leaving almost nothing for the people of Peru. well, the U.S. pays more then any other country, and Alan was making lots of money during his role as president. Faby told me she remembers when Alan was president, her and her mother were standing in long lines for up to six hours just for one potato kilo, or one rice kilo. one kilo is about a half a pound. not to mention the fact that Alan likes to change up the money and if you don't have money in the bank, well, you just got broke again. if you had a pocket full of money, it was worthless, because the banks would not except it. some choice. no wonder Faby is not letting me know just who she voted for. Ollanta says this, if you are against him he will kill you. there have been several clips on TV. about him giving orders to kill citizens of Peru. and when he was questioned about it, because some of the people were trying to take him to court . . . . he just said this-I have no time for your silly games, I am about to get the government, if you are against me, I will kill you. then he left the scan. some choice. Faby is looking worried. she says come four o'clock, we will be locked in our home for the rest of the night. no matter what the out come, its going to be a riot out there. luckily we do live in a peaceful street, how ever, we hear a lot of what is going on in the avenue. right after the first vote, we were almost caught up in a riot. in where there was gun fire, and beatings, we hid in a small corner store, they-the store owners, closed up shop with us inside for a while, until the screaming stopped. Faby told me tonight, we go no where.

Tuesday June 13, 2006

Crazy to start with, a nun-penguin, out of envy, killed another one in the catholic house-not church, the nuns house. why, because she was the favorite, always getting first choice and the best schools to studied in. any way, the penguin that did the killing went to jail. she just killed one. Ollanta Humala has killed hundreds and tortured thousands of Peruvians. not just regular citizens, but also the police and basically any one who is against him. the courts did call him in for a trail, but the police will not arrest him. there was a reporter that even questioned him on TV. and his re-ply was, "I have no time to play your silly games, I am about to get the government. if you are against me, I kill you." well, I did not hear that, I just heard a bunch of Spanish, but I seen Faby take a deep breath and put her hands over her face, so I asked her what happened? that is what she told me. there is a news caster I told you about in some earlier letter, that got her program started in another country, she still broadcasts in Peru but from another country. and here lately she has been telling all the Peruvians that can to get out as soon as possible. and she is still making fun of Humala. now for another good one . . . when we left, I just knew I locked up every thing . . . I was waiting for my chocolate milk for a long time . . . about a week any way. I was asking Faby just how long that milk would last in the fridge, and she told me about fifteen days. when we got back, the kitchen door was open. at first I could not see any thing missing. and Faby and I went to the internet to let every one know we were back and ok. it was late. we were tired, and when we got back to our apt. Faby asked me for some of the milk, well its chocolate, I want some too. I was tasting it, was looking for it . . . couldn't find it, I was about to turn the fridge upside down . . . and Faby tells me to settle down. I was saying I know I locked the door. I just know I did. [mom, you raised me, you know I lock up every thing . . . that is what you do all the time!!!] I just knew I locked the door. Faby says, I know you will not lie to me. you did lock the door. this morning, our next door newborn, who lives in 3-A just across the hall from us told Faby that the second floor woman-yes the hooker-was making lots of noise in our house . . . our neighbor said she was looking, and couldn't see Faby any where, but he hooker got the kitchen door open and was in side our kitchen. I ain´t happy. Faby has told me lots of times we can not afford to have a scandal-like police re-ports. be it us or some one else doing the re-ports. we can not report her. no since in trying to fight her, she would not understand any way. so what do you do when a crazy invades your house and believes it to be theirs? not only was the milk gone, but the mozzarella cheese for our lazing was gone and fays chilly souse was gone. I miss my chocolate milk. nothing more we seen is missing that we can tell. just a few things that is really irritating. maybe ill do the same to her, then again, maybe not, some times she leaves an awful smell in our living room and it does not even have a roof on it. well I guess this is Peru and that is the way its done here.

Wednesday June 21, 2006

Gasp you just might not believe the process we have to go through. but what is worse is the fact that the U.S. Embassy has been treating me like an outsider . . . . I sure was not impressed by them at all. the last time I was there, I was told I need three copies of every thing, then before I could pick up all my papers, I was told to leave, and she called up some one else, he was pushing me out of his way, and they were of course speaking Spanish, while I was trying to pick up my papers, then she says (pick up you stuff and sort it out over there), like I was just in the way . . . . we just are not real sure if it will ever end. I told bob this yesterday, if you know him, you already know what he said, I will not repeat it, but it did make me laugh. we are running and running all over the place. we are trying to get things done, and we hardly have any time to rest. just a note to let every one know what is going on

Saturday June 24, 2006

Last Night, oh, well . . . for about two weeks or more, there has been some milk being sold for only one soles a bag. the bags are eight hundred mills. coca cola cans and bottles are usually five hundred mills, what ever a mill is. any way, the milk usually sells for around two soles a bag. and every time I wanted to buy that milk Faby was saying no. don't need it, don't want it. it was chocolate milk, I really wanted it. but she said no until last night, she said she wanted ten bags. guess what, last night they were not one soles a bag any more, they went up thirty centimos. she was not happy. we only got five bags. BUT THATS NOT ALLL!!!!! no this was double feature. Natalie and Carola last night and this morning. last night, when we got home, Faby and I realized we needed a couple things, and the corner store usually had those things. I tell natty and carola to wash the dishes in the sink and we-mama and me—will be back shortly. natilia started crying. carola just sat down and started pouting. Natalia followed ann down the stairs. I just shook my head and grabbed Carola by the wrist, she started to fight, I told her, if she resisted, I would drag her. when we hit the street, natty was jumping up and down and even side ways, she was so happy. Carola was almost crying, or at least trying to. I told natty a few times to stop the jumping around, but she did not listen. when we got to the store, Carola was still fighting me a little, Natty did not slow down. and there was some real expensive clay peaces on display there.(handy crafts) getting the picture. a couple of soles of items we were only expecting to buy? I tried to tell natty to stop bouncing around, and instead we wound up buying seventy soles worth of handy crafts. Natty cried for about thirty minutes, Carola started hugging me-she did not break any thing, she was happy. and when we got home, they both did a few dishes, they refused to do them all. so this morning, when they were looking for utensils, I told them to look in the sink, they just sat down and started eating with their hands.

Tuesday June 27, 2006

More on Faby

I do not know who all are saying what, I really don't care. What bothers me the most is Faby, and I'll tell you why.

Faby's health . . . some believe Faby stays mad all the time. well, its like this . . . her liver is almost gone, when it works, it does not work right most of the time, and that has brought so much stress to her heart, that she has needed a new heart for a few years now. Being mad all the time is not very healthy for her.

About three weeks ago, Faby got the news that two of her closest friends died. that was not easy for her. the hospitals and doctors all knew those people were sick, but do to the fact that they were not rich enough to double the doctors paychecks, they were sent home. one was forty, one was thirty four, maybe thirty five. Faby is thirty three. Just last week, one more of her friends-Monolo- called her. we were at a corner store to get some avocados . . . at first he thought he was talking with his father . . . saying he was in the hospital. he realized he was talking with Faby and said he was fine, and hung up on her. I seen the look on her face, I just grabbed her. she said to me, "I just lost two friends, now Monolo is in the hospital and he will not tell me what is wrong."

I have seen Faby go through these attacks, they are like small heart attacks. I really don't know what else to call it. I see her chest pounding, she can not hardly breath. some times it will knock her out. I have seen these attacks lasting all night long. her chest pounding for up to ten minutes, so hard it was like she was bouncing, flopping around. she would get up to fifteen minutes of rest before going through it again.

After she found out she lost her two friends, she did have a small attack. when she got the call from Monolo, I thought she was going to have an attack right there in the corner store. I held her and said, lets go home, eat lunch, rest a bit, and in thirty minutes or so, we will go to a pay phone and call him. in church several months ago, after a discussion of some kind, me not knowing the language, of course I didn't know what was being said, she had a small attack. it did not knock her down, but she could not hardly breath for a while. I found out later what was going on, some of the people in the church were, you could say "yelling", at Faby for being very rich and refusing to give more than she was giving. and why was she going to this little church, she should be going to the mother church in down town Lima. and finally that Faby was going to that little church just to show off and flaunt her wealth. that stuff was bad enough . . . . when the church was chasing ollanta humala all over Peru, saying they are for him no matter what he does, Faby finally said, we are not going back to church as long as we are here.

Are you getting a Picture of her Yet? the last time we were on mirc. Faby and my self. remember? it was ten thirty. internet closes at ten thirty. in fact all internets her in Peru close at ten thirty. some times they are not real quick to kick people out at closing, but some times they are. the internet closed and those people wanted to go to bed. and some of the family were talking about how mad Faby was. Faby is mad about some thing again, or still mad over some thing. she seen some of that before I logged out. she cried half the night, asking me why my family hates her so much, and she did have a small attack that night. come morning, she told me she did not want to go on family chat again. a few months ago, we ran in to her real doctor. the one she grew up with. the one that told her she would not see thirty, because of her condition. that was when she was fifteen, her liver went bad. she has gone years with out seeing her doctor. when we bumped in to the doctor, the doctor was very surprised! saying, your still alive? those tests I did. you can't be. how are you. things like that at first. well any way, you know I don't know the language. Faby was telling me about it after words. her doctor told her the hospitals only want Faby in there because those machines make the hospitals money. people with the liver condition like Faby. the government has funds for the hospitals that help people like Faby. the only problem is, is the fact that the longer you are hooked up to those machines, the more dependent you became on them, and what will happen if the government decides not to pay??????????? and about the I.V. bag of medicine? her doctor said not to go on that until she puts the I.V. in Faby her self. her doctor told her to take two kinds of pills. first one kind for a while and then call her, well she has done that, now she needs the other one. which is costing around 80 dollars. and Faby is more worried about running out of money in doing this process than getting the medicine she needs.

Her doctor put it as plain as this. Faby is living on borrowed time. she could die at any moment. any one of those attacks could be the last one. Carola really tries to help Faby along in her fit throwing. and natilia takes a turn once in a while. I just hold her some times I shut the door of our room and turn the T.V. up and start brushing her hair saying not to worry. we did call back. to Monolo. he said his cell phone was stolen last month. when she called the number that was on her cell phone, she got a nurse. the nurse said Monolo was doing fine, and she would be happy to let Monolo borrow her cell phone again. and he told her, not to worry, he is fine. he is very sorry for calling her because she does have a heart condition, and is very sorry for worrying her. she told him she just lost two friends and a call like that did not help her condition at all. he said again please don't worry, he is fine. but she is worried, he refuses to tell her what is wrong.

Faby can not afford to go around being mad all the time. or upset. it could kill her. her doctor has stated she has out lived her expected life expectance by at least four years. and the only real reason for Faby being alive for so long is the fact she is happy. a few good pills could help out a lot, but the most important thing is her happiness. stay away from up setting situations. the more upset you get, the more likely you will have an attack. the more attacks you have, the higher the chance it will be of being your last.

I don't know if or when we will be going back on mirc. I do know for those of you who are writing us, we will write back. we will let you know when we get your letter. the more letters Faby gets, that are addressed to her, will help her when she goes to the embassy.

Wednesday June 28, 2006

Natalia

This may sound familiar to some one . . . . Natty was out of school for a month. On the day of return, last Monday, her teacher-the problematic-gave the whole class a test on what they learned for the month. did not give natty any time to study. just a quick re-view along with all the rest of kids. then the Test. Well, only one kid got an "A D" the highest grade. like an "A +" for the rest of us. the next score was a C. Natty got a 100 percent, the next kid got a 60. and why am I talking about this now? the mother of the kid that got the 60 was very upset and was almost attacking Faby today. saying, how is possible, my kid goes to school every day, does all the work assigned. your kid misses a whole month and all the assignments and still gets an AD . . . how can that be? over all in that class, natty has a one hundred, the next kid has a fifty five. so far this year. any way, as I said, these girls will not except any thing less than an A. Carola is an actress, she can read a book and start quoting it back to you. Natalia, can not do that, she studies and studies very hard, to keep up with Carola. we just had to share that with you

Thursday June 29, 2006

Natalia yesterday was not very nice. the kids have a four day weekend. at the end of class, just before the teacher left . . . Natalia had to remind her to give home work. saying we will be out of school for four days, and we need to have home work. Natalia friend told us first, saying to Faby that natty is still writing. Faby asked the friend why she was not writing, was she done? no, she said she don't like the home work. and natty has to bug the teacher to give home work. her and a few other students did ask Faby to teach Natalia on how to stay quiet. one other thing. two days ago, I thought the teacher was being unreasonable, still do to some extent. any way, for home work, the teacher gave the kids forty words to look up in the dictionary, write the meaning done for each, then put each word in twenty sentences. yesterday Natalia was the only student to give her home work completed to the teacher. plus the fact of catching up with one month missed, she has until Monday to catch up. But to ask for extra home work when she has plenty to do? I can almost see why the teacher might be a little irritated. Faby and I don't know when natty did all those sentences, she never asked for any help at all. she did run out of pages in her note book though. we did have to get her a new one.

Wednesday July 5, 2006

Tradition

I have seen people watering the side walks and paved streets here. ann tells me its tradition, keeps the weather calm. personally, I think some of them have hidden cameras . . . to water a side walk every day that is well traveled? get for real. I have slipped on many of them. ran right in to parked cars, walls, and even hit the side walk full force a couple times. I have said "its a conspiracy, they are all out to get me" Faby just laughs saying "its tradition, to keep the weather calm" well, I have been around Peru a little bit now, and I have seen where watering the side walks and streets do come in handy, as for keeping the weather calm, well, it keeps the dust down, because there is no pavement or concrete. there wind, but no rain. I have not seen it rain here yet, been here for six months. not a drop of rain. one guy I know is 80 years old. he says he has been here for 14 years. he told me in the 14 years he has been here it has not rained one drop. he said it rained once 15 years ago. that rain destroyed about half the buildings in lima area. he said he seen the after math 14 years ago, they were still re-building. here, the bricks are made of mud, but then again the cement holding them together is nothing more than mud. sounds real inviting don't it? it does hold to gather. they build some real tall buildings out of mud. the side walks are made of real concrete, they are always watering the side walks.

I was just talking with mama, or papa, not sure which, before I started this note. one of them reminded me of this. I was wondering, can watering the paved streets and concrete side walks have an affect on the weather, or do you think, like I do, that some of those people have hidden cameras? personally, I think there are some that get quite a kick out of watching people BITE the concrete. 15 years? no rain?

Saturday July 15, 2006

On Line that was interesting. Monday Faby and I went to get a phone line and internet connection. they told us two weeks. ya, three days of visits, and the woman that took our order told us not to come back and she is working on it. we got the phone line in Wednesday, we went back Thursday, and before Faby could say any thing, that woman said she was working on it, and if we are not home when the worker shows up, that it will be two months to get connected. the problem with that is we would have to pay for the internet for those two months. well, so we called her on Friday, teehee. and today we be on line.

Wednesday July 19, 2006

Visa well, to day is the 19th. yesterday the 18th was something. I was not feeling very good either. Faby went to talk with the Peruvian consulate with out me. she told me they said a minimum of five days, usually takes ten days, could take up to fifteen days to get a permanent visa to her husband, ya, that did not set too well with Faby. they opened at nine am. by noon, three hours later, I had the permanent visa to Peru. next step is getting a Peruvian I.D. card. that way I can work in Peru with out too many problems. which will be helpful.

Faby just told me she is getting cut off. they have her aunt birtha believing that I am a million air. Faby use to be getting 400 soles a month from her aunt and her adopted father. now she says she may only get one hundred soles, if she is lucky. the rest of the family say they are broke and starving, and Faby is married to a north American. she does not need any money, she is rich. not only that, but her father sent her clothes, shoes, and sent some to me. her aunt only had half the things he sent for the girls-Natalia and carola. nothing for me or Faby. the family needed those things worse than we did, we are million airs according to them. well, any way, I am doing every thing the U.S. Embassy has told me to do. almost, I still have to get a Peruvian I.D. card. and yes, this helps get Faby a visa to the states. me becoming a spousal citizen of Peru will help get Faby a visa to the states.

that does not mean I give up my U.S. citizenship, Peru will not except me fully. I have met several north Americans that have tried to get full citizenship to Peru, and Peru just laughs at them. as for today, I finally got Faby in the pacific ocean. her first ever boat ride, the first time I ever paid for a boat ride. and after, we went walking on the beach and picked up shells. I think I am rubbing off on her, because she even got wet this time. all the way up to her knees-in the water. our last trip she would not even touch the water, saying its dirty. but this time she got in.

Monday July 31, 2006

Second Floor Woman

for those who have not heard yet, well, that woman came in last night at a quarter to eleven pm. you know, the middle of the night. has she no respect? Faby says she has no education, as well as, met her manager? you would probably know the word better as "Pimp" well, last night, I was aggravated, belly hurting, head hurting-when will I be over this thing?—plus the girls were upsetting Faby. that too was upsetting me. and to top it off, that woman, with out knocking, just comes in, like she owns the place . . . so, ya, I yelled, screamed, and cussed. she says pardon? I was saying "do you know what time it is?" pointing to my watch, and her actions was not impressive, like a big question mark on her face. so, yes, that to was upsetting. I started saying "GET THE *   *   * OUT OF HERE!" so, she calls the land lord saying I was beating her. well, Faby also called the land lord, and told me he said he already talked with her. and she is going to report me to the police for beating her. I don't know how well that is going to go. but coming in in the middle of the night, and stealing our things? come on, some thing is got to give. I'm also going to demand my TABLE TOP back . . . that was ridicules! stealing Faby's table top, left her frame, just took the top. that was right after she moved here. want was unforgiving was my chocolate milk, I still ain't over that one. just who do she think she is? she thinks she is problematic, I'm learning.

Tuesday August 1, 2006

Languages here is a funny one. we went to the natives community yesterday. talked with one of Faby's friends. she is having lots of problems, one is her house. I seen it, it don't look good. any way, there is a group of people there that build houses for free, mostly French, based out of France. and when we were leaving, we ran in to them. Faby sent carola to get her friend, and Faby and her friend went to the group. there were four French and two Russians. Faby started talking, her friend was too scared to ask for help, any way, in Spanish, the French guys were looking at each other and started speaking in French, so Faby went off on them in French. the four French guys just dropped their jaws, the two Russians tried to answer Faby in French, but had a real strong English accent, so Faby spoke English to them. she blew all their minds. they asked her what she was doing there if she knew all those languages, she said she was just trying to help her friends. they said they would help build the house for her friend. this one I thought was important to share with every one. Faby knows five languages, well five that she has admitted to so far. 1,english, 2,spanish, 3,french, 4,itilian and 5,quechue-native Peruvian language. she catches them coming and going. Faby has told me she likes to speak to other on their own level, as in other words, she speaks to people in their own language in stead of telling other they have to learn hers to speak to her. now don't get me wrong. I am meanly stating a fact that I have run in to so many wet backs, that would scream at me in Spanish, and once in a while would say in English that if I want to talk with them I have to learn their language. I have met a few Mexicans that I got along with just fine. them speaking Spanish, me speaking English, we communicated just fine, they would try a little English I would try a little Spanish, but we finally spoke our own languages and we got along just fine. well, I think I talked this one to death. I tired.

Wednesday August 9, 2006

Papers well, it took a while, but we finally got them all, I mean all sent off. so far, its costing us over five thousand dollars for all those papers. I have not added up what Charce will do, wasn't thinking of that when I sent them to her, one hundred and ninety dollar money order for each packet, and there are three of them = thirty dollars short of six hundred, which will make the whole thing around six thousand two hundred dollars, give or take a dollar to two. Faby did add some money in to that sum. any way, in about two weeks, Charce, you will get the package, there is a letter in there explaining what to do, PLEASE, be so very careful with it-them-all three of them. you will receive one package, in side are three of them. one has pictures, the others don't, they don't need them, the other two are Carola's and Natalia's packets. so I am asking to please don't mess up the packets, if the pictures are loose, just look for the one that has the most paper work in it, its the one with Faby's name written on most of the papers. that sure was a lot of money, and most of it went strait to different branches of the Peruvian government. Peru says they are bankrupt, BULLLLLL S"#$%&/ ())==??¡¡]]]]]]!!!!! any way, they got over five grand from me, and who knows just how much they keep taking from others all the time. talk about money hungry, but that is only the government and different branches of it. any where else, its a lot cheaper to live here than in most places in the world. I have met people from different countries saying the same thing.

Thursday August 10, 2006

What to do?

Carola started off the day ok. when I asked her to help, to carry some papers, she said some thing to Faby in Spanish. I asked what was being said, I ask her do some thing and she speaks like I am not even there. Faby said "carols says she is not going to carry those papers because some of them are for me." I said fine, I'll remember this. carola started crying, talking in Spanish out loud almost to the point of screaming. I held Faby and said to carola to dry it up, I did not want to hear it. carola is a real good actress, if you did not know her, she would make a believer out of you real quick. well, we just happened to be passing by a school for hair styling, today they were learning how to cut hair, and were looking for volunteers to practice on. carola was not happy, she use to have long pretty hair. well, its about three or four inches shorter now. to start with, carola was crying so hard tears were streaming down her face like a water fall. the student was afraid to even touch her. I seen Faby grab Carola's hair, and show the student how much to take off. Faby did not pull Carola's hair from what I seen, but carola just screamed. I was watching Faby looked at me and said, don't listen, don't pay attention, she is an actress. and started talking with the student again and they went in to the back rooms.

I waited for a few minutes, then went back to check, carola had cried a puddle on the table she was leaning on while the student was just combing her hair-was long. Faby told me carola stopped screaming because she told her if the student didn't trim her hair, her head would get shaved when we got home. her hair don't touch her shoulders any more.

Carola was so mad, ouch. I told her if she thought that was bad, mommy was being very nice, you should ask aunt Charce and grandma how they would have cut your hair, with the way you are acting. carola quit speaking to me for almost the whole day she was so mad. mad at Faby for translating what she said, mad at me for not defending her. probably mad at the world for not revolving around her, but that is another story-funny one too, may write that one later on tonight if I don't fall asleep first

Friday August 11, 2006

Pay attention, The other story. yes, Carola really believes the whole world revolves around her. she don't need to watch where she is going, every one has to move out of her way. was kinda funny when I think back. about a week ago, Faby and I were almost yelling at Carola to pay attention, watch where you are going. look forward. what did Carola do, head to the side, not paying attention. ran in to four or five men, I mean slammed in to them. hit I don't know how many others, just running in to them. but the funny part, was right after she slammed in to a big guy, he almost went right over the top of her. Faby and I both yelled at Carola to watch where she is going, me speaking in English, Faby half English half Spanish at this point. what does Carola do??? head snapped to one side, with the "hummmph" sound and takes off like a shot. you know about those two inch poles sticking out of the ground with lights at the top? they don't give much, I don't think they even care. and before Faby and I could even say any thing, because we were still catching our breath, Carola went right in to one full force-side of the head. slammed!!! the red mark from her jaw to the temple. she started to cry and Faby started screaming in Spanish, I was screaming in English. "how many times do we have to tell you to pay attention? watch where you are going, now look, you are bruised. you did it to your self." oh we screamed for a few minutes. carola went from almost crying to being very upset. she was mad at us for while for that one. as in other words we should have told her there was a light pole there. thinking back on it, sure was funny. reminds me of Bill Cosby when he was talking about how at night, when some thing is out to get you, and your body has turned and is making tracks, but the head ain´t paying attention. the head is off in wonder land looking back at what it was.

Monday August 14 2006

Last night that sure was some trip. an hour on the buss. Faby and I thought it would be better if we paid for three seats, the girls are small enough to share one seat. the first ten minutes, they had three different people sitting with them, of the first two, one went to the front of the buss, and the second went to the back. the third was with them for about ten minutes, then got off the buss. those two, kept fighting, driving Faby up the walls of the buss. I was holding her saying don't listen, they are just trying to upset you. any way, they were by them selves for about twenty minutes, until the fourth came along. she lasted a few minutes then went to the back of the buss. and right after that t'was—"gargantuan" about as tall as Faby but about five times as big, I mean to say, it looked as if each cheek needed its own chair plus one for the tail bone. I first seen her head bending down, facing the floor, I turned to see the girls- there eyes, was some thing, almost like the cartoons-popping out, mouths wide open, then they both tried to become part of the side of the buss, and that when I see those cheeks coming at the girls. I looked at Faby and Faby was just laughing. that one stayed the last fifteen minutes. as much as the girls squirmed and tried to fight, she was not paying any attention, and didn't give them any room to move. boy she was BIG! I said to Faby "those penguins don't put up with much do they? she laughed saying, "she is no penguin, she is from a religion that say all men are Gods." I asked about the kids, she says "kids don't matter, if they act up, they get sat on." ok, explains the wide bottom . . .

Tuesday August 15, 2006

A short story

one day last week, while Faby was shopping for some things, carola and I were watching a little girl running around. I do mean she was running. her mother called her, and she came running like mad, not watching where she was going. ran right into the glass display case. she started to cry, but the mother rattled some thing off and she just stood there with a sorry look on her face. I looked at Carola and said "does that look familiar?" Carola said "that's not funny daddy!"

Friday August 18, 2006

Restaurants burgers, pizzas, chicken? McDonalds is really the best. only one problem, they have the smallest burgers. well, Burger King is the same size. how ever, one thing we noticed was this, McDonalds is usually four times bigger then Burger King, plus Burger King is always connected with Pizza Hut, and some times or K.F.C. as well. when all three are in the same building, K.F.C. is got more customers. we were just there yesterday. almost every one was eating chicken. last week, we tried a Burger King/ Pizza Hut, after McDonalds-which was two stories and four times as big, with a line out the door and wrapped around the building. get the picture? any way, we went because Burger King had the Garfield Two toys. ann got a happy meal, gave me a bite of the burger, I told her I was full after that one. I did try one fry. not very good. then we noticed, that the place was only half full, and over half the people were eating pizzas. I was joking with ann about going back to burger king, she said only if I eat every thing bought, she wasn't going to go through that again, and the girls won't eat that stuff either. in case you are wondering, some times its just as cheep to eat out, because they run lots of specials here. when we were in Chile, we ate at McDonalds all the time, they were cheaper then buying at the black market, grocery stores. I don't get it, but we did love it.

Friday August 18, 2006

New School the girls started a new school yesterday. the teachers were surprised on how smart the girls were. their old school was planning on failing them, Natalia's old teacher mainly. she has been trying to get both the girls kicked out of school and making them repeat their grades. when she found out we were moving the girls, she went to the new school to make problems. the old school refuses to give up the girls papers. the director of the new school told us two days ago, that if the old school refuses to give the papers, the next day- yesterday-to bring the girls in any way. well, their first day was very impressive to their new teachers. the new director told us that the reason the old school is making so many problems is the fact the girls are so smart. Natalia's teacher is the main problem maker. natilia was the only kid in her class that was passing. and she wanted to kick Natty out of school, but refuses to let her attend another school, and she is trying to prevent carola from moving as well. oh, well, the new director also said, that if a teacher looses too many students in a year, the government will check in to how she teaches, and she may be removed. not fired, just moved to some other school, not of her choosing. as in other words, make life very hard on her and try to make her quit. firing is not an option once you have a permanent job for life, but they can try to convince you to leave on your own.

Good One Saturday August 19, 2006

today Faby called her adoptive father. she tries to call him once a week, some times she misses a week. any way, today, she was crying her eyes out after the call. well, the last time she was questioned by her adopted father about money and gifts he was sending, he did not believe her, and she came up missing for four years. what happened last time, was some one in the family told her father that all the gifts he was sending, Faby was selling in the street, including the clothes and toys he sent to the girls. Faby told me if it wasn't for the fact we are waiting for the response of those papers, we would leave today. we have a chance to get a half acre for 80 soles, yes that right, 80 soles. no house, just land. there is power and water in the community. plus, no one will know where we are. well, today, she was questioned again. only this time it was about three thousand dollars. the family says Faby received it, Faby said she knew nothing about it. as well as over half the things he sent this time. remember, she only received about half of what he sent the girls, nothing else. and the family says she got it all. well, her father says he will call around this time to see what happened, and Faby has to call him back tomorrow morning at 9 am sharp. Faby is not happy. 3,000 dollars, is over 9,000 soles. some one sure had a good day. Faby wants to leave right now, but is stuck because we are trying to get the visa to the states. in fact, we are stuck here for at least six months if not longer. now you may be wondering why he sent the money. he knows how expensive all that paper work is. and he has been asking Faby how much I have, what I own, well, she does not lie to him. I never told her to lie to him, so he knew we have no money left. he said he wanted to help us. Faby has told him lots of times, ever sconce I got here, not to send us any thing because the family steals it before Faby gets a chance to even see it. but the family says she does receive it. she told me she said to her father she never asked for any money, he said, you need it, I sent it, the family says you received it. Faby said, she never seen it. now what??? just letting you know what is going on it has been a real upsetting day today you know, when Faby come up missing for those four years, the family was hurting, Faby was not calling her father, and he was not sending any money or gifts at all. he was ordering all the family to look for Faby and make sure she was ok, or he would not send any thing to any one. it took them four years to find her. she is really thinking of doing it again, what about the embassy though? the U.S. Embassy that is?

The New School Monday August 21, 2006

today the girls met their English teacher, ya, ok, after they corrected the new teacher a few times each, they told the teacher their father was north American. I am getting to the good part. at the time to pick up the kids, her comes Carola's teacher, with some one by her side, we didn't pay any attention, just Faby was talking with the teacher about the manicure things, and Carola came by and hung on mommy, the other woman started walking backwards, grabbing the teacher like they were late for some thing, finally they left, and after that, Carola said the other woman there was the English teacher. she really opened mouth and inserted foot with Carola and natilia. she comes to the school once a week to teach all the classes English, and has had no one to correct her, until today. I can only imagine what was going through her mind when she seen me. she already tried correcting Natty and Carola. finally gave up when they said their father was north American, and their teacher confirmed it, yes the teacher already met me. any way, this is a two prater, part two coming up

I mentioned carola had an experiment she had to do today, on family chat last night, and the only thing I could come up with was a couple coke bottles. gluing the lids together and drilling a hole in the lids, creating a whorled pool, or tornado, which ever you want to call it. well, after we got it together, and tested it out, carola wrote a report on it, and guess what happened? out of every one in the class, you'll never guess who was the top winner???

BOB, JODIE, THANK YOU THE IDEA!!!!!!! well, last time I talked with Bob, he said volcano with baking soda and water. but then I started thinking of Bob, the shop, Jodie, and what they were doing. then about the shop and the two bottles together in the main waiting area and sales counter, with the water in them. and the fact that both Bob and Jodie told me about that thing. well, any way, thank you both very much, you won Carola first place in the experiment, plus she has to go to school early Wednesday morning to show it again. school for the girls start at 1:00pm after noon, Carola's has to be in the school Wednesday morning at 9:30 am morning time to show her project again.

I just had to tell every one the two good parts that happened today, now for the other . . . well, also today, the old school finally gave up the papers, with last years grades. yep, they are still fighting. they are loosing the two smartest kids in the school and they are not happy. the new school said its a start, they can get the kids registered with what we got today, how ever, they still want the girls grade books. its a fight, and carola old teacher don't care, her students are good and learning, she is not fighting, its Natalia old teacher that is fighting, and is trying to get the girls to repeat their grades-fail them, and have them removed from school for the rest of the year. well, at least the new school says differently. maybe tomorrow, Wednesday, Thursday, Friday, or next Monday, one of these days we will get what we need.

Some short stories Tuesday August 29, 2006

Carola mainly for two or three days now, Carola has flat our refused to eat breakfast. both girls tend to go with out eating and go to school hungry and tell every one we are starving them. not only that, it took carola three days to do dishes, about half a kitchen sink full. she can be very stubborn. tonight, Faby told both the girls to go to bed at 8pm. and told them again several times after words. come 9pm, I told them to go to bed. what did they do, lay on our-Faby's and my bed. Faby was talking with mama, so I asked mama to tell the girls what time I had to be in bed when I was growing up. 8pm. carola was not happy with me when she seen that.

Aunt Linda Hats today, Faby had to make a phone call at 1pm, the girls had to be in school at 1pm. so Faby stayed home while I took the girls to school. after I took them to school, I went to the post office. the woman there told me it would cost 30 dollars to send the hats. I thought not too bad, but I better get Faby. when I got home, I told Faby what it would cost, she said hmmm, uh huh, lets go and see. when we got back to the post office, there was a different woman in there, she told Faby 15 dollars, half of what the other woman told me. some charge more than others, but when they see gringo, they try to double the price. any way, they are on their way, will take two to three weeks to get there.

Plants on the way home, we stopped of at a metro store. to see if we can find any plant food fertilizer sticks. they got them, 30 for 13.45 soles, and 50 for 16.70 soles. well, we don't have much money left. so we went to a plant lady that Faby knows. she said those sticks will not do aloe plants any good, what we need is real fertilizer street from a farm. one kilo for 1.50 soles. ok, so I replanted three plants today. I'll be keeping an eye on them, if they do good, I'll be happy, if not, in a week or so, guess I'll go and get the sticks.

Birds got two pigeons, and two sparrows getting real brave. well, one pigeon mainly, comes right down and lands on the table, while I am in the bedroom in the morning usually, stares at me for a moment, then goes around cleaning up any thing that was left on the table the night before. he don't land softly, I hear him coming in and he stomps the table good. when I look out the door, he looks back for a couple seconds then tends to his business. that's a white one with brown spots on him. there is also a blue-gray one that comes in once in a while. as for the sparrows, well, they dive bomb me when I am in my living room, then land on the roof and yell at me. when I am not in my living room they come right on in, if the kitchen door is open, they go right in. I have been sitting at the table, and watched one a male sparrow, fly right in, land on the floor, and go in to the kitchen while Faby was cooking. a few times, I told Faby she has a visitor. I heard her saying "who invited you in. you must to leave." and the sparrow would hop right out, not too worried. the female is not as brave as the male. I have seen them both on my dinner table before, and Faby and I both seen the male take his girl friend in the kitchen. what happened that day, well, the girls refused to get up, so Faby and I were eating breakfast, and I thought I seen a bug flying through the room. I looked again and seen the sparrows sitting on the window sill. I told Faby to look. we watched the male hop to the floor, then chirp at his girl friend, she then hopped to the floor. he went right in to the kitchen. then he started chirping. came out and went to the female and really was trying to talk her in to going in the kitchen. Faby and I were eating breakfast watching the show, he was really talking to his girlfriend. finally got her talked in to going in side the kitchen, took him about five minutes. Faby looked at me and said "I don't believe it." then said a little louder "that's my kitchen, you don't belong in there." the male came to the door, chirped and turned around, went back in. I started laughing too hard, I went to the puter to play solitary. I couldn't watch any more.

Tuesday August 29, 2006

The Apartment well, there is a roof over our bedroom, the bathroom, the girls room and the kitchen. the living room has no roof, and I have to shear my living room with the hooker on the second floor. she hangs her soaking wet laundry in my living room, I do mean its soaking wet, I have watched her take her clothes out of a bucket, large bowl, what ever it was, and it was full of water, her clothes were streaming water from the clothes line to the floor. remember one night I told every one she killed my potato? I went to store to get a couple of items, when I got back, her panties had water draining right on to my potato, yes, she comes in what ever time she wants to and gets my living room floor soaking wet. well, she use to, I broke my door, sort of, the glass any way, she came in at mid night and I threw her out. she tried to get me throne out. instead I got my rent raised. and she still comes in, but not after 10pm and not before 7am any more.

Tuesday August 29, 2006

Natalia today, well, just how many titles does some one need? Natilia has earned the title of the most intelligent in her class. her teacher said she is setting the standards for all the kids in the class. and she has only been in this school for only two weeks! she is letter perfect and number perfect. plus the fact she makes strait A's on all tests and home work. now she is also teaching her teacher, not the English teacher, her classroom teacher English as well. today, there was a vote on different kids for different titles. Natilia won the most intelligent in her class. guess what else she won, also the most friendly, how ever, the teacher said she could not hold two titles. well, it does make since, give some one else a chance to shine as well. but Natalia was disappointed any way, asking why she can't have both titles, she wants to be every ones friend. her teacher said that she really earned the first one, and she really must let some one else have the most friendly title, one child can not hold all the titles, that would not be fair. a little on carola, I am guessing carola likes mommy painting nails better than selling icy pops, gelatin stick, or cakes. because she talked her teacher in to letting mommy give her a manicure today. her teacher was very happy, plus another teacher came in to watch and seen all the U.S. items, and was impressed. this happened at 3pm during break time. and Faby barley got finished when the break was over. just maybe another teacher will ask. we be hoping any way.

Saturday September 2, 2006

Hopeful tomorrow, well, um, today, some thing like that, any way, its a Feria, some thing like a first Mondays, flee market, and/or on the road barging items place. we got a place, or hopefully we got a place. one guy running for what we, the states would call "Mayer" is putting on a Feria, and his people told us we can put a stand up to do the nails and faces things. maybe we can advertise a little more. that was the good news now for the other Faby's aunt Murugha, next door, how ever you spell it, that is how it sounds, is making problems again. I mentioned Faby can not have any police reports, or bad reports. maybe I only told mama, not sure, I am tired, its only 1.45 am right now. well, that woman has put a denouncement-police report, in on our land lord. not good. she has three floors, only had permission to build two floors. the land lord has three floors, how ever, the third floor is not quite finished. the out side walls facing the aunts house is not covered properly and she is saying he has to fix it, how ever, she will not let any strangers in her house. the only way to fix the wall is to be on her property, and she will only let one person in that knows how, and he charges. well, the land lord may do a police report on her for the third floor. he already wrote a letter saying this third floor has many years, like ten or so years, and she never said any thing until now. he is thinking of writing another letter, he is a lawyer, he knows how to write good ones, on her third floor. if he does that, she may do another report on him about this third floor not having a roof. and guess what? WE MOVE if we have to move, the petition for Faby and the girls gets canceled. the U.S.Embassy will say Faby canceled hers and her girls petition to get a visa to the states, and if that happens, they-Faby and the girls-may never get a chance to get a visa to the states. why does the petition get canceled? the embassy has this address. if we are not here to get the letter from them, they say we are not interested, we can fight if we do not move, how ever, if we move, the embassy will say we are problematic, not being able to stay in one place. why hopeful? hopeful things go well tomorrow and the fight between the aunt and the land lord does not excel, we can not afford to move, we can barley afford to stay. if it ain´t the second floor woman, its the aunt. the land lord is some thing else, I am still paying for a room I ain´t got, and I ain´t happy about it. and the birds keep visiting, woke me up this morning, screaming for their daily bread.

Monday September 4, 2006

Different Story yesterday was fun. for the first few hours, they moved us around, four times. why complain, we just moved and were thankful they let is be in the Feria. we made 32.50 soles yesterday, about 20 soles today. yesterday Faby and I were talking about the Feria, I asked her if she wanted to join the group. Faby just told me they did not want us, the treated us poorly. she was a little sad last night. but, by morning, lots better, we got ready, packed up and out the door by 8:30 am. first thing when people started showing up, we got moved a few times. again, why argue, we were happy being there, doing some thing. well, I was helping put up tents, and we were told, that all tents were taken and we would not get one. oh, well. the whole time yesterday and today, Faby never lost her level-as she puts it-her education, her bringing up. any way, I noticed the boss us the Feria talking with Faby, I can't understand any thing, and does not get excited, or sad, keeps her posture. after the woman left, and was out of site, Faby got excited. telling me the boss of the Feria wanted her to be a member of the group. Faby was saying she can not be a member, but she would like to be part of the group. I asked what the difference was, members have to be able to vote in the group. Faby can not vote in pueblo libre, her address on her id card says san migiell, some thing like that. any way, the woman, boss, what ever you want to call her, told Faby, that she-the boss-is high society, and it is so hard to talk with people not on her level, but Faby is on her level. the main reason she wants Faby in the group, so she can talk with some one on her level. that is only part of it, she also mentioned the fact of moving us around so much and we did not complain one bit about it. that in it self shows a high level if education. she was impressed with us over that. she has a job to place every one in their proper places so it looks right. some times her job is not real easy, especially when there are people looking for a fight, there were a few today. its real doubtful those people will be in the next one. she did tell Faby that we were invited to next Feria, and to be in her office Monday afternoon to get the details of the Feria. what she told us is its a medical Feria. and she wants us there for the kids.

I don't think I mentioned what group this is, its a political group, they try to do things to help get their people elected to office, and this next election is for what we would call the city "Mayer" he is friendly, his wife is nice, Faby painted his daughters' face, and they all three were pleased with it. now for the building, it was not the aunt, turns out it was the uncle. what happened? his neighbor got him. he did not have the side of his house finished. so, he was just passing the buck. Pueblo Libre is a medium high society neighborhood. and its unheard of to have an unfinished building. the uncle said he had to finish his house, so the land lord has to finish his house, and if the land lord tries to make Faby any problems, to let him know, and he will, with Faby, take the land lord to the public records place, and show just who is responsible for this building, as in other words the land lord has no right to bother Faby over his building in which the law says he has to have looking a certain way. if this was low society, or one of the natives communities, then there would be no building specs. how ever, being in the high side of medium high neighborhood, there are plenty of laws, lots of head aches. I just hope this fight don't escalate too much.

Sep 7, 2006

Peruvians ya, Peruvians. there is a real famous actress from long ago named Valintina Lines she is 90 some years old. she did a film with carola back in March. that is how English met her. we also met her son. some son. a little history on Valintina, she was a diva. a Peruvian super star, movie star. she always had money, or rather when she was young, and looking good she always had jobs and lots of money. never saved a dime. and time went by, she got old and lost her looks, and producers and directors went on to younger models. I'm getting to it. Valintina was found living in box, she lost her house, her husband left her, and so did her son. up until last march when some collage directors wanted to make a film, and found her, then asked if they could do an autobiography on her. carola played Valintina as the little girl. during the making of the film, her son found out, because the collage kids put in their web site and the actors syndicate, that they were doing a film on Valintina Lines. So, guess Who showed UP??? and it was not a happy re-union. when they brought out food for Valintina, the son ate every bite, when they brought out drinks for Valintina, the son drank every drop. she did not get any thing to eat or drink, plus the money she got paid, he took and left her with nothing. a woman over 90 starving, can not walk, and he treats her like that. she was skin and bone. there was nothing we could do about it. I am building up. that is how the majority of the Peruvians are. out to help them selves no mater who they hurt. carola is loaded full of it!!! a few days ago, i felt like a walk, only a few miles, Faby did not complain, well she should have, but she did not complain. we got home, she did not feel very good at all. she rested for about an hour, then made up some dinner-soup. the girls had big bowls, i had a tiny one Faby did not have any thing to eat-which i did not know at that time. my little bowl was gone quickly, Faby asked if i was still hungry, well, yes, i just had a mouth full. so she made a box of mac and cheese. not some thing she does, she makes her mac and cheese from scratch, so when I seen that I really knew she was still feeling bad. but does she complain? no. well, you know how much one box of mac and cheese makes, not much. Faby divided it up for the two of us. what does carola do? talking in Spanish, so sweet, then Faby says in English, "carola, i am not feeling well, I am hungry and tired. its 10pm you should be in bed. go to sleep." carola starts screaming in Spanish something, and before I could say any thing, Faby screamed in English "go to bed, i am not doing any more for you tonight!" carola ran out of the room screaming. Faby told me after that scene, carola said at first "mommy, I want your plate of food, you don't need to eat, i do." then when she was screaming, "you must feed me, you are not allowed to eat, you have to feed me!" Peruvians-ya just got to love um. I miss my toy

Sep 11, 2006

Feria, flee market, side walk sale-same difference this time we got forty soles to last the week. last week, we got thirty soles, we went with out any bread for two days. Carola was not happy about that. telling us we need to buy bread, when we don't have any money to buy bread. here the bread is ten cents a bun, almost as big as a burger bun. the loaf bread, small cheep loaf cost 5.00 soles. which is about one fourth the size I am use to seeing back home. the bigger loafs, which are about one half the size back home cost from 8.00 soles to 10.00 soles, depending on if you want bad bread or good bread. so it really is cheaper to buy bread by the bun. if it wasn't for aunt Linda buying those hats when she did, we would not have internet, or a phone. its not like the states, where they give you a few months of warnings, nope, if you don't pay by the date due, the next day you could be shut off, that is if they are in the area working, they will turn you off right away, then it will take at least one month to get the phone turned back on, and at least three months after that to get the internet back on. its kind of funny, I spent over six thousand dollars in paper work. I got less then five thousand dollars for my land. where did the other bit come from? Faby. I am not real sure how much she was getting, some where from four to six hundred soles a month, from her adopted father and his wife. last month that was cut down to two hundred and fifty soles. the phone and internet bill was three hundred and fifty soles. Charce sent me one hundred and thirty dollars. Faby and I were talking about what to pay, the phone and internet, or the rent? we decided we can not move, too much against that. so we paid the rent. looked at what we had left, not enough for the phone and internet bill, and its not like the states, were you can pay a little and they leave it on, nope, you pay a little, they will turn you off. so we bought a little food, trying not to spend too much, and some tomollies-we have a few customers that buy tomollies from us. we pay fifty cents a peace, and we sell them for one soles a peace. only no one had any money and the dead line was coming up fast. then Aunt Linda came to the rescue. bought two hats from us, thank you. we got your hats off in the mail, and with what was left over, was just enough to pay the internet and phone bill, one day before the dead line, talk about cutting it close. THANK YOU AUNT LINDA. well, the bills were paid, and no money left at all. we were invited to join in the Feria that weekend, our first one, we made thirty soles. the first day, the girls were not happy. at first Natalia was excited. she has a dragon costume, and she wanted to wear it. Faby let her, then painted her face. she started walking up and down the side walk while Faby painted Carola's face. when she was done, she told Carola to walk with her sister, advertise a little. Carola got a real sour look on her face and just sat there. natilia seen that and sat down right beside carola, both staring at Faby. Faby tell them again, and again. three times to walk around and advertise the face painting. they refused to move. Faby finally said, "fine, you don't want to help, you both can go home" so I took them home. by then, we were moved to twice. two different places in the feria. when i came back, we got moved two more times. we didn't argue, we were happy to be there. that day we made about 20 soles. Faby had me buy some film to take pictures. we are working on yet another web site. that was 12 soles. the next day the girls stayed home. we went out, Faby painted some kids, and did some nails, I took pictures. and we make 22 soles. that was the thirty soles we had for the week. come Thursday and Friday, we did not even have a dime to buy one peace of bread. Friday Carola stayed home, while Natilia went to school. we are on the free milk program. how ever, its not just street milk. they add oatmeal to the milk and cook it. carola just hates the idea of oatmeal. she believes it to be low society meal. only the poor and low class eat oat meal. she has in the past told her teachers and class mates that we are starving her. and well, you can tell when some one is hungry. their attitude, body sounds-stomach growling? during the science fair, some woman, a mother of one of Carola's class mates was yelling at Faby to feed her child. well, we had oat meal for breakfast, and carola flat out refused to eat, so I told Faby to take Natalia to school and carola will not move until she finished her breakfast. she received it at 8am. school starts for them at 1pm. we leave by 12:30pm to get them to school. four and a half hours of saying its a low class meal and she is not going to touch it. she cried for about two hours, solid tears streaming down her face when Faby and natty left. carola loves school, and hated missing it. I was not going to let carola go to school hungry again to tell every one mama was starving her. this weekend was a little different. we make about sixty soles this time. the girls went with us, but this time they just played in the park behind the feria. not sure what natty was doing, but carola was breaking the flowers that stood over six feet tall. I know, I was watching her. we showed up early, I helped put up the tents the first day and helped take them down after words. the second day, I put up three of them by my self. the real workers that were suppose to do it were arguing about missing peaces . . . . ya, well, after I put up three tents, they were tearing the fourth one down, well, I started putting it back to gather. so what if it was missing peaces, ain´t you never heard of "niger-riging?" I got it up they were all amazed, now comes the fifth tent, I put it up in the middle of the street, no help and cars wanting to run over all the peaces. almost forgot, I did have help, Natalia and Carola. after we got it up, they the workers, came out of the building to take it to its place. going back a day, Faby was talking with the head of the feria, asking if we could sell tomalleys the next day. she said scenes we are so much help, not a problem. she will make room for us for two spots. so, Sunday, we sold tomalleys and cakes, as well as nails and face painting. we made sixty soles. could have been more, but Faby had a couple of problematic customers, and lost out on a couple of kids. plus she wound up painting two kids for free. which was not the plan. that woman lied to Faby. it was pay four soles for a kids show or paint her two kids. she painted her two kids, and then Faby had to pay the four soles for the kids show. that's ten soles. we could have had seventy soles if not for that. may have been more if not for the problematic customers. these past two days were a killer on me. the sun came out and slapped the doggie out of me!!! last night during the chat, i sure was in pain. I was home all day today resting, didn't even get dressed, all I had on all day was my bath rob to go to the rest room, just incase our uninvited house guest comes in. speaking of last night, just before the chat . . . is the reason of telling this whole story in the first place. we are broke . . . barley able to eat, but we are eating, that's about it. what happened last night to bring this on? besides having my head pounding, body hurting-do to the fact that the feria workers refuse to do their jobs, so, I get to-got us another spot any way. i was getting yelled at just before the chat. natilia wanting me to help her with multiplication-which i know very little of, and carola wanting me to teach her division, ya, division here is the same as there, but back words. that in it self did not do my head ask much good. and carola kept saying "I don't understand" the girls were wanting help, so who was yelling at me and why? apparently I am suppose to be writing letters to people I don't know. a post card to mail cost 5.40 soles to send to the states. a small letter cost the same. believe me, they weigh every thing here. at the cheapest, a letter cost 5.40 soles. try adding photos, the cost goes up. and I didn't even have a dime to buy bread, but I am suppose to be writing to people I don't know. I'll get to writing the letter and sending the post card, but my first priority is paying the rent. if we move for any reason, or get kicked out, Faby's visa process is canceled, and all that money we spent is for nothing. my second is food. we need to eat. third, well, try internet and phone, so we can try to keep in touch with every one? or at least those who care to keep in touch with us. so, when i get about fifteen soles that I don't need, i will send a post card, a letter and some pictures. that is about what it will cost. Faby might get it cheaper, if I stay out of sight. its a quarter to nine pm, my head ask is finally going away, but now I also have an uninvited guest in the house watering my floor. one head ask going away, and another one comes in. I MISS MY TOYS!!

Sep 13, 2006

Last Room

I got it. I know, some of you may say, "took you long enough" or, "why did it take you so long to begin with?" the last month and a half I have been paying for this room, and the land lord has been saying he is looking for some one to buy or some place to store his stuff. he would give us a day that he would get his stuff, then for some reason, it got delayed. well, today was the last day. I waited for a while, 12:30 came along, time to take the girls to school. speaking of which, Carola. she believes for some reason that oat meal is a low class meal. food for the very poor and uneducated people. come lunch time, she still had her breakfast-the oat meal milk we get from the free milk program, its not free, cost one soles a week. any way, Faby made some rice and vegetables. carola was very excited, running in to the kitchen with her plate. I said, "you still have your breakfast to finish." she got a big frown on her face. then I said, "are we going to have a re-play of last Friday?" she walked to the table and stared at her cup. sorry, I just don't give in no more. natilia brought out all our plates of rice. carola looked at her plate and I told her as soon as you finish your breakfast, you can eat your lunch. she was not happy, but she finished it. now for the second part of Carola she is telling natilia that this last room is for her-natty, and there is monsters in there. bad things happened in there. just all kinds of things. natilia came running to mama several times crying, telling her-mama-Faby what carola is saying. Faby translated to me. well, finally Faby sent carola to bed, it was 8:30pm, she did not even fight about it. I told natilia to wash all the dishes before going to bed, its her week any way, plus, by the time she finishes, carola would probably be asleep. I caught natty a little while later, or rather she caught me, and told me carola told her, they she- carola would get what is the kitchen, and natty would get the last room. why? because, carola is the oldest and carola gets to decide. ok, little does carola know, mommy and daddy have already decided, and its reversed. hope those stories she is telling her sister don't back fire to scare her. back to last room Faby believes the land lord herd me moving things out. well, I wasn't real quiet about it. he has a display case, like for displaying your fine dishes, that stands about six feet tall. and I wanted it up against the wall right next to the windows right beside the door. you can't see through the glass any way. but the locks for the windows are metal and rusted and were sticking out too far, so I took a hammer and started pounding away. ya, i made lots of noise-yes on purpose. shortly there after, he arrived. i had about half the room empted out in to the living room. he looked around, went in the last room and looked around, then told me in English "Cecil, please give me a moment" his English is not real good, but is better than my Spanish, by a long shot. so I took about a thirty minute break. just as I was about to start throwing things out again, he comes back with some one to take some of the things out. well, he took all the metal-bed frames, curtain rods, and some tools. filled his three wheel bike up twice. it has a bed in it about the size of a small pick up. the land lord kept trying give us his furniture. Faby wants nothing to do with any of it and i can see why, termites. I swept out a whole lot saw dust. it took me about a a half an hour of sweeping, it was full of saw dust, and dirt, cob webs and dead bugs. I got it all swept and mopped. I sure had a long day today, but i got my room. now all I need is to get lights installed. ain't real sure on how to do that yet, but I'll figure it out. first I need the money to get the parts to install.

Sep 15, 2006

A few stories the girls have their own rooms now. carola was not happy. she has been telling Natalia ghost stories about that last room, then telling natilia "you will get this room, I am getting the kitchen room, i am the oldest, I get to decide" ya, well, didn't quite happen the way carola was planning on.

I found out there is power in the last room, so I put a lamp in there, and it is now Carola's room, what use to be the kitchen is now Natalia's room. as for the kitchen sink, ain't no such thing here. this apt. we are in has two large rooms, two small rooms, one bathroom and sink in the community room-living room-which has no roof, except for what I put on, that I don't get to use any way-grrrrrrrrr. getting the picture, like a ghetto, get it? yep, the way some land lords do is rent small rooms from 50 to 100 soles a month, and the big rooms from 100 to 200 soles a month. and the renters have to share the bath room and sink. after the land lord got some of his things moved, he was talking with Faby. when he left, Faby told me what he was saying. he wants me to make some improvements. ya, sure, so he can raise the rent again, I don't think so. I am guessing he wants me to make the improvements so he can raise the rent to try to make us move so he can do the above thing and make more money per month. the most I will do is add windows, that room is just too dark for my taste. Faby is thrilled over her new kitchen, lots of space to work in. we sure did have fun getting the girls things moved out of there. we just need to add one more plug and find some one who has a power drill, so we can move the microwave over. its on a shelf high on the wall, and Faby wants it to remain that way. no space for it any where else, we don't have a counter. it is a fact of live, once you don't have some thing you sure do miss it. simple things like a counter top, kitchen sink, running hot water, cabinets and cupboards. oh, well, at least we have some space now and Faby is happy with that. the best part for last Natalia after only one month, has proven her self to be the best in her class. an A D student, we would call it an A +. not only that, but has been voted most popular, and the most friendly in her class. what am i getting at? this, she is going to be driven around in a car during a parade (I think), shown as the schools second grade princess. this is for the spring time thing they have here. she needs a sash saying her name, a crown and a staff / wand—silver. this will happen on the 30th of this month. what does the school provide, the car, we Faby and I get to buy every thing else. any how, there is no way we can deprive her of this. she has really worked very hard. in her last school, even with every thing against her, she still came out on top, and the teacher was not rewording at all. and in this school, she just got put on a pedestal. i just had to share that with every one

Sep 17, 2006

Feria it was kind of funny, they have so many problems in setting up the tents. me, I just come in and can put it all up with out any help. the woman in charge of the Feria had her husband set up a tent today. Faby and I were an hour later then we usually are. we showed up at 10 am, we are usually there by 9 am by the latest. when I showed up, he left the seen. before 10:30 I had the last three put up, and tied together, had to rig it a little. did most of it by my self. now they want me to be fully in charge of the tents. Faby told them no. we will not be responsible if any thing happens to those tents. we have our own. they love the way I can put the tents up with out them falling down. I just told Faby I use to go camping a lot. today carola stayed home. why? because of what she did yesterday. now, how many of you would just stand around and let some one make fun of your mother?, then make friends with that person, and go along with what that person is saying about your mother? and disobey your mother, doing what she says not to do? Carola did this when I went home to heat the tomalleys again. and to top it off, when I was gone, natilia told me that her mommy fell down. she tried to help mommy get back up, Carola just went to the park, did not care that mommy fell down. that is why carola stayed home today. not only did she let another little girl-her own age-make fun of her mother, she to was saying bad things, then went in to the park with out permission. she was told by both of us not to go in the park. for various reasons. the biggest one is the fact tooooo many people around, she could wind up missing real fast. there was a little girl that almost came up missing today. that was when we were tearing every thing down and most of the people left. she screamed, got the other kids around screaming, when the two guys seen all of us—the ones working there—looking at them they dropped the little girl, and stared back. they did not move. they just stared for a while then sat down. they were there when Faby and I and natilia left about a half hour later. boy those people sure do get upset with us when we run out of tomalleys. we went there today with 29, we had 2 left over. Faby had one, the girls split the other. no one wanted a manicure or face painting today, our biggest money makers. just wanted the tomalleys today. at least we had enough today. yesterday and last week, they got mad at us for running out. we did not make very much this time, we only have forty soles to last the week. we will survive, thank you AUNT LINDA, we will survive.

Sep 17, 2006

Telephone we may be with out a phone line for a couple months. don't know when it will happen. Garcia-Peru President-is saying he wants competition in the phone company. there is only one phone company here. after you pay your bill, you only get fifty minutes, and you have only 20 days to use the minutes-local calls only. the last ten days, you can not make or receive calls. if you don't use the minutes, you loose them. the only way you can keep in touch with any one is if you have internet. you can go on line but you can not make any calls. funny, you can make calls and receive calls when you are on line.

Garcia is fed up with that. the telephone company said Garcia can not put any other company in Peru. they have all the rights in Peru. they say they will cut up all the phone lines if Garcia puts in any more companies in Peru. this is what Garcia said "you may be with out a phone line for a couple of months. I am negotiating with a few telephone companies. they say they can bring you service for much cheaper prices. right now we have the highest phone bills in the world. and what's worse, we can only make local calls from our homes. this has to stop." well this is what Faby told me he said.

Sep 20, 2006

Quakes?

I am guessing every one might have heard, we just might be home for the fourth. anyway, Faby and I were talking last night. I remember lots of times she told me about earth quakes here. I have been here for nine months. have not even felt a trimmer. she told me its unusual, they get little quakes here all the time, at least one every other month. then I remembered Florida. I spent a year in Florida. i for get how many hurricanes were predicted to hit. some where from eight to twelve that year. I kept saying I went there to crash a hurricane party. I guess they said i was not invited, and went to the Carolinas. one week after i left Florida, two of them hit back to back, then the next week, a third hit and took out a power plant which started a fire that lasted I think my friend said one month. the fire trucks could not put the fire out. with that in mind, what is going to happen when I leave Peru? I remember just before aunt Linda took us-mama, Charce and me-out of Texas. the news stations kept saying they were long over do for a hurricane. what happened when we left? Connie was screaming at us. she told us it sounded like three freight trains running through her living room. I have been told by a number of people that we left Texas just in time. and I have been told by lots of people that I left Florida just in time. REALLY? if that is what every one wants to believe, its fine with me, i am wondering about Peru? will it be a hurricane, or a very big Quake? what do you think?¡

Wed Sep 20, 2006

Peru

Remember, I mentioned once before, some time back, that it did rain here about fifteen years ago. not just a little rain, it was a real storm here in the Lima area. and it destroyed about half the buildings. oh, well. what I am getting at is this, when we left Texas in 1983, it was rough on all of us. i mean for my self, mama and Charce. when i left Florida, i was having a bad time there, I was not happy at all there. and both places got hit real bad with the hurricanes. now the last time i was in Texas, I was on the farm, very happy. I don't think any thing happened. other than the usual weather, very hot . . . now for Peru, Faby and I are not very happy here right now, we are very happy being together. but as for our situation, well, that is another story in its self. like her family for one, the laws, the general way people do things around here. it really gets to us from time to time. now for the question, what will happen here? earth quakes happen here all the time, from what Faby tells me, only none have gone on scene I have been here. not even a trimmer. the funny thing about Florida, is the fact, not one hurricane hit Florida when I was there for one year. not one, they came close, one went over the top of Florida and hit Georgia real bad, the rest of them tore up north and south Carolina. I just remembered it, I was working as a security guard, and it was being tracked by satilite-vea internet, by one of my co-workers. he said he could not believe how fast it went over the top of the state. in which of course no damage was done to Florida. I do remember lots of radio announcers saying to get ready here comes another one.

I can see mama saying earth quake, when her family finds out about it, we don't plan on telling them till after we are there. what made matters even worse for Faby, is today we went to her university to check on her papers. she studied there four and a half years. working on her masters when she was forced out-do to the blood sucking leaches-family getting the money from her father and keeping it for them selves instead of paying the collage fees for Faby like they were suppose to. ok, I am getting to it. working on her masters degree ok, today she was just told this, "you will have to go back to the 4 grade" which is redoing the second year of her studies. she was not happy about that at all.

Sep 26, 2006

wluvia to start off with, this is a plant, flowers. when Faby and I were walking around Metro, we went to the plant section. this plant was really talking to Faby. Faby said to me, "am I imagining this, this plant is moving!" I looked, sure enough, it was. Faby took a few steps away and it stopped. got closer and was barley moving, she touched it and it really was moving. it came home with us, we had to get a pot for it. it seems real happy now.

Yellow Bean not real sure what the real name is, unless that is it. any way, Faby put it in a cotton ball, with a little water, last week, and it sat on a shelf type wall in our living room for about five days, it barley grew, but is alive. the last two days, its been in our room, and has tripled its size. Faby has been talking to her bean every day now for the past couple days.

Avocado my fist one has a single root about an inch and a half long coming out of the bottom, nothing coming out the top yet. it has a real big crack in it, looks like its almost in two peaces now. I am guessing its doing ok. so, when do I plant it?

Onion three days ago, Faby told me if I wanted to grow some thing, try this onion, it had some green stems a few inches long coming out the top. ok, so I planted it, now the stems are about six inches long, boy is it happy.

Plants in general, the land lord said we are not allowed to have any plants. Faby told me today, what the land lord said the other day when we paid the rent. she said she did not want to up set me too much in one day, which was this, he said if he seen any plants in our home, he would destroy them. they are in our room, with the dead bold lock which some one has tried getting in to a couple of times, and failed so far.

Rent went from 80 dollars, to 100 dollars-with an extra room, now says we are using too much power, saying the power bill went up by 20 dollars, and we have to pay that bill. he is trying to make Faby believe the computer is using that much power. can you believe that? he said you will pay or you can move. we can not move.

Feria that was a good one. Saturday, well, we did not sell very much of anything. the girls taking turns causing problems, if it ain´t one its the other. we made close to 40 soles, sold about ten tomalleys, did a nail thingy and a couple faces, some thing like that. Sunday was different, sold the last fifty tomalleys did one face, and one nails thingy. made sixty five soles Sunday. also, the sauce Faby made, was a big hit. Faby said she was going to try to hurt the people, by making the sauce very spicy and hot, lots of onions, peppers, and other things,

I tasted it, and it burned from my lip half way down my throat. and the people were fighting over it. when we ran out of tomalleys, they were using our sauce on other things they bought. then one of the women selling next to us wanted our bowl, we threw it away, she pulled it out of the garbage asking us permission to keep it her self. how could we say, no you can not have it. we just said, its yours. the girls just don't like to obey. instead, they want to be fiends with a girl who tries to destroy our things. she broke Natalia's soccer ball water bottle, and natilia got upset because that girl did not want to play with her. didn't care that, that girl wanted to steal her bottle, or that she put a hole in it. Natalia got upset when she and carola refuse to play with her. after she cried for a while, she went running all over the place. now her toes hurt her. as for carola, she was trying to give every thing away. or is turning the manicure and paint faces boxes upside down, side ways, just messing things up real good. those girls tend to chase away customers at times, some times they help us. not very often. we can not take them to the ferias, and we can not leave them home.

Store we tried to go shopping Sunday night, that is when natilia was complaining about her toes hurting. she was not just complaining, she was crying, screaming, and sitting on the floor, just making a very big scene. people were staring, some spoke to us, I don't know what they were saying, but we did not have hardly any food in the house. we had to do some shopping. well, before we got very much, we had to leave. as i said, in previous stories, some times natilia has to take a turn in causing problems for us. so we went shopping today while the girls were in school, or was it yesterday? 2:am, Tuesday, my watch says, it would not lie to me, my mama gave it to me. so it was yesterday, Monday while the girls were in school we went shopping. we were ten minutes late picking up the girls, carola was at first upset that we were late, but then seen the cab, and all was better, she loves the cab rides.

Friday Sept. 29, 2006

Hello letter 1this is Faby today in the morning I found a page about a Peruvian woman that got married with a north American guy and she was explaining all the process she is doing to get her wife visa Cecil and me want to share the info with you. So you will know how is the process and the requirements step by step they ask for a primary evidence:

PRIMARY EVIDENCE: Es de tipo documentario: pases de abordar, entradas y salidas en el pasaporte o como las provea cada país, recibos de estadías en hotel, recibos de retiro de dinero en los países del beneficiario, bills o facturas de servicios en caso de que vivan juntos (teléfono, energía, luz, agua, lease, convenios de renta, etc. i will translate what this say because this woman wrote most of the requirements that she had to do in spanish

NOTE:THIS IS A 2006 PROCESS!!!
Primary Evidence: is a type of documents: boarding tickets. Stamps of the passport every time they are in and out of the country hotel tickets(in case that Cecil was here in a hotel) bill tickets, like bank vouchers, tickets of power, water, rent, etc (in our case I have saved the western union receipts in order day by day)

SECONDARY EVIDENCE: USCIS define como evidencia secundaria todo lo que pueda "complementar" a la evidencia primaria, pero que por ella misma no podría demostrar lo que se afirma, asegura o jura en los diferentes casos: fotografías, cartas de amigos y familiares, y algunos boletos de tren o bus que no demuestran nada certeramente.

SECONDARY EVIDENCE:USCIS take as secondary evidence everything that will be a complement of the primary evidence . . . that by themself will don't show what is prooved . . . in this cases PICTURES(i have saved the cecil s pictures before he was here the first time, and some others that you family sent us) FRIENDS AND FAMILY LETTERS:(we have mama & papa, Charce, aunt Mary, aunt Linda letters in their mail envelope with dates) SOME TICKETS TRAIN OR BUSS THAT DONT SHOW NOTHING CERTAINLY: we have Cecil's plane tickets and some buss tickets of our trips

Fotos que comprueben la relacion amorosa—indicando fecha y lugar en el reverso, indiquen si aparecen amigos o familia. Pueden mandar desde 3 fotos hasta las que consideren necesarias.(del compromiso, con familia, con amigos, de vacaciones, etc). Nosotros enviamos 100 fotografias y mucha evidencia primaria.

PICTURES THAT SHOW THE LOVE RELATIONSHIP: showing dates and places in the back side of every picture, writing also if we appears in the pic with friends or family. we can send at least 3 at all the pictures we consider necessary(the engagement, with family, with friends, vacations, etc.)on her case she sent 100 pictures and lots of primary evidence

Pases de abordar/ tickets de avion o de tren

Recibos de hotel o viajes juntos

Sellos del pasaporte mostrando fechas de visitas entre ustedes

Copia del recibo de anillo de compromiso. es opcional.

Copia de bills de telefono o celular mostrando sus llamadas

BOARDING TICKETS,TRAIN TICKETS OR PLANE TICKETS
Hotel tickets in case to travel together Passport stamps showing the dates of the visits(Cecil have his stamps) Engagement ring receipt copy . . . is other option Phone bills copy . . . showing our calls(in our case we dont have)

Copia de mails, cartas o correspondencia entre ustedes enviadas por familia y amigos *Mejor aun si muestran sello postal y fecha.

COPY of e_mails, letters sent by friends and family. better if show the postal stamp and the date(we have the letters you sent us in date order) SUPPLEMENT FOR QUESTION XX. Corresponde a la respuesta de COMO CONOCI A MI PROMETIDO es una respuesta digna de muchisima atencion y muy importante. Es mejor detallarla. *fechada y firmada. Las parejas que lo han explicado con todo detalle han recibido menos RFE (request for evidence) que las que escriben media hoja

SUPLEMENT FOR QUESTION XX: talk about how we meet . . . is an answer that need to pay much attention and importance is better with details,signed and dated.The couples that explained everything with details got less RFE(request for evidence) than the ones that write half page.

PROCESS:
1- Send the petition to the homeland security(we already sent)
2-Notice of Action 1. Indica que el pkt fue recibido.Da un numero de recibo

NOTICE OF ACTION 1. say the the petiton package was received and give a code number(we already got the Notice of Action and we have our code number) 3-Request for Further Evidence. Llega en caso de que USCIS solicite evidencia adicional

Request for Further evidence:we will got this in case the USCIS ask more evidence(we don't get this yet)

4-reply

Se envia la respuesta si fue requerida
REPLY: we must to send more info in case they ask us(we don't get this yet)
5-NOA 2 significa la peticion aprobada

NOA 2:they send us a letter letting us know our petition was aprooved (we dont get this yet) 6-Paquete Recibido por NVC en seguida el pkt se envia al centro nal de visas. after the step 5 the package go to the national visa center(we dont get this yet)

Fri Sep 29, 2006

Hello letter 2 here i continue:
7-Paq. Sale del NVC

Despues de su revision, sale del centro nal de visas. Package leave the national visa center after get checked the package leave the NVC(no yet)

8-ePaq. Llega al consulado

Llega al consulado de la ciudad que le corresponda al extranjero

Package go to the consulate,the package go to the consulate where live the foreigner(in this case Peru)(we don't got this yet)

9-Pkt.3 se recibe el extranjero recibe este pkt con instrucciones de lo que sigue

WE receive a package with instruccions to continue the process(we dont get this yet)

10-Pkt. 3 se completa el pkt debe completarse y enviarse

Package 3to complete we must complete the package and send(nothing yet)

11-Pkt 4. Letter appoinment se recibe carta de la cita para entrevista

LETTER APPOINTMENT: is get the date to the appointmet in the us embassy here(nothing yet)

12-Entrevista ese dia se define si se recibira la visa o no
APPOINTMET. these day the us embassy say if they give us the visa or not.(nothing yet)

Para los que hemos esperado muchos meses después de recibir el numero de codigo En mi caso han pasado 156 días desde julio 10 de 2006 he recibido un paquete que me pide un documento nuevo mas NO me pide mayor evidencia de mi relación. El documento que nos han pedido es una pequeña forma a llenar que USCIS requiere desde Febrero de 2006, debido a la nueva enmienda llamada IMBRA: "INTERNATIONAL MARRIAGE BROKER REGULATION ACT". Este documento es para verificar si la pareja se conoció a través de un "arreglista de matrimonios" this is her case . . . she say: to the ones that was waiting lots of months after to get the code number . . . on her case was 156 days waiting for an answer since July 10 2006 . . . she got a package asking for a new document . . . is a file to write that the USCIS ask since February 2006 . . . for a new rule called IMBRA: INTERNATIONAL MARRIAGE BROKER REGULATION ACT . . . this document is to verify is we meet by a marry agency . . . in other words if we married by contract(only to get the visa) (we don't get this paper yet) T I P S

Expliquen detalladamente cada una de las piezas de evidencia que enviaran en una hoja de papel.

Guarden las etiquetas del equipaje si contienen nombres y fechas. Si no tienen recibos de hotel o rentas en las visitas del americano a sus países, expliquen detalladamente en hojas aparte que el se quedo en la casa de la familia, uso los bienes de la familia, etc, por tal motivo no hay recibos. Si hablan o se han conocido por internet, guarden todas sus conversaciones de chat, e mails, etc. Si usan fotos digitales es bueno que tengan fecha desde que las sacan. Guarden todos los recibos de compras que tengan que ver con su relación de prometidos o esposos. TIPS: explain with detail every one of the evidence pieces that will be sent in a paper save the baggage tags with names and dates(we lost this) is we don't have hotel receipt or rent receipt on the north American visit to here . . . explain with details in papers that he was on the family home, and was using the family home things, etc. in that reason doesnt exist receipts if we talked or meet by internet, save the chats, e-mails, etc. if we used digital pics . . . we must have the dates since we get the pics save all the receipts of shopping that have to do with our marriage relationship

Sep 29, 2006

Hello letter 3 the appointment day these day the us embassy will make us a lot of questions our us . . . one by one . . . in apart rooms

QUESTIONS:

1) How long do you now your fiancé?
2) How did you meet?
3) Have you ever been to USA?
4) When is the last time you have seen your fiancée?
5) When will you leave for the US?
6) When did you meet in person?
7) When did your fiancé propose?
8) Why was your fiancé's first marriage not working out?
9) Does your fiancé have any kids? How many? How old? Who do they live with?

10) When did your fiancée divorce?
11) What is your fiancé's birthday?
12) Does your fiancé have any brothers and sisters?
13) Do you have any brothers and sisters?
14) Where do your fiancé's parents live?
15) What does your fiancé do for a living?
16) Where does your fiancé live?
17) Where was he or she born?
18) What do you love about your fiancé?
19) When are you going to leave?
20) When is the weeding?
21) Have you ever applied for a traveling visa?
22) Where did your fiancé visit when he was here?

What are your fiancé's hobbies and interests?
What are your hobbies and interests?
What does your fiancé(e) do for a living?
What do you do for a living?
Do you know if your fiancé(e) was married before?
Does she have any children?
Will there be a problem with the children from her other relationship?
Did you know that your fiancée was divorced in 199-?
Does this matter to you?
Where do you plan to live in the United States?
When and how did you meet your fiance(e)?
How long have you been corresponding with your fiance(e)?
Do you have any wedding plans?
Are you planning to have children?
What is your fiance(e)'s religious background?
What is your religious background?
Does your fiancé(e) speak and understand your language?
Do you speak and understand your fiance(e)'s language?
How do you two communicate?
Why do you want to come to the United States?
What is your fiancee's name?
How do you spell her name?
Are you a terrorist?
When do you plan on entering the US?
What are your fiancee's parents names?

Does your fiance have any brothers or sisters?
Where does your fiancee work?
Did you know that your fiancee was divorced?
Have you ever been to US? If so, what type of visa?
Have you ever met your fiancee's father or mother?
How often do you talk to each other?
How old is she?
What are your fiancee's parents names?
What does her father do?
When are you planning to get marry?
Where are you going to get married?

The Consular Officer can ask questions about the documents.
What's the name of your fiancé?
How many times have you met?
How did you meet/know each other?
When was the last time you met?
How long have you been with each other?
How long have you been with each other last time?
What are the dates of the visits?
What have you done when he/she came?
Where did you go?
When did he/she come last time? When did he/she leave?
Where does he/she live? Which city/state?
What does he/she do for a living?
Where does he/she work?
What is his/her phone number?
Do you know how long he/she has had this job?
When and how did you meet?
When are you planning to have your wedding?
Questions about the pictures; when, where and who.
What does your fiancé do for a living?
Where will you live?
Have you met his/her family?
Where do his/her parents live?
Questions about fiancé English; do you speak good English?
How do you communicate with your fiancé?
How do you keep in touch?
What language do you use to communicate with your fiancé?

How many times do you two talk on the phone each month?

Are you willing to marry him/her?

Why do you want to marry him/her?

He/She is much older than you. What do your parents think about this?

Do you love him/her?

Does he/she own or rent his/her home?

Have you set a date for the wedding yet?

When/where do you plan to marry?

Please tell me about your wedding plan.

Are you going to hold a wedding?

Are your parents going to be at your wedding?

Do you know you must marry within 90 days of entering the US?

How much does he/she earn?

Write his/her full name?

How do you spell his/her last name?

Have you ever been to the US? When, how, for how long and where did you live?

Do you have any relatives/friends in the US? Where do they live?

When do you plan on entering the US?

What are your fiancé's parents' names?

Does your fiancé have any brothers or sisters?

What are your fiancé's hobbies and interests?

What are your hobbies and interests?

Do you know if your fiancé was married before? How many times?

When did he/she divorce his/her ex-wife/husband?

Does he/she have any children?

Will there be a problem with the children from his/her other relationship?

Did you know that your fiancé was divorced in 199?

Does this matter to you?

Have you married before?

Do you have any wedding plans? Are you planning to have children?

What is your fiancé religious background?

What is your religious background?

Does your fiancé speak and understand your language?

Do you speak and understand your fiancé language?

Why do you want to come to the United States?

Do you know if your fiancé was married before?

Do you have children?

Does he/she have children?

How old is he/she? What is his/her birthdate?
When and where was he/she born?
Do you speak and understand your fiancés native language?
Have you ever met your fiancé's father or mother?
Have you ever met your fiancé's family?
Where and when were you engaged?
What are your fiancé's parents' names?
What do you do for a living?
Where do you work?
When do you plan on entering the US?
What do you plan to do once you are in the US?
Do you plan to work in the US?
Do you plan to study in the US?
What company does he work for and what is his title?
What is his/her favorite food?
Where did he/she work in the past and for how long?
What color are your fiancé's eyes?
What color is your fiancé's hair?
Did you fill the form yourself?
How much is his/her salary?
Has he/she any brothers and sisters?
Are his/her parents alive?
What are the names of his/her brothers/sisters/parents/children?
How old are his/her children? What are their names?
Which university did you graduate from?
Which subject you have studied?
Have you been in the military? Talk about your experience in the military?
Please tell me more about your fiancé? this is the first part of the appointment same question to Cecil in a different room

Sep 29, 2006

Hello letter 4 here more question for the us embassy appointment

The Consular Officer can ask questions about the documents.
What's the name of your fiancé?
How many times have you met?
How did you meet/know each other?

When was the last time you met?
How long have you been with each other?
How long have you been with each other last time?
What are the dates of the visits?
What have you done when he/she came?
Where did you go?
When did he/she come last time? When did he/she leave?
Where does he/she live? Which city/state?
What does he/she do for a living?
Where does he/she work?
What is his/her phone number?
Do you know how long he/she has had this job?
When and how did you meet?
When are you planning to have your wedding?
Questions about the pictures; when, where and who.
What does your fiancé do for a living?
Where will you live?
Have you met his/her family?
Where do his/her parents live?
Questions about fiancé English; do you speak good English?
How do you communicate with your fiancé?
How do you keep in touch?
What language do you use to communicate with your fiancé?
How many times do you two talk on the phone each month?
Are you willing to marry him/her?
Why do you want to marry him/her?
He/She is much older than you. What do your parents think about this?
Do you love him/her?
Does he/she own or rent his/her home?
Have you set a date for the wedding yet?
When/where do you plan to marry?
Please tell me about your wedding plan.
Are you going to hold a wedding?
Are your parents going to be at your wedding?
Do you know you must marry within 90 days of entering the US?
How much does he/she earn?
Write his/her full name?
How do you spell his/her last name?

Have you ever been to the US? When, how, for how long and where did you live?

Do you have any relatives/friends in the US? Where do they live?

When do you plan on entering the US?

What are your fiancé's parents' names?

Does your fiancé have any brothers or sisters?

What are your fiancé's hobbies and interests?

What are your hobbies and interests?

Do you know if your fiancé was married before? How many times?

When did he/she divorce his/her ex-wife/husband?

Does he/she have any children?

Will there be a problem with the children from his/her other relationship?

Did you know that your fiancé was divorced in 199?

Does this matter to you?

Have you married before?

Do you have any wedding plans? Are you planning to have children?

What is your fiancé religious background?

What is your religious background?

Does your fiancé speak and understand your language?

Do you speak and understand your fiancé language?

Why do you want to come to the United States?

Do you know if your fiancé was married before?

Do you have children?

Does he/she have children?

How old is he/she? What is his/her birthdate?

When and where was he/she born?

Do you speak and understand your fiancés native language?

Have you ever met your fiancé's father or mother?

Have you ever met your fiancé's family?

Where and when were you engaged?

What are your fiancé's parents' names?

What do you do for a living?

Where do you work?

When do you plan on entering the US?

What do you plan to do once you are in the US?

Do you plan to work in the US?

Do you plan to study in the US?

What company does he work for and what is his title?

What is his/her favorite food?
Where did he/she work in the past and for how long?
What color are your fiancé's eyes?
What color is your fiancé's hair?
Did you fill the form yourself?
How much is his/her salary?
Has he/she any brothers and sisters?
Are his/her parents alive?
What are the names of his/her brothers/sisters/parents/children?
How old are his/her children? What are their names?
Which university did you graduate from?
Which subject you have studied?
Have you been in the military? Talk about your experience in the military?
Please tell me more about your fiancé?

Sep 30, 2006

Parade

Natalia was the spring princess of her class, the number 1 in every subject! Carola is number 1 in math, and really did not want to go. oh well. at first both teachers said we are all walking. ok, I don't mind. then Natalia's teacher said for Natalia to get in one of the trucks, they had 8 trucks there for the spring prince and princess. the carola seemed upset, natilia gets to ride and she has to walk . . . until Carola's teacher told her to get on one of the trucks, then she was a little bit happier, still did not want to be there. then guess what happened? Carola's truck kept stalling out- stopping do to the engine quit running, several times. one time we wound up it seemed to be a couple miles away from the parade. wow, what a run. Faby almost hurt her self, she was very worried for natilia. we stayed with Carola-she refused to get out of the truck, she did not like the idea of walking. when they got it started, they took off like a shot, leaving us behind. there was a teacher and three other parents there on the ground, about fifteen or twenty kids, not sure of the number of kids, in the truck, with carola. it was interesting. Natalia had a great time! She was Spring Princess of her class. we got her a crown with flashing lights, white see through with flower decoration gloves-I don't really know the name of those gloves. I think that may be the reason carola was not happy being there. Carola is always telling Natalia "I am beautiful, you are ugly. I will have all the opportunities, you will have nothing. I have a white completion, you have a dark complication. no one likes the darkies, every one loves me, because I look white. no one likes you because you are dark." she is always saying things like that. today Carola was very quiet. we did not hear Natalia crying about how she looks today at all. I got pictures, will post as soon as I get developed.

Oct 2, 2006

Feria this weekend was not real good. Saturday was ok, but Sunday, nothing much happened. the girls were not real happy with me. I really kept them under control, every time they tried to go some where, I just guided them back to their seats. there was also some puppies there this time, some people were trying to give away their puppies. one problem with them, covered in flees. guess who else was covered in flees? Carola. she was mad because we did not bring a puppy home. we kept telling her not to play with them, but does she listen? well, she was covered in flees and then gave some to Natalia and Faby. we tried to tell her that when we get to the states, we can have dogs, cats, and what ever else we want. I own land. this renting is DRIVING me NUTZ I ain't kidding. Sunday was easier, the kids went to pastor David's house. and Faby and I were in the Feria, we ate more than we sold. not only that, but there were four or five women really wanting to know Faby's secret on her onion sauce. her sauce did not change color, even in the sun. they were amazed. the customers would buy other things and fight for her sauce. one woman that was selling with us, Faby said she was a chef, was really studding the sauce trying to figure out the ingredients. she bought one tomalley, to take home. ya, ok. she was also talking about different things about the sauce. saying the onions were carefully picked out, just the right amount of salt, vinegar, lemon, and some other things. Faby just didn't have the heart to tell her we found a box of the cheapest onions we could find and bought them all up, added a little salt, peppers and a few lemons-that was it honest. also, the fact her being a chef was really scaring Faby, Faby has lost other inventions to chefs before and threatened with jail time if she kept making what she invented. so I don't blame her for not wanting to talk with the chef. I mentioned to Faby if they pay her some money, I mean like a lot of money, then maybe she could talk with them? Faby just looked at me. didn't answer, just looked at me with a blank look. I am guessing Faby don't want to deal with any more chefs. there was one nail thingy on Saturday, that was bad. Faby has a design brush for nails. it has a solution to keep the brush clean and in good shape. the woman Faby was working on was not nice, and kept moving around. knocked over the bottle for her design brush spilling out almost all the fluid in there-we really have to find more, and did not even say she was sorry, just kept saying to Faby that she was doing a bad job. Faby lost a lot of pain trying to design her nails. then the woman asked Faby to wash her fingers and to the cuticle thing. Faby told her she only paints nails, and for five soles, nails is all she will do. Faby is still talking about that woman and how mean she was. most of the time for five soles nails, Faby has them done in five minutes, that woman took Faby for one hour. and not to be joking, that woman was a big as a horse . . .

Oct 2, 2006

Hair cut

Carola was crying earlier today. she did not go to school today either. she was not happy. Faby was having problems with her hair, yes Faby's hair. Faby really looks different now, short hair, I was not happy about that, but her hair was really bothering her. as for Carola? last Saturday, a couple days ago, there was some puppies that some people were trying to give away. they were covered in flees, badly covered in flees. Carola wanted a puppy, she got covered in flees and before we knew it, Carola shared the flees with natilia and Faby. Natalia was smart enough not to argue, she did every thing mama told her to do with out question. as for Carola, well, the way she was acting all day long Saturday, even in to the night, then Sunday night. well, it was settled. it was carefully planned. "Faby went up first today, she got a real short hair cut. she really looks different. then told the hair stylist to trim up Carola, just a trim. Carola went to the chair not knowing any thing, taking a comic book to read. just before the hair stylist started, Faby tapped her in the hip. then motioned with the hands, one hand like grabbing a whole lot of hair the other hand in scissors motion, cutting. Faby then did the open hand thing closing the first finger and thumb like she was saying make it very short. saying out loud, "just a trim, all around her head, just a trim." well, the hair stylist did one side, and about half way through the other side when Carola dropped the comic book and looked in the mirror. she started to fight, then I said, that hair stylist has razors, I will have her shave your head if you give her any problems. Carols was not happy at all. she was trying to kick the counter, she pulled the apron off and threw it on the floor. she got hair all over her face, neck, front and back. what made matters worse today was the fact that Carola had to take another shower. took one last night, one Saturday night and one this morning. she was not happy about that at all. then again today at noon to get the hair off of her. Carola's hair is a lot shorter than Faby's now. I wonder if she will ever trust another hair stylist again

Tue Oct 10, 2006

Close one . . . you might think I would be talking about the Feria . . . well, it went ok, Saturday, the girls were not happy with me again, I would not let them run around wild. so, Sunday, we took the bike to let the girls ride, that ain´t going to happen again. Carola took the bike in to the park with out permission and let other kids ride it. to top it off, at closing, both girls were out of sight. Faby went to the store to get some supplies. and i lost a tent leg to my tent. I had way to much help and no one was helping me. i was not happy. when Faby got back, we went looking and did find it. now to the story of tonight . . . the girls really don't care. Faby is taking classes. the class is called Tell Tellers Workshop. from 9am to 12 noon. today we were told that I and the girls could not be in the room. so the girls and I went walking around for a while. I thought the class was over at 11am. by ten thirty, we were back at the building, in side the fence there was a bench in the shade where I was resting and the girls were playing. come ten minutes to 11am, the girls wanted to go in to the park that was across the street-different park. different place in lima. i told them no, I felt safe here, they have plenty of space to play in and no one is bothering us. what did they do? got mad at me and started fighting with each other. ok, ok, lets go. we went in to the park and the girls left me to run around. right after they were out of sight, a police man appeared. made a "B" line street for me. I was getting scared. he approached speaking in Spanish. I said, I'm sorry, I don't speak Spanish. he spoke in English saying show me your pass port. I said, I don't have my pass port. he said, hum, huh hu, we have a problem. then I reached in my pocket and said, I have an I.D. Card. he said, show me. I opened it up and showed him. he looked at it for a minute, then looked at me, so I folded it up started to put it away, then he said, what is your nationality? I said north American, then showed him my card and pointed where it said U.S.A. he said huh ha, then I said my wife is in the Spanish cultural center-pointing behind him, then I said I am waiting for her to finish her class. he said no problem. he walked past me, taking two steps, and I almost ran to the building. where were the girls? I don't know, I was too scared. I never let go of my wallet. I was holding it so tight my finger tips were white. if the girls seen, they did not care that I almost came up missing. I never gave him my card. Faby told me over and over if I give up my card to the police, they would destroy it and make me so many problems. to the point of beatings, trying to get money, if they find out I am broke and family is not million airs, then I am dead. the police for the most part here are worse than the drug growers. I am sure every one knows how dangerous they are. if you want protection, you make friends with the drug dealers. you have no idea how scared I was today. did the girls care? not one little bit. I walked in the building five minutes to eleven am. ten minutes later, I noticed the signs on the wall, saying the classes go until 12 noon. I was not going back out side for any reason. the girls were running around in the park. from what natilia said, they were also talking with strange women as well. one of which was offering candies and asking where their parents were, and where they lived. did the girls care. no. they did come in the building about 11:30, I guess they were looking for me, but then they left again after about ten or fifteen minutes. I was not going near the front door, I was still nervous. come five after 12, the door of Faby's class room opened and the students come out. Faby looked at me and asked what's wrong. she seen I was scared. so I told her every thing. she said the girls left you alone in the park? and the girls appeared. Faby looked at them, and said do you know what almost happened to your father? Natalia started talking, and when she starts, there is no shutting her up. I just walked away, a few feet to lean on the wall-I was still shaking. that's when Faby found out about the strange women that they were talking to. Faby told them about me and what happened. and they did not have any reaction. like they really don't care.

Faby was looking on the internet a little while ago, news on what is going on here, and she found out from January till august one hundred north American have come up missing for a while. so far of those one hundred, fifty have re-appeared. saying the police took them, beat them, destroyed their documents and demanded money. the police were making them call their relatives in the states to ask for money. that is how they were released, their relatives paid the ransom. as for the other fifty, well, who knows. and that is what almost happened to me today. I don't know any one who is a million air. we found the ambassadors house today. well, I seen the U.S. Flag flying on a big building, and we went, after the class was over, to see what the building was, and the guard told us. Faby also told him what happened to me. the guard said so far he has had about 80 north Americans in the past few months come to him for help because of the police in that area. and the ambassador was on a trip, out of country for a while. THAT WAS SCARY TODAY!!!

Faby called her uncle today, a police captain. he has told her from time to time not to let me walk along any where. to dangerous. he told her to night, that he has been in different cars with his own police and they would say to him look a gringo, lets get him. and he would say, no not him, he is my nephew, he is married to my niece, you can not mess with him. but he can not be every where all the time, plus he is only in charge of pueblo libre. he did say that if I ever do get picked up, to call him immediately. he may not be in charge of other districts, how ever, he is a captain, he can pull strings in our favor. and told her tonight again that its getting way to dangerous for north Americans and don't ever let him walk alone again. he said he would always be looking out for me, but he can not be every where all the time. he also told Faby that if I ever get questioned by a police man again, to get his name, badge number, and vehicle number, if he is near one. and then let him know as soon as possible. that way, he can respond. basically he would say, don't mess with that one, he is my relative. I am guessing, I really don't know what he could say to some one out of his district.

Oct 16, 2006

A Few Stories

Friday the thirteenth. didn't know what day it was until we got home that night. what a day, what a trip, what a headache. well, it started like this, and its not finished yet. Faby's father sent her his Peruvian I.D. card. it cost him around three thousand dollars. why? because the laws changed here again, its law for whom ever picking up a check must have the I.D. card to match the check. Roberto-Faby's uncle has had the power to pick up her fathers check, but now because the laws changed, he needs her fathers id card. her father is reluctant to send him the card, so he sent it to Faby . . . . sorry, Faby don't have it, I do. and sent her the papers of power for three months, those papers go to Roberto. along with a letter saying for him-Roberto—to give Faby six hundred soles as soon as he gets the check, then two hundred soles a month after that . . . ya, right. Faby called her father that night, it wasn't funny at all. Roberto had already called him crying his eyes out. he has three sons, 20, 22, and 23. all living with him, not working, just living off of Faby's fathers retirement checks. each check is one thousand and five hundred soles. Roberto's retirement check is only three hundred soles. his sons, don't work, they are Peruvian. they refuse to work, and make Roberto provide for them . . . . so . . . . what happened was this, Faby's father heard all that as well as the fact that he-Roberto-also ran up a large bill in her fathers name. he said if he can't pay the bills, he will say, its not his bill, its Faby's fathers bill, the bill is in her fathers name. which means, they will do a court process on him and force him back to Peru to pay the bill. Roberto was laying this stuff on real thick on Faby's father. and when Faby talked with him that night he said, not six hundred soles, but three hundred soles, and not two hundred soles a month, but one hundred and fifty soles a month. then Roberto calls saying he has no money and we have to pay for the papers to be legalized. BULL S!"#$%&/()=?T. any way. Saturday the fourteenth was some thing. Faby was not feeling very well, so I was not trying to push her out of bed, it was about 11:30 am. and the phone rang. one of the women in charge of the Feria was calling, Faby had three women wanting their nails done. Faby tried talking her way out of it, but they were insisting, so we went. I was crying, those people don't know how to set up those tents-i have photos will share when we get them out of the photo shop. I mean it was all taped up. really taped up good and falling down, almost hit a few people, including me. hit Faby right over her right eye. she has a knot on her head where the tent part hit her. we made about 20 soles Saturday. Saturday is when Roberto called us telling Faby she had to pay for the legalizing of her fathers papers. it was some thing. Sunday the fifteenth we were there early at the Feria, Faby had six paint faces to do right away. plus there was a parade that the Mayer want to be was putting on. the girls went, I went, Faby stayed in the Feria. I was really crying at the start of the whole thing, I was trying to put up tents with missing peaces and cutting off miles of tape (still pealing tape off my shoes) and too many people trying to help-the wrong way. one went to get tape, I was trying to say no, but that was not working until I caught him in the building and held my hand up in the "stop" motion, shaking my head from side to side. I went in looking for peaces that were missing, sure enough, I found them in opposite corners. they were trying to tape every thing up, I was screaming no, stand still and hold. I had to show them what I was saying. finally got it all up, and what do you know, it stayed up with out the tape. amazing . . . . ain´t it?????? they could not believe it worked with out all the tape. oh, well,. on with the rest of the story, the parade was ok, went all over the city. after words we went to the natives community.—I'll really be crying next week—those poor tents. we made about 22 soles Sunday. the natives community. there they have a French community there. they have been there for four or five years now. they are like a help center. they have been stationed in Peru for fifteen years now, and Sunday was their anniversary. they invited Faby to come and celebrate with them. Faby went with her paint faces kit. she painted about thirty faces in the community. they were happy. they love Faby, and she loves them. it was no charge, just for the fun of it. sorry, no photos, no film. its all in Spanish any way, so I was not paying too much attention to it, looked like a miss something contest to me. any way come Monday, today, the sixteenth. Roberto called again saying he has no money, and we have to pay for every thing, sorry we don't have any either-buss fairs, and lunches. then uncle Romolo, aunt Murujhaws husband-next door neighbors. came knocking. saying that the letter her father sent is good, means what it says. she is to get six hundred soles right away, and then two hundred soles a month. why? because mama birtha retirement check is going to pay for the bills that Roberto refuses to pay. is that good news, or bad . . . how much was she getting before I came here? about six hundred soles a month. after I came her the first time, it got shortened to four hundred a month, now, its two hundred a month. when do we leave??? we are ready any time . . . and its not over yet, Roberto has not come over yet to get the papers legalized he says he has no money, and his sons are upset with him because they are hungry and its all Faby fault for being problematic. when Faby told Roberto that I would go too, he has not come back yet, still demanding Faby go with out me, sorry, that ain't going to happen. the poll closes December first, if you have not voted or feel like changing your vote. I just can't imagine the mess Peru will be in when we leave. I keep thinking of Texas back in 83, and Florida back in 97, oh what a mess. got to go bake a cake.

Oct 16, 2006

GRRROOOUUULLLLLLL!!!!!!!!! its well documented how much mommy Birtha don't like Faby. from giving her three hundred soles a month, down to two hundred and fifty, then to two hundred soles. now its nothing. yep, its right, Faby is cut off from mommy Birtha's retirement check. she says its because there are too many bills to pay. Faby calls her aunt birtha. BUT, even though she don't like Faby, she really hats Roberto with a passion. they have a bad past. when Roberto was an air line pilot, he was doing very well. Faby's adopted father and his wife on the other hand, was not. Roberto, and his wife never let them in their home. Roberto did give them a house and a pickup-along with the bill. they had to pay it back. but, as for money, food. nothing, they slammed the door in their faces. Birtha remembers this all too well. what Faby's father remembers is the fact that Roberto gave him a house and a truck. the fact that he had to pay for it was beside the point. and Roberto reminds him of this fact every month, saying "when you were in need I was there to help you, now I am in need, you must help me." ya, some story so far ain't it?

Faby talked with her father today, as well as mommy Birtha. boy did she get it to day. an ear full. both mommy and daddy on the phone at he same time. yelling at each other this time. daddy defending Roberto, and mommy defending Faby . . . what a switch. Faby said she could not believe what she was hearing. birtha may not like her, but she really hates Roberto. well, the sum went up again, Faby is to get six hundred soles as soon as we all get to the bank, and then Roberto has to give Faby two hundred soles each month. this power is for six months. if we are still here in six months, Faby gets the power, and the whole check, and Roberto gets only one hundred soles a month. Roberto has six months to pay his bills off after that, sorry, he is getting no more. unless we leave before then. because now to pick up her fathers check, his I.D. card is required, or so we have been told. we will make sure of this as soon as we can. sounds good don't it. as I said before, we are ready to leave as soon as possible.

Tue Oct 17, 2006

a short funny while walking through the store the other day, Faby and I heard a couple kids crying, well sort of, the kids were wanting some toys. well, the father said, in Spanish, Faby translated, "you two start getting 20's and I will start buying you presents" well, we can't do that. not with these two. That is all they make. The highest score on tests is 20. Thu Oct 19, 2006 the other half well, some of it any way. I really have not been telling you the whole story of what goes on here. not even half of it. here is some of what I have not told you. at the school. Natalia's teacher gave of her own money twelve soles to Natalia's uniform for some kind of holiday game thing. she was thinking that we, Faby and I, would gladly pay her back. (we still owe the school 100 soles for the girls enrollment) one of the fathers went with all the money to buy the uniforms. never bought natilia uniform. instead bought one for some other girl. he and the other parents were saying that I, me, Cecil, was a million air. and some kind of U.S. government spy checking on the public school systems in Peru. why else would these two girls be in the public school. two public schools this year. he can afford to buy the whole class top class uniforms. he can pay you back and get his daughter a uniform that cost more then all these put together. plus they were saying that we lived in the rich side of town. all the big houses. some said they followed us home and told the teacher where we went. all lies of course. the teacher called us last night around 8pm with this story. you see, we missed a day of school, or maybe two days, and the stories flew about us. they were saying things like that maybe I was looking for another school to spy on or some thing like that. and the teacher would like her money back, and I still have to get Natalia her uniform. double the money now. but that is how the Peruvians think here. I am a million air and now a spy. about the Feria. the woman that is suppose to be in charge of it. she took our Styrofoam box, its big enough for a six pack with some ice, just a small box. saying she would sell our jellitons for us. we had the party to go to in the natives community. yesterday, that woman told us her daughter sat on the box and destroyed the lid. just sat on it, ok, sure. how many people have seen or had these type of coolers? you know the lids are tougher than the sides. much thinker. the sides are ok, but the top broke when she sat on it. then she said it cost her more to do the favor to sell the jellitons than what they made, so she is not going to pay us for the jellitons. she said will try to find us a lit for our box. but you know, I am a million air, I can afford millions of these little things with out no problem. so why make any scandals. I am ready to leave any time.

I better not go any further right now, its upsetting. just releasing a little steam. better this way then what I dream of. remember I said a while back, Faby, before I came was getting six hundred soles. after me, it dropped to four hundred. then down to three fifty, then two fifty. it is now, only two hundred soles a month now. the soles to the dollar—it is usually 3.30 soles to 1.00 dollar, some times it goes up and some times it goes down the rate changes every month. mama birtha has cut Faby off completely now. her father has ordered Roberto to give her the two hundred soles a month. right now, up front, he has to give her six hundred soles. four hundred to pay the land lord-one hundred dollars rent, and the other two hundred soles to pay the phone and internet bill. we may have this month covered, not real sure though, the land lord is still trying to raise the rent. what about next month. oh, ya, Faby's money now is just for her chocolates and purses, and shoes. things like that. her whole family still believes just like al the other Peruvians, that I am a million air. they can not believe she is paying any of the bills. as for my self, sounds like I am just wining and crying. but I can not get a job here. if I do, I have to get a Peruvian tax number, and inform the U.S. embassy. the embassy may wind up taking my whole check before I get it so they can take out any U.S. taxes I owe, then of course, I have to pay the Peruvian government taxes for working here. that part is not as bad as if I wanted to leave. it would only take one day to get a tax number. it may take up to three months to deactivate the number. and before I can leave, I would have to have the number deactivated. so, we are stuck in a rut here. almost looks like no way out of it.

Sun Oct 29, 2006

Passports it sure took a while. but we finally got the girls their passports. Carola's passport took one day. each passport cost 70 dollars each, which is roughly 230 soles. well, the birth certificates were not good enough, which was another 20 soles each. no, the passport office wanted the hospital script, the written report of live birth. Faby never put the fathers name on either of the girls birth certificates, for various reasons. any way, the passport office said they will find the father and talk to him. ok, go for it. as I said, Carola's was easy. she was born in the home, so her script was in the,—what we would call the court house. it cost one hundred soles, and took almost an hour to get. we were watching the guy look through the books, those were some big books-looked almost like two foot by two and a half foot, some thing like that. and the scanning, that in it self was a show to watch. you ever try to put a book that big on top of a copy machine? any way, we got the papers and the passport for carola in one day.

Natalia, was a different story. she was born in the hospital. her paper only cost 20 soles, and was suppose to take five working days. we got it in four working days, and it cost us another hundred dollars-photos to be added later. why? no father. if Faby would have had another two hundred and fifty dollars, my name would have been on Natalia's script. but we didn't have quite that much. and I thought carola was expensive. not only that, but the cab rides, about five soles each time we entered a cab. first, the hospital made one tiny mistake, so they whited it out and stamped with their seal, then made another tiny mistake. one tiny line said Natalia was born in 2006. passport office caught that right away. so back to the hospital for the correction. then back to the office. then they said, nope, the paper can not have any mistakes on it. the paper must be perfect. no folds, no nothing, perfect in every way. back to the hospital for a perfect page. then back to the office, only to find out we were just minutes late. well, that was Friday. come Monday, we showed up at 8am, the office opens up at nine thirty am. you should have seen the line. you know how big a block is, well a city block, the line was wrapped around the building almost. we skipped the line-teehee. we went in the front door. passport door was in the back of the building. and Faby does have a friend in the passport building. I waited in the waiting room for her. she told me later what happened. she was suppose to go in the back of the building,,oh, well, she went to her friend, cutting in front of every one. she said they were screaming at her that they were there at four am waiting in line. not only that, but the law got changed, now you have to wait until the next day to get the passport. well, it took Faby a couple hours and we got natilia her passport that Monday-last Monday. one good thing about that, Faby did not have to give him any extra money or get in line. sure does pay to have friends in high places. Faby has known this guy for years. he lives right in our neighborhood, and we say "HI" to him once in a while when we see him. well, these passports sure did cost enough, but we finally got them.

Faby called her father and told him, she sure was happy to hear that. he understands the fact that we just can not tell any one when we leave, or even let any one know we are planning on leaving. he just told Faby yesterday, "I am getting old, I just want to know you three are in the states. I would like to see all four of you in my home before I die." well, he said lots more than that, she was on the phone with him for about an hour. he is not doing well right now. at least the news about the passports cheered him up.

Sun Oct 29, 2006

just a little funny some thing Faby said to me yesterday, then I thought about it last night, after i turned on the puter-played one hand in solitary, then laid down on the bed. then this morning, I got up at 6 am, to post my note, took me a while to just wake up, so, I played lots of games- solitary. Faby got up, went to the corner store to get some bread, she came back, I didn't notice until the girls told me its time to eat. I told them I'll be there in a minute. I finished my note, go and eat, come back to lay down. its ten minutes to three pm now and Faby is making chicken sandwiches to sell at the Feria—getting the picture?

Faby told me yesterday "Some times I just can't believe we have a T.V., telephone, or best of all, a Computer."

I do get some time on line. when she is sleeping or cooking. it started out great, I was on line almost all the time, she would not touch this poor thing at first. I guess she was thinking she was still dreaming, afraid to touch it thinking it might disappear. and as time goes by, she sure has claimed it.

I have told her I like to live comphortably. just wait till we get to the states. she has told me she will never drive a car. well, its probably because she has never really had to drive. with all the taxi's and busses around. not only that, but there is no where to park with out charging lots of fees. plus the gas prices are five dollars a gallon and higher, well 15 soles a gallon. plus insurance, and then there is the police that pull you over just to ask money, and if you don't pay them, you get to go to jail for what ever they make up. so its safer and cheaper to ride a buss, and about half the taxi's, the ones caring special stickers. the other ones, you don't want to mess with. well, its about time we went to the Feria, we are suppose to be there at 3pm. well, better late then never.

Mon Oct 30, 2006

Faby to answer Connie, yes, Faby has her passport. we got hers shortly after her new I.D. I guess I never shown that one yet, so i will load it up shortly. the story went like this we already had fresh copies of her birth certificate for doing other processes, so all we needed was copies of her I.D. card. after going through several lines, and paying the seventy dollars, she was told to go home and come back tomorrow. Faby was not happy. her papers were all messed up, and she was a mess her self after a couple hours of being shuffled around. I was with the girls, and I finally sneaked in to the waiting room. that really drove Faby nutz almost, we were not where she left us. the security guards ran us off. when she finally found us, she said she was told to come back tomorrow, today was a lost cause, but also she said she seen a familiar face and asked me permission to go see him. at first I was baffled, I really didn't know what to say, so, I said, I guess so. I watched her go and stand by an open door-right across from the waiting room. she stood their for about five minutes, when he looked her way, he waved her in-by-passing the line-a very long line. she told me later that the people in the line was saying she needs to get in line, and wait like every one else. her friend said, this is my friend, you wait your turn. and more started saying the same and worse about how that woman was cutting in front of every one. and her friend screams out loud "if you continue making problems, you can come back tomorrow. I will not see any one who is yelling at me." ouch, they all got quiet. Faby told him every thing that was going on and that she was told to come back tomorrow by several people. he said, here is your problem, let me fix this. striated up some of the papers, added a few more, then told her to get in to another line to get her picture taken. then to come back to see him in an hour and don't bother with this line, just wait at the door like you did before. she did just that, but before going back, she was told not every thing was correct and to come back next week. that is what she told me before going to see him. she told him, and he said really, give me about an hour, you wait in the waiting room, I'll call you if its earlier. sure enough, he found it, took him about thirty minutes and got it processed. told her to go up to the third floor and wait till she was called. we all went up, we were not their very long, and there was her passport. we went in on the 6th of June, her pass port was dated 12 June, for the date of issue. no wonder they told her to come back next week.

Sat Nov 4, 2006

My Turn

Nov. 2, Thursday. sense I have been here, Carola was first, she did a part in a movie. then came Faby, she did a commercial for a talk show for the Spanish Peruvian channel in the states, here in Peru. Thursday was my turn. not real sure what it was all about. I still don't understand the language. but I was in a commercial. I was one of the primaries. well, that is what Faby keeps telling me. I was in the front row in the audience. she said I was getting lots of close ups. Faby told me they took pictures of my eyes and put my eyes on some one else. a woman who was taken by aliens and transformed. her natural eyes were brown, after being taken, even her eyes got changed. the director was telling Faby that I was doing so well, he may call again. Faby found out that the director was doing a little spying and liked what he seen. the fact that I was not hanging out with all the other extras around the area. he even sent in the main star of the commercial to sit with Faby and me at our table to see I was talking with any one else at the table. his report was this, "the gringo was only talking with his interpreter."

I did lots of clapping, a surprised look and some pretend talking to a china guy. what was it all about? I really don't know. it may take a few weeks or a couple months before its out.

Mon Nov 6, 2006

Not leaving with out Faby!!!!!!!!!!!!!!!!!!

I went to the embassy today, I wanted to check on some thing we found on the internet. the possibility of Faby and the girls going to the states before the visas are approved. wasted trip. may be the next one too. does not mean I will not keep trying. this time, I was seen by a north American woman. she helped me the second time I went to the embassy. she was just as polite as the first time I seen her. we were separated by a counter, and very thick glass, with a little tray just big enough to slip papers through. not big enough for your hand, it ain't going to fit—I wonder why??? she told me three times that I had to be in Texas to do this process, that I have no business being in Peru. three times I told her, and each time I got louder, "I'M NOT LEAVING WITH OUT MY WIFE!" I am guessing the last time I really screamed it, because she took a couple steps back with a wide eye look, and the glass was fogged up. then I looked at Faby, she was in the far corner of the room, trying not to be seen. then the woman said very softly, "you can check with home land security" I said, I am not calling Texas just to have them tell me I have to be there. then she said, no, next window, only they work Tuesdays, Thursdays and Friday from 1:30pm to 3:30 pm. but you have to call for an appointment first. then she said a fourth time, only this way, "they too will tell you, you need to be in Texas for this process." I took a deep breath, and she said, "please call them, come back tomorrow, or Thursday or Friday, but call them first for an appointment." and I was shoed away for the next one in line. now why do I have to be in the states to do this process? well, I have talked with lots of north Americans here, from time to time. found one on line that has been fighting for ten years to get a visa to his wife. well, some have said this. while in the states and trying to do this process, they are discouraged in many different ways. not only that, but here in Peru, they will discourage the spouses as much as they can. it is the job of the embassy to stop Peruvians any way they can. if you think the questions I posted are difficult, try being separated and drilled those questions over and over. department of home land security in the states, does not mater what state, is connected with the embassy. and they are in constant communication. so all answers are check, and one mistake, no visa. that is just one part of it. there are other parts, and questions, like why do you have to marry a foreigner? can't you find some one here? sense you were married in a different country, the U.S. will not recognize it and you can marry again with out a problem. different things like that. what do they do with the spouses? this paper is not right, come back tomorrow. this paper has a mistake on it, mistakes are not expectable, come back tomorrow with another one. if they make it in to an appointment, they get drilled on, why do they want to leave Peru. isn't Peru good enough for them? you'll never amount to any thing in the states because you'll never be a north American. they do every thing they can to stop Peruvians from going. still some do get to go. why are they doing this? at last count, there was forty million illegal Peruvians living in the states. there is no way to move a mass that size because they have banded together. how did they get there? visitation visas, schooling visas-like collage, foreign exchange student program, temp. work visas, temp visa for a child of a permanent resident. there are many different types of visas to get, only thing is, most of the time they go, and never come back. how would you move forty million people with out starting a fight?

Ok, screaming at that woman probably was not the best thing to do. But she did not have to keep telling me over and over to go back to Texas to do the process. every time I go to the embassy I have been told, "go back to your country to do the process, there is no reason for you to be here" I just wanted to find out more info. on some thing I seen on line that said some thing about getting Faby and the girls to my county quicker. only thing is, it also said on line that you have to go to the embassy for the paper work. And That is what I Ran in to. But, wait, this is only part one if today.

Part Two when we got home, we were caught by Faby's brother, Gustavo. he was sort of yelling at Faby about how poor Romolo and Marouhaw is, and how poor Roberto and his whole family is. he was also saying that Faby should be giving money to every one, because she is a million air now. not only that, but he also told Faby how bad she acted, on taking trips to Chilly, and dropping her kids off with Soladot. then not even being thankful for Soladot taking care of her kids. and Faby could not even spare a candy to be thankful. after he left, our sweet aunt from next door came over, and caught us before we went in. and she sure was crying how poor she is and how hungry she is. and why can't Faby help her. I did not know what was being said, they all were sounding so sweet. smiling and all that stuff. we go to the internet, to make copies of what we found on line to show the embassy and ask how to get the quicker process done and wait for the permanent visa to be approved while in the states. we get there, and to our surprise, no computers. phone is free. so Faby calls her, or tries to call her father. got mama birtha instead. oh poor Romolo, oh poor Roberto, you are a million air, why can't you help them. you don't need any of my retirement check, they need it more than you do. you need to help them. mama birtha also said, the family has been calling them both there in north Carolina, saying they are worried for Faby, that maybe I, Cecil, only wants Faby for a servant. she did not tell me this or the above until we were on our way home. well, we got on a puter, and got the copies. on the way home, Faby was telling me all about what was being said. that crossed with the embassy, the land lord, second floor people. I am so ready to leave. but not with out Faby.

Tue Nov 7, 2006

little histories

Oven in the photo folder, our home, there is a photo of my cake, "Cecil's cake" the cake is setting in our oven. a real Dutch oven, I am guessing. our dear sweet aunt is calling us at least once a month begging for our oven. she is also begging for our propane tank and stove. along with a few other things.

Propane tank Faby has gone through three propane tanks so far this last time she has been here in pueblo libre. the first one she got was stolen right away. no one seen it, just disappeared. the second one, well, the woman living on the second floor of her house, her house is the third floor of the building, made such a scandal of how Faby stole her propane tank, that Faby just gave her the tank. the third tank came in later. we sold the that tank with the sandwich cart. our dear sweet aunt-next door-don't know that and is still begging for the tank.

Stove well, sense we did not have the propane tank, we really didn't need the stove. and with our aunt constantly calling and begging for it, we finally gave it away. sort of. our tamale guy. he was very thrilled. he gave us thirty tomalleys for it. Faby said its only worth about ten soles, thirty soles new. the guy said, he was very happy to receive such a gift. his stove was falling apart and it was very hard for him to cook. thirty tomalleys sounded fair to him. ok, why argue, I ate good for a few days, and we sold about half of them to boot.

Kitchen set cabinets with ceramic doors, and kitchen desk. by order of Faby's father, those items belonged to Faby. the family made such problems fighting over them they broke some of them. one table top was ceramic, and was broken. Faby said they were even fighting over the broken peace. their biggest argument was the fact that Faby and the girls had no use for any of it. like she has no use for the stove, propane tank, or the oven.

Faby's first oven, big one with four burners on top. big fight over it in her house. uncle Roberto stole the door of her oven. and finally our dear sweet aunt next door hired some one to cut it up in peaces. I am guessing she sold it for scrap right from under Faby's nose.

Mirror
Faby has a very big mirror in the bath room. our dear sweet aunt is begging for it. its broke. in several places. well, chipped any way. Faby just told me that is one of the things our aunt is begging for. they, the family has been dividing up Faby's things sense January. when Faby needed help, they did every thing they could to get money off of her father, but to help Faby, that did not happen. so, what will we do with the things we can not sell? who knows, but if you think any thing will go to the family, think again. we will give to the ones who have been nice to us, before we even think to sell to family members here.

Nov 9, 2006

Embassy

I think every one knows this, the U.S. Embassy is the biggest and most protected Embassy in Peru. If you don't know, well, you know now, it is. It has guards all around the fence. the fence it self is a solid wall. the guards are the police, very heavily armed. that is the Peruvian police. ya, the U.S. Embassy pays them, so they will do their job. those police probably get paid more money than the ones guarding the capital of Peru. so, what am I getting at? I am going to do another poll question.

Can any one guess which Embassy is the least protected in Peru? on one of our walks, and buss rides, doing things . . . we have seen embassy's from around the world. some looked pretty sharp. none looked half as big as the U.S. Embassy. there was one that really caught my eye. no fence. no guard. open door. no one any where around it. looked like there was a guest book in side the door, but we did not go in. Faby told me it is a real embassy, but no one cares about it.

Thu Nov 9, 2006

Good news, or Bad? this morning, when we were leaving to get extra copies of our pictures, we seen a letter to our land lord from the municipality think we would know it as "city hall" or "court house". any way, we, Faby and I, don't have to tell any one the unlawful acts the land lord is doing. uncle or aunt next door may have done that already. our land lord has six months to empty the building. he has no permission to rent. he had no permission to build a third floor. not only that, but he owes one thousand dollars in back taxes for the building. the tax is one hundred soles a month for the two story building and has to be paid every three months. that's just under a hundred dollars every three months. he has not been paying any thing. the city ain't too happy about that.

I am not trying to scare any one. it looks like the land lord may try to raise the rent even higher now to try to force every one out. right now, there is no place we can go. most places don't allow kids, and the ones that do allow kids charge about five times more than we are paying right now. the excuse is "kids cause too much damage."

Sat Nov 11, 2006

No Subject

I could not thing of what to name this one. I for get who all I told, but a couple years ago, when Faby first said she might come to the states, she told me the place she never wanted to go was north Carolina. as caring as he is, she sure does take the cake of being well, you figure it out.

Faby called her father today. he says he believes she will be in the states very soon. that was about the only thing nice he said. Gustavo, one of his sons, Faby's brother, I wrote about him before. he helped Faby and me to get married by law. he did not pay any thing for it. it cost me about a thousand dollars total cost. he just took a lunch break, did not loose any time in his job. well, it was an extended lunch break, how ever, he was the main boss, number # 1 in the hospital. as in other words, no one there could tell him what to do. he was telling Faby's father how he helped us get married, that he lost several days of work, and he spent over a thousand dollars for the marriage it self. well, Gustavo got his thousand dollars today and caught a plane back to where ever he came from. Do you remember Gustavo? he went from being the number one man in one hospital to a simple employee in another one. I think I titled it some thing like "You know what my answer would be" or some thing like that. he was also the brother that was sort of yelling at her a day or two ago for being a million air and refusing to help the family. that boy still owes us several hundred dollars, he was promising to pay back the next day, then the next check, now we are monsters for refusing to help the family. I am repeating my self.

Faby told me as we were leaving the internet today, "if there was any way I possibly could, I would remove every Latino from north America STARTING WITH MY FATHER!!!" Faby was on the phone for about a half hour today with him. no sense in telling every thing, its just too upsetting, so, I'll leave with this note,

Nov 13, 2006

Family of Stars? we will find out. I think 18 December is when she airs. Natalia went on, or, in front of the camera today!!! don't know how well she did. but the production crew really loved the way she acted, conducted her self off camera. she did real good at the first part of her scene, but at the end, she was suppose to be screaming. took three takes to get her to scream. the little boy, who happens to be one of the main stars of the show, took a real liking to Natalia. I was not close enough to see any thing at first. Faby said the little boy was being so very rude with another little girl. her mother kept demanding to him to let her take a picture with her daughter. he was not happy about that at all. well, any way, Faby said when Natalia walked on the scene, the little boy went right over to her and started talking with her. Faby tried another little approach. after a while of those two talking, Faby walks over and asks very politely, may I take a picture of you and my daughter? he get a big smile on his face, puts his arm around natilia and says yes, she is my friend.

Faby and the boys Father talking: he is ten years old. been on TV, movies sense he was five. his mother left him when he was a week old. his father had to quit his job, loose the home and every thing he had. he was living on the street, started selling candies on busses. just doing every thing he could to survive and keep his little baby alive. when his boy started walking, he dressed his boy in a clown suit and he too dressed as a clown and did tricks at stop lights to make some money. one day, when the boy was around 3 yeas old, there was a production agent looking around for new talent. rounded up some street clowns. he was one of the clowns that got taken for a series of tv shows. he did not like being on TV. did not like acting at all. but his son loved it. he did five shows, then went back to the street. his son wanted to go back on TV. well, he did make a few friends, and tried over and over to get his son a casting. finally at five years old, he got a break. he was an extra in a movie. and went on from there. so far, the boy has done three movies, five TV shows, and three major commercials. this last TV show, he was only an extra, very small part, just like natilia did today. the little boy stole their hearts, stole the scene, and later on, stole the show. his mother? well, when he got on this show, he had been on TV for a while. the mother tried to convince the production that she gets the boys paycheck. the father was smart enough to know that he could not fight alone. he got one of the production managers-a woman who was single, and very rich, with no kids of her own. what he did was tell her the story of what was going on. well, she said, really, we'll see about that. she has a panel of twenty lawyers. he the father, signed over legal guardian ship of his son to her. she told the mother, sorry, he does not get a paycheck, I am responsible for every thing he does. then she sicked her lawyers on the mother. needless to say, the mother lost the case for the boys paycheck. and yes, the boy still gets paid. he bought a circus and his father is still a clown. only he is the head clown in the circus. he says he is smart enough to know what he can and can not do. now the mother is trying some thing new, saying she misses her little boy and is suing for custody. the father just says, we'll see what one lawyer can do against twenty lawyers. one thing Faby and I noticed is the little boy was very well mannered. for being a street kid, he sure does not act like one. how ever, the first run in that Faby had with his father was not a good one. Faby is a professional, he was not. when he seen how happy his son was with natilia, he changed his tone with Faby. I am not real sure what all was said or happened, but I got the high lights. he mentioned some real famous actors and directors, and Faby told him she was an actress for 14 years, graduated from the school of dramatic arts, and yes she knew those people. he says, oh, ok, he is not an actor, he is just a clown. his son is the actor. then Faby told him, now we are communicating. he went on to ask permission for our phone number and where we lived. he said he never seen his son so happy with any one before. he was very strict with his son. he liked the way Natalia acted around his son. so at the very least, natilia made a friend, a very important friend today.

Fri Nov 17, 2006

HMMMMMMM GOOOOOOOD

Peanut butter, yes, it got here yesterday. its a nice big jar. when we got the notice, the mail man said it has been sitting in the post office for almost one week. Faby said they were trying to figure out a way to steal it, if they already had not done so. we went right over there. while in limbo—waiting. Faby and I seen three people in front of us whom the post office sent to the bank. a woman had to pay for a business letter, it was a big one. I guy in the Peruvian air force had to pay two hundred dollars for an electronic thing-looked like a fancy car radio. we did hear the guy complaining, I guess he was not happy. the third guy, don't know what he got, or how much he had to pay, but he got a bill and he stomped out, I mean he was not happy at all. any way, when Faby was called up, the post office guy asked her what she was expecting? she said peanut butter. he says uh huh, why? she says, for my husband, pointing at me, saying, he does not eat breakfast unless its peanut butter. the post office guy did the "pss" with his exhale in a humph, saying, I'll check to make sure. he emptied the papers all over the table. picked up the peanut butter, looked at it, I was almost over the counter, Faby holding me. no, he didn't see, his back was to me. he put every thing back in the box. then came back over to us, stamped our voucher, saying to Faby in a grouping tone, go sit down and wait.

Faby said he was just mad because it didn't cost enough to send us to the bank too. some times it good to be generous with those people, but when they are being rude, we just grab our stuff and run!!

It got here, Thank you sooooo very much. I carried it all over town in my cargo pocket, it barley fit.

Fri Nov 17, 2006

Post Office???

I was just thinking, about the post offices there in the states. on how some of the postal workers are complaining on their low pay? if they only knew how much other postal workers got paid around the world, they would be very thankful for their JOBS . . . as I said, the average Peruvian makes around 200 soles a month. the hours are well, 6 to 10 days strait, minimum 10 hours a day up to 18 hours a day. and if you complain, you are fired and replaced the same day. lots to choose from. what I didn't tell you, was the starting out was 100 soles a month, you have to work up to the 200. so if you are wondering how the all survive? Tips. the nicer you are to the people, the more chances you have in making a living. I don't think I ever told any one this . . . the majority of the Peruvians here are skin and bone. not because they believe fat is bad, but because they don't make very much. its 3.30 soles to one dollar. most places here charge rent in the dollar amounts. what's worse is, the renters know how much the people are making, so they make sure they charge just enough to leave you with barley enough for a few snacks, if your lucky. they start out charging twenty dollars and say you can only sleep here. then it goes up to thirty dollars, inflation. every time you are do for a raise, so goes the rent, they stay right with you all the way. which means if you want to eat, you are very pleasant with the people on your rout. come to think if it, Faby and I go to metro a lot, its right down the road, just a few miles or so. any way, the metro employees, I thought it was funny at first, when the free samples of cakes and pies were set out, the first in line was the metro employees, they would run in grab hand full's and run out again. I mean they were running. Faby told me, if they were caught off their duty station, they were fired, but if they were running arrons? its a different story, which means if they are running, their chances are better. So, next time any one hears "Strike for better Pay" try saying, "look at some of these other countries" maybe they'll be more appreciative of their real situation . . . plenty to eat . . . plenty of time off . . . can you really ask for more?

Sat Nov 18, 2006

Couples

Today was some thing. all I could do was hold Faby and tell her that is not the way real north American men act. Well, to start out with, Gerald and Sandra, I never heard of or seen Gerald hitting Sandra. And Mama and Papa, as long as they have been together? I can not imagine Papa hitting mama, or even putting time limits on her absents, like saying "you have only 15 minutes to go to the store, and don't be late." How about Jodie and Charce? Calvin and Vickie? John and Connie? Well, I can't go and name every one I know. What happened? The kids went to Pastor David's house today. his wife had two bruises, looked like from knuckles, on her jaw. Her left side bottom jaw. I stayed home during the morning while Faby took the kids over. Andrea said her son had a birthday party to go to, and her daughter had no one to play with all day. They way she was talking, Faby thought David was not going to be there, so Faby took her nails box. She was thinking she would have time to paint her nails, and talk a while. Ya. Well, first thing Faby told me was this. she was sitting in the living room and Andrea was in the kitchen. then pastor David came down screaming "ANDREA, ANDREA" as he was walking down the stairs. he seen Faby and then got real calm saying "Faby, I didn't know you were here, how are you, we have not seen you in a while, how is your husband?" ok, enough of that. he told Andrea to go to the bank because there was a problem with the credit cards, and they kept putting him on hold. so much for painting nail. but get this. he puts time limits on her absents. Faby went with her so they could talk. they get to the bank and there was a long line. she was very scared saying, he is waiting for me, I only have fifteen minutes. they talked to the guard there explaining Andrea was only there to ask a question. good, they got past the line, lots of Peruvians very upset saying "go home gringa" as well as other things. and on the way back, Faby said lets stop for a coffee. well David called for another arron to do and she got very nervous telling Faby there is no time, and dropped her off here at home. Faby told me all this when she got here. I was surprised Faby got here only after a couple hours. at first Faby thought i was mad at her for coming home so early. The girls were suppose to be there until 7pm. well, Andrea called asking if we could get the girls a little early, because they have so much to do. ok, we get there at six pm. I seen for my self, the bruises on her jaw. and she was so happy, laughing and smiling. saying the girls were having so much fun, she just hated to see them go. I don't know how long that site will be stuck in my head. but there is nothing any one can do, if she wants a life like that, what can any one do? All I could do was hold Faby saying "that's not how typical north American men act." well, granted, I only hang around country men, still that's not how we act at all. as far as I know any way. I can't get over that. how many women have time limits in my group? how many men will beat their women if they are one minute late? I mean giving fifteen minutes to go to the bank. twenty minutes to go to the store? what happens if the line is a mile long and problems with the register? ok, i know those are loaded questions, but really. I just held Faby saying, that's not how I was raised. that's not how things are really done. a couple women going out to share a coffee, and do a little shopping, that's at least an all day thing, not a fifteen minute deal. If any one has any thing to say on this, Please do. Faby does come in the group any time she wants to. when she comes on the puter when I have been on, I don't close out my group if I have it up. and I do see her looking around in it, mainly looking at all the letters. she did ask permission the first few times, I have told her over and over, its her group too, and I will not hide any of it from her. its after midnight now, 12:45 am here now. I think I better go. sorry mama and papa, I didn't sign in, it was late by the time we got in, and I have so much on my mind.

Mon Nov 20, 2006

Bemboe's some thing else happened yesterday, besides the other story, or is it now two days ago. any way, after Faby got dropped off, we went shopping, got photos. well, after that, got the girls, and on the way back, realized we still needed some milk. well, plaza vea is on the way, and the plaza vea buss-a free buss, leaves us almost at our door. well, the store clerks were having problems with the credit cards, so we were waiting in line too long and missed the buss. had to wait an hour now. next door was Bemboe's. well, so we go over there, and the line was out the door. we push our way in. the girls go and play in the kids play area, like a jungle Jim sort of thingy with tubes and stuff for them. we find our usual table, its full of trash. Faby hollers at one of the employees to clean up the table for us. I say to Faby, "this is a fast food restaurant, they don't have waiters or waitresses" she just looks at me, after he got the table cleaned up she says to him, "I want three ice cream cones and one yogurt with fruit" I say again "this is not a type of restaurant that has waiters. I really don't think he is coming back." he came back, saying some thing to Faby, she hands him some money and he goes and returns with the ice creams and yogurt and fruit. Faby says to me, "I will don't make a file, we come here all the time, they know that. they will treat us with respect or we will go else where."

Thu Nov 23, 2006

Spoon, Fork?

When I first got here, Faby was giving me a spoon to eat spaghetti, and a fork to eat soup with. ok, now, as long as I have been here, I have seen how the Peruvians refuse to change, get progress. Peru is between three and four hundred years older than the United States, and is still in the stone age. when I first got here, I really thought Faby was playing with me. but today was funny. I just said "it figures" we went to Reana's, a friend of Faby who owns a store, for breakfast. we got yogurt and cereal. I asked Faby if she asked for spoons. she said yes. in walks four forks.

Sat Dec 2, 2006

The correct answer on the Embassy Its Panama. no fences, no guards, no nothing, why, because Peruvians don't care about it.

Sat Dec 2, 2006

Next Door

Ok, there are two houses I talk about next door, because both are next door. our dear sweet aunt, and her house, and Faby's fathers house, which he built a three story house and divided it up-Faby is part owner of the third floor. one of Faby's friends-a small store owner a block and a half away, and is full of "cheese may" I call it "B.S.", told Faby yesterday, the first floor of her fathers house was sold last week. that's not the best part. from what I catch, the munisepaladad here is like city hall in the states, and the munisepaladad security guards are like city inspectors in the states. ok, now the first floor of that house has a door way in to the hall way that leads to our deer sweet aunts house. the first thing she says to the new owners is "you need to buy bricks and close up that door leading in to my hall way, or I will go to the munisepaladad and open you a process and have the security guards come and see that you are invading my privacy." if that was not enough, she caught the new owners trimming the little peace of lawn in front of their house. Big No No. she said, "you can't do that, the whole street has hired a professional gardener to do that, you have to pay him, you can not do such a thing. it is insulting!" making a big scandal over that.

Faby told me this last night. this afternoon, Faby told me there was a "FOR SALE" sign in the window. Faby and I are both guessing our deer sweet aunt and the crazy old woman and her daughter who still live in Faby fathers house have been making too many problems to the new owners. what Faby believes is the crazy old woman and her daughter is making problems to the new owners inside the house and our deer sweet aunt is making problems out side the house.

Wed Dec 6, 2006

Bob while listening to Faby, I thought it was a little funny, so here it is.

Bob, not cousin bob, one of Faby's friends, and the girls call him Uncle Bob. he is sixty years old. he has been in lots of trouble here. some Peruvians saying he hit them for no reason, some Peruvian women saying he promised to marry them and give them a visa to the U.S. well, bob learned his lesson real hard. now he fights, but he also says "I am a missionary, and this is the Hand of God! if this hand hurts you, its because you don't believe"

Bob is a missionary, a non catholic missionary. here in Peru, there is catholic missionary and non catholic missionary. first few times things happened, poor Bob got in to lots of trouble, but being a missionary, he had some help. now, he has gotten mean. Faby says she has seen him just playing with some of the people in the dream center, the place he is a missionary in, and in just playing, he has put them to sleep. her words were "Bob moves his hand, and smacks a woman, she fall down and don't move for hours" Faby has told me as mean as he can be, he has never even raised a hand to her or Natalia or Carola. now it is customary for women here when they great some one to give a hug and a small kiss on the cheek. bob don't go for that at all. if a Peruvian woman gets too close to him she gets the "Hand" Faby has told she has seen total strangers-women-greeting bob and then going to sleep for hours. when they try to make a report to the police, Bob fights with the police as well, the police don't like messing with him.

Faby has another friend, Larry. he met and married a Peruvian in the states. they came back to Peru, he got a Peruvian id card, and made the process to get his wife a visa to the states. she got the visa, and moved, gave the power of attorney to her family here and told them to sell the house and put Larry in the street. bob knows Larry, and knows the story. Larry has been here for about ten years. bob has been here for three or four years. any way, one day, Larry's wife came back to Peru. she and Larry ran in to bob. Larry introduced them, and she hugged and kissed Bob like Peruvian women do, bob growled. she got very rude, saying things like this is the kind of friends you have. and worse, well, bob didn't take too well to that and as he turned around, caught her right in the upper side of her head sent her flying. Faby said she was asleep for hours. when she woke up, she went to the police station to make a report and try to get bob in to lots of trouble. well, the police filled out the papers and told her to go home. she said she is Peruvian, and that man had no right to treat her like that, and the police must do some thing about that mean man. the police said, they are Peruvian too, and they have their health to think about.

Tue Dec 12, 2006

Good, Bad, and Scary starting off with yesterday picking up the girls from school. when we got there, didn't see Natalia or Carola any where, we were about ten minutes late. one little kid told Faby that Natalia's teacher would not let any of her students out. some one stole two kids, one girl and one boy from the school right when the bell rang. we went right to Natalia's class room, and Natalia was safe. the teacher confirmed, two kids were taken-kid napped. we went to Carola's class room. we knocked, no answer. there was a crack in the middle of the door. I looked in told Faby I seen chairs on the tables and no one in side. Carola's class room is on the second floor. we looked over the four foot wall and did not see Carola, and Faby started beating on the class room door and yelling for Carola. between doing that, and peeking over the wall, Faby seen Carola's teacher on the ground. she was making a B-line right for the teacher, but wearing high heels, was not to fast on the stairs, I got down first, and you would not believe where

I seen carola. right by the schools front door with the door wide open. when Faby got down stairs, I said not to panic, I see Carola. Faby got to me just as carola got to me, and the big door shut. every one probably knows carola don't care. but remember, Faby does. Faby was asking carola where she was, and carola would not answer. I did tell, I was trying to get carola to understand that was not the safest place to be. on Sunday, Faby was talking with a woman who had her own school. she was from Finland I think, retired here in Peru trying to help the needy. primarily educate the underprivileged. any way, Faby told her she had nine grade in the university. but could not finish her degree. the woman told Faby to try to get at least her seven grade certificate. ok, in the U.S. you have two semesters per grade. here you have two grades per year. Faby was working on her masters degree, she was half way through it when she was forced out by her aunt and uncle. her aunt still works as a teacher, and her uncle in one of the assistance directors at the university. yesterday, on the way to the school, Faby was worried. how would she get the certificate. if she ran in to her uncle it was not going to happen. I for get if I told you about the last time we were there. he said to Faby, that because she went so long with out studying or teaching, that she was reduced to the third grade. he would give her the third grade certificate, but only if she started the third grade that week. and if you are guessing he wanted money, you are right. him and her-the aunt-got about three thousand dollars from Faby's father in the states, and forced Faby out of school. ok, I will continue . . . we get there, its about five pm. we are told the director will show up between six and six thirty pm. so we decided to wait. the girls were with us. well, the girls were hungry, so we went to the snack bar, where Faby ran in to one of her old class mates running the snack bar. that was a great little reunion those to had. after a while, she-the snack bar woman-had to run some arrons. and after some time, came back and told Faby that the director was here. we went to the office, she went in to his office. they were in there for a while. his office is surrounded with glass windows. ok, now the school is like this. it is a high class, high level university. not just any one can get in to this school. you have to be smart. it is a pre-paid university. the graduates get real good government jobs. Faby was telling me that she was number one in the university from grade one to grade nine. she came out of the office, she was happy. telling me that the director was one of her old teachers, and remembers her personally, saying that she was the best in the school. told her to go to the accountant and see if she would give her the seven grade certificate. so she goes, but then comes back with a very sad look. saying, the woman in charge will not give just the seven grade, but all, one through seven. at forty dollars each. that's two hundred and eighty dollars. Faby was trying to say all she needed was the seven grade certificate. well, the woman went to the director to talk with him, then went back to the front. Faby turned slowly and went to find out what was said. she did come back very happy showing me the certificate. she needed to make a copy and give it to the director to get it certified. he is also a government employee who hires government teachers. he also got Faby a government teaching job for three years, and he said those three years will help a lot. and it is his own signature on her papers. now a little bit better. he said that because she has been out for so long, she may have to start in the third grade, but because she was such a good student, she could probably get her degree-the masters degree-in one year! how is that possible? she takes a course in the third grade, and one in the fourth grade, after a while, takes a test, if she passes, she goes to the fifth and sixth grade, takes a test, and so on and so on. ok, he has to go to his government office and find Faby's government papers where she worked for the school, plus he is certifying her seven grade certificate. he also said he had to look up Faby's university papers to have ready and proof on how good a student she was. he said if it was at all possible, he would start Faby out in the eight grade classes, how ever, she would still have to take the courses in the other classes, short courses. Faby said to him, if he does that, she would prove to him she is still the best student in the school. he said to her, I know you are the best student I have.

I was your teacher. if I can get you in and start the eight grade classes, you don't worry about the money, we will work out a payment plan. and then told her to come back this Thursday to find out if he can get her back in to school. and he would have her seven grade certificate certified for her. last night Faby was so very excited. I don't know how long she was up, I fell asleep. she was talking with mama, papa, and I don't know who all else. I remember her squeaking. I woke up and seen her tapping her chest. I got to her just as she fell. me being about half asleep my self, it took me a while to get her in to bed. she did not hit the floor. and she did walk, I was holding her, she took about five steps before she clasped again, but at least that time she was her side of the bed, the side she likes any way. problem was her knees were hanging over the end of the bed. I finally got her striated out, and she was having a pretty good attack. I didn't get back to sleep until after three am. I do remember that. Faby can not handle too much excitement, weather it is good, bad or scary. today, Faby wanted to walk. she wanted to get some exercise. we had to get some papers legalized, at the renick office. while in the office, today, she had another attack. at least this time her chest was not pounding. there was a medic out side giving blood pressure tests, he came in and checked her. there was a fire man in side that called the police and an ambulance. Faby was on her feet and trying to leave just as the police came in. they escorted her to the ambulance. Faby was telling them she was not sick, some other woman in the office fell down. the police went in to try to find the other woman, but by then the medics got a hold of Faby and was giving her blood pressure tests, and listening to her heart. he told her she needs to get to the hospital. her heart does not want to work. he said it sounded like her vessels were about to explode. he had the stethoscope-thingy-on her chest for about ten minutes, really listening her. he also said if she does not go to the hospital, for her to be on bed rest for at least one month. no excitement of any kind. it could kill her. one more thing he said, was this, there was a surgery for her, but it does not exist in Peru. he said it does exist in a few countries, he noticed that I was north American, and specified that the U.S. has the best doctors for her condition, and it would be advisable for her to go to the U.S. as soon as possible, but until then, "Bed Rest" is what he said.

I think I said enough for now. its getting long. so, I will inform you again on Thursday about the answer. Faby really wants her degree. and she is afraid her aunt and uncle will screw her out of it again. I just keep telling her "your no dummy" I don't know what else to say.

Wed Dec 13, 2006

Medals

Natalia did it again. only this time she was the best in the school. Natalia was the only one in the school that got three first place medals! two for running, and one because her class won the soccer tournament.

Wed Dec 20, 2006

Today's Embassy Visit

The time was nine thirty am when we arrived in the little room. Faby got a window ticket number, we sat down. I just stared at the floor, didn't even give them a facial expression. nine forty five Faby's number was called. fifteen minutes later, ten am, Faby sat down. she told me the woman told her three times she could not find my pass port. the last time Faby pulled out the e-mail from the senator to us. she told Faby to have a seat and she will find my pass port.

Forty five minutes later, I mean, at ten forty five, that woman called Faby up to the window. a couple minutes later, she sat down and we looked at the pass port page by page, no damage. so, we left. down the street and several blocks away, do to the cameras all over the embassy, the cameras pick up people out side the embassy as well, Faby told me what she seen and what she thought. first, what she seen, was three pass ports get run through a machine that left big holes in them, then returned to the people who had them. I did not ask if she knew or heard what happened. second, what she thought, that the embassy people were trying to get me on camera being rude to them. ok, lets see, every time I go up to those windows, I am being told to go back to Texas to continue with this visa process. that I have no business being here. because I have not lived here for two years, I have to be in Texas, and when I say I don't want to leave with out Faby, I am being rude to them. time be for last time, I was completely out of line when they took my pass port, threatened to cancel my citizen ship because I owed child support, when I said, "I hate coming to this place, they all treat me like dirt." I also said some thing about wet backs being treated better than north Americans, I don't remember my exact words, Faby was telling me to be quiet and pushing me through the door. I am serious, you speak English in that building, they give you a dirty look and rattle off in Spanish. and I am being rude to them.

I guess the e-mail from the senator made them a little nervous, but not by much, it still took them forty five minutes to produce the pass port after seeing the letter. at least it was unharmed.

Thank You Senator Stevens

Fri Dec 29, 2006

Diploma today was a long day. we first went to the post office to mail that letter to the child support office, that was 22 soles. then we went to the school to pick up the girls qualification papers. we find out Natalia was getting an award, the first second grader ever to get a honorary Diploma. back to the house to pick up the girls and return to the school. the school said they are starting the ceremony at 10am, we got the girls there at ten thirty, I keep forgetting, Peruvians say one time, they mean an hour later, or an hour and a half. it started a quarter after 11. it was over at 1pm, two hours in the blazing hot sun. there was at least one child in each class that received a certificate of achievement. the sixth graders going on to high school received diplomas. Natalia received a 100 percent over all grade in her class. plus she received a 100 on the government test, the reason for her diploma. Carola received an over all score of 99 percent. how ever, every one here should know how carola is by now. she don't kiss up to any one. Carola did not receive any certificate, the kid that did was a girl who's score was 74 percent. why? because she was always kissing up to the teacher, bringing in snacks, drinks and some times lunches to the teacher. Carola's real teacher is vacationing in the U.S. and her now teacher is a substitute that missed most of the school. she would put her brother in, or would show up an hour to two late for class. and get this, that teacher is fighting to get a permanent job there, she wants Natalia in her class next school year. she is trying to get Natalia's teacher fired-the reason is Natalia's teacher lives too far away, two hours away. and fired does not mean she looses a her job, it means she gets transferred to another school closer to where she lives. the school director does not have a lot to say when the board of education steps in. it don't look good for Natalia next year if that happens, unless we can manage to get Natalia to skip a grade, which is possible because of the government test she took, and passed with flying colors. oh, ya, Natalia was asking if she passed the grade or if she has to repeat the grade. and she was being serious. as for Carola, she didn't care at first, but then after we were telling Natalia she got the best scores in the school, and yes, she did pass, Carola started getting upset. we asked Carola if she knew why she did not get a certificate. she just shook her head no. then we asked how nice she was to the teacher, did she give the teacher any presents? bring any candies, drinks, or lunches? did you do any kissing up to the teacher? Carola just gave us a look that said, "I don't kiss up to any one" we told her we are very proud of both of them. we have the number 1 and the number 2 students in the school. Carola don't like P.E. that's why she got a 99 percent, the second highest score in the school.

Sat Dec 30, 2006

Hat

I mentioned last week that Faby sold a hat. a U.S.A. soccer hat, one of four that Charce sent us. what I didn't mention was how she sold it. there was this guy that just hated the U.S. and all north Americans. Faby was asking him why. he said because they are all rich, they can go any where and do any thing they want to, I am stuck here. and of course, me being north American, he was really pointing some anger towards me. well, Faby tore in to him. saying, do you have any idea how many north Americans live here, do you know why they are here? most of them can not work, or own any thing. the government will not allow any of them to own a house, or a car. there are fifteen thousand north Americans living in Peru. do you know how many illegal Peruvians are in the states? forty million illegal Peruvians living in the U.S. putting north Americans out of work because they work for less then half the normal pay. by the time she got done with that poor guy, he bought the soccer hat and poured me a glass of Champaign for a toast of getting along in the future. he shook my hand and wished me a merry Christmas. oh, ya, it happened on Christmas eve.

Thu Jan 4, 2007

a few short stories

Pencil one woman asked Faby if she had some kind of designer eye liner pencil, Faby said, "no, I am sorry, I don't have that kind of pencil, I have a Canada pencil" showing the woman. the woman asked how much the pencil was, Faby said "five soles, but I don't sell to Peruvians, I only sell to Canada and U.S. people." we got the Canada pencil from the U.S. and Canadian independent celebration day picnic. which brings me to another story Mabellene while painting nails of one girl, a woman who worked for Mabellene of Peru walked up, asking for prices. Faby said three dollars, she said, I heard you pain for one dollar and a half. Faby says no, its three dollars. the woman said, I have all this stuff in my home, I work for Mabellene of Peru, I only put the best stuff on my nails. Faby says, you have all this stuff in your home, pulling out one of her bottles of polish showing her. she said, "where did you get that? that stuff does not exist here. you must paint my nails." Faby said, "I'm sorry, I don't do Peruvians." Faby had a line of women waiting, they all started laughing. Faby don't like it much when some one starts acting high and mighty around her, if she can, she puts them in their place. Soft Drink it was really hot yesterday, trying to get the package Connie sent us, yes we got it yesterday, but that's another story, any way, it was hot. we stopped in a little store to get a cold soft drink. after cooling off a bit and finished the drink, the store owner said it was three fifty. well, Faby did not have three fifty on hand, but had a twenty soles bill. the store owner said she could not break that. I got up asking what the problem was, Faby told me, so I started helping count the change. yep we had three fifty-including four nickels. the store owner said "I don't except nickels, that is for drug users, I am not a drug user, here is the change for the twenty, give me the twenty back." The Package the post office where we usually go got shut down. Garcia said there are too many post offices, too may employees doing nothing. we had to take two busses and it took two hours to get there. I can not read much Spanish, but I did understand the price list. it said for every package you have to pay seven soles. under ten kilos is an extra fifty cents, over ten kilos is one soles per kilo. which means, if a package is ten kilos, its going to cost seventeen soles. the post office has a bank installed, where you have to pay for you packages. we know the routine now. step one, get a paper and fill it out from one line. step two, get in another line to present the paper. step three, fall asleep waiting three hours to be called. during the wait, we seen a guy working there that was in our old post office. he was not the inspector, he ordered the inspector to open the packages . . . and this one package contained a package of chocolate drops. the inspector showed him, he took the package to the window asking the guy if it was really candy? the guy said yes it is, he said he has to check to make sure, and opened the package, pouring the chocolate drops in to his hand. he said, yep, its candy. he put it back in the package and taped up the box then presented the guy with the bill. then another package caught our eye, because one guy was almost making a seen. the postal employee opened up his cookies package pouring all the cookies in his hand. the postal employee said he has to make sure the package only contains cookies. of course, this is not looking good. lots of charges, lots of goodies getting handled, literally, physically. after a few short naps, Faby was called up, and to our surprise, it was our friendly neighborhood postal employee. Faby says to him "you look familiar" he says "yes, I got transferred here, and I ain't too happy about that." well they chatted for a bit, he ordered his inspector to open our package. he took out the shoe box and opened it, our postal employee went to look, then told him to put it back, don't bother checking any more, these people are his friends and are good people. he resealed the box and told us to go to the next window to pick it up. we were thinking (what, no charges, lets not ask)it was two more lines, we got the package and ran. several times I was temped to scream "GO BACK TO MEXICO YOU SORRY WET BACK!!!" Faby kept telling me that is how Peruvians act. they just cut in line, and scream at you in Spanish. I tell Faby, that is how the wet backs treat the north American in north America and that is my reaction, and of course Faby has to tell me, "we do have a level. lets not lower our selves to their level." sounds familiar, don't it maw? the good news is, we got the package with no extra fees this time any way

Sun Jan 7, 2007

Couple of things

I was acting again, another commercial. this time it was for cell phones, I was back ground scene. I did have fun, I walked and talked at first, Faby said it was too far away to get hardly any pictures, our little camera just ain't strong enough, and our bigger one is broke. and the second part, I got to ride a bicycle, I went right be hind the main actor, after he almost walked in to a car, I rode past him, he and I looked at each other. not sure what kind of scene it was, but after about twenty takes or so, they finally got the look they wanted . . . most of he takes wasn't because I messed up. most of the retakes happened before I got in front of the camera. to tell you a little bit of the commercial, we start out in Lima Peru, and are transported to Paris France. I am guessing its almost like a "can you hear me now?" type commercial. about the film, to start out with, it was a low budget film. no one got paid very much, except for the camera crew-they got hourly wages. as for the actors and actresses, well, one guy was an hour late, he got paid a whopping 13 dollars for the day, the average pay was 15 dollars, I along with four others got paid 30 dollars. the five of us may have been just extras, but we have been established as just a bet better then the average extra. there was this one guy who looked like he was over seven foot tall. he tried saying he was French, until a girl from France showed up and was speaking to him in French. then he tried saying he was from North America, until I showed up, well, its only too obvious, he kept his distance.

then the translator showed up and was directed to him, she was speaking to him in English, and he could not understand, he tried saying he was from Australia-you know the country down under where the croc. hunter was from? saying his English is real bad. Faby said he was more Peruvian than the huaro potato. its a real Peruvian potato. and if you think that was good, there was a girl there saying she was French, and she did not want to work with a north American capitalist-I am sure you know the rest. when she found out i could not speak any Spanish or French, she was having fun, the real French girl did speak a little English to me, not much. the producer told her she can work with me or leave. not to worry, Faby knew what she was saying, remember, French. any way, Faby told the producer, she was not going to let me film with just any extra, it would hurt me and boost her, the director agreed and put her with two others who were very new to acting. and if you are wondering, she along with the others she was acting with, received 15 dollars, except one guy who showed up an hour late, he got docked 2 dollars. come to the end of the film at pay time, the one pretending to be French, well her parents showed up. dead give away, Faby said she was more Peruvian than the seven foot guy. its kind of funny, we were suppose to be there at 7 am, I got there at 8:30 and received my full pay of thirty dollars, but I have an Ace in the Hole, "FABY" she is a professional actress, and she will not be walked on. we didn't start filming until 10 am. it may be a couple of weeks to a couple of months before it shows up, when it does, I will let every one know and put the link right here in the group so ever one can see and enjoy.

Faby sure is some thing. she asked me when I first arrived in Jan. last year, if I wanted to be on TV. I told her not really, who in their right mind would even look at me. well, she didn't believe me, I finally told her, that I do watch a lot of TV, I love the movies, and I do dream of being an actor. she got me in front of the camera twice now.

Tue Jan 9, 2007 high prices

Garcia is at it again. he is exporting all the fruit he can. bananas use to be five for one sole, now are fifty cents each. apples were one sole and fifty a kilo, now six soles kilo. we just heard on the news. we really hope this process hurries up. letting every one know what is going on. we have not been to the store lately, so we don't know if the prices increases hit yet, but the news stated the prices are going up because Garcia is exporting all he can. Faby told me during Garcia's last run as president, he tried to close Wong down. Garcia don't like the China people. Garcia failed last time. Wong expanded after Garcia left the office, now is also Metro and Eco stores. Faby told me Garcia will probably try to run Wong out of Peru again. if you are wondering how, he grabs all the fruits first and exports. then he puts limits and taxes on the imports. and in this little battle, he winds up starving about half his country. Its not just Wong he tries to shut down, he tries to shut down all forging business, how ever, he really don't like the china people.

Fri Jan 12, 2007

Inheritance

This is a good one. remember, I told every one that one of Faby's aunts died. her husband is the police captain. well, in her will, she left Faby some clothes, a few dresses, stuff like that. a few weeks ago, Faby was talking with her uncle, he said he was going through his wife's things and doing his best to respect her last wishes. he told Faby to come over two weeks ago to pick up the clothes his wife wanted her to have. well, Faby called him just before going. he said it would not be a good idea to come over, the crazy old woman is over there begging for the clothes his wife wanted Faby to have, and to come over last week. once again, Faby called to see just what time would be good, our dear sweet aunt was over there this time begging for the clothes. he told Faby to come over this week, this morning in fact. Faby called at 8:30 am. Guess What? Both of them were over there fighting over who is more deserving, and both saying that Faby is not deserving because she is married to a north American. she is a million air, and things like that. he told Faby maybe next week. He said he could not call the police, because he is the captain of the police and his officers would laugh at him, not only that, but there is no such thing as problems in the family. Can you believe the extent that some of these people will go just to keep Faby from getting some thing? Not only is her uncle police captain, he is also a lawyer. he said he is bound by his word to keep his promise to his wife, and one day, sooner or later, he will make sure Faby gets what his wife wanted her to have. some thing like that.

Mon Jan 15, 2007

Fit

I threw a fit today, Faby just smiled and stayed in the bedroom. I got tired of running in to the clothes of the second floor whore, and threw all the land lords chairs on the roof, photo in group in "home" folder.

I told her the dresser, the stove, and the china cabinet are next, she said, "tomorrow" while smiling and sitting in front of the puter. the stove is a bit heavy. got a nice shiny solid top to it. it just became our new cooking table. as for the other two items, well, we'll see. still thinking about it. I did throw more than a few chairs up on the roof. the chairs do stand out.

Wed Jan 17, 2007

Uncle Roberto

This happened yesterday, we were not happy about it. Uncle Roberto, as every one probably knows, has his brothers-who is also Faby's adoptive Father—power to pick up the retirement check. The checks are issued on the sixteenth of each month. Uncle Roberto always comes over on the fifteenth to make sure we well be here, do to the fact that Faby holds the paper with the power on it . . . I keep a close eye on it and will not let them leave the bank unless Faby gets it back. Uncle Roberto never showed up on the fifteenth. come the sixteenth, we waited and waited. Finally, mama Birtha, Faby's adoptive Fathers wife, called to see how Faby was doing. That was about 10am. Faby said we were waiting for Uncle Roberto. Come to find out, Uncle Roberto is in Cuzco, and will not be back till March. In fact, Uncle Roberto left for Cuzco last month after giving Faby only two hundred soles, telling Faby how broke he was, and how painful it was for him to give her so much because he needed it so badly. he knew he was leaving, and his brother, Faby's father, told him to give her six hundred soles and tell her he was going on a trip. Faby's father was paying his trip, and hotel bill. PAID IN ADVANCE!!! and here we are waiting and waiting. Birtha told Faby there is nothing left, it all went to Roberto for the trip. She did say she would try to send Faby some thing, saying she might be able to scrape up about fifty dollars. it would probably take a couple of weeks, then she would send it down. as for the sending part? she and Faby's father do not believe in bank transfers, or western union or money grams, no, they find some one who is flying and send down that way. Faby is not holding her breath. every time they send some thing to Faby, she does not get any thing, her two girls some times get up to half of what is sent, but Faby does not get any thing, the family some how makes every thing disappear then tell mama and daddy that Faby got every thing that was sent, as for how I know, I was here the last couple times they sent Faby things, and Faby got yelled at by her parents because the family said she received what she never seen.

Wed Jan 17, 2007

Peruvian Justice

On the news the other day, what we heard was some thing else. I wrote a long time ago about how Ollanta Humala was treating people, how he tortured and killed people who were against him. in one town alone he tortured several hundred and personally killed over a hundred people. that one town kept pressing charges over and over. they would not give up. finally they got him in court, and convicted him of murder. Ollanta is on record as a Peruvian Prison Inmate. Guess What??? first, he is still receiving five hundred soles a month retirement check from the Peruvian army. second, he is only under house arrest. and the best of all, so far he has been to Bolivia, Venaswala, Columbia, Cuba, and Russia. what the news reporter was asking, was, if ollanta humala is only receiving five hundred soles a month, how can he in one month travel to all these countries? not only that, but how as a Peruvian prison Inmate, can he even be allowed to leave Peru in the first place? Faby says it only happens in Peru. I told Faby if he was a North American, he probably would be President of the United States.

Sat Jan 20, 2007

drug dealer yesterday we bumped in to him. our local major drug dealer. what was funny this time? well, as usual, he was very happy to see us. he bought us all an ice cream. he looked happier than he usually does. showing us the rosary and the picture of the mother Mary he was wearing around his neck. he said he started talking with God. he use to say he was talking with the enemy-the devil, saying the enemy was his friend. but yesterday, was a little change in his attitude. he was hugging Faby and the girls and was shaking my hand.

Sat Jan 20, 2007

Can any one Guess???

Three days ago, it started. while the hair dresser people were shooting possible clients of Faby away and just trying to as Faby puts it, "make impossible my life", the wind came up from no were and blew down their sign. once, twice, three times, then they, or a couple of them, went out there to stand by the sign. no wind, and no one around. funny??? Two days ago, while the one who paid for every thing . . . first let me tell you, the owner of the hair solon is a woman. she is the lover of the guy who bought her all the equipment for the hair solon. he left his wife and baby for this woman and her three kids. he is still married. any way, he was yelling at Faby saying once he gets his video store going, he will not allow Faby to be on the side walk, it will make his store look bad, or some thing like that. after he got done yelling at her, his T.V. stand he had mounted high on the wall fell down, coming with in inches of hitting the T.V. Yesterday, while they were at it again, telling possible clients that no nails are being done here, it happened again. a big crash back in the gallery. i went to look, and there it was, a big picture of a hair design-about a foot and a half wide by two foot long, fell down and the glass from the picture went every where. Faby looked at me, and I said it wasn't me, not me at all. she said to me, it wasn't her either. she said every time some one asks her about the hair salon, she sends them back saying they do good work. she tells me if you have bad thoughts, or with bad things or put bad spells on some one, then bad things come back to you. I have told her, I do believe that as well, and its not me. so, can any one tell us what is going on and put Faby's mind at rest, she is a little worried. what made her more worried was after what happened yesterday, they were in the hall way just rattling good. I asked Faby what they were saying, she said, they were talking about what was happening, and its not just a quensedence, it happened for a reason, they seen Faby was listening and went further down the hall.

Fri Jan 26, 2007

Life in Peru

We have a couple friends here named Juanita, its a Spanish name. one is our laundry lady, the other is our hair dresser. our hair dresser don't talk much, how ever, our laundry lady loves the "cheese may", as Faby calls it, the rest of us would call it a B.S. session. our laundry lady was over talking with Faby in front of the girls, and Faby was translating to me. telling what is going on, in her life and our hair dressers life. what a role reversal that is. Our hair dresser don't have a husband hanging around, but her son still lives with her, he is twenty years old. he is always calling her obscene names in front of her customers, and if she tells him to be quiet he hits her. he is twice her size at least. I have seen him, he is a big boy. she rents the space she lives and works in. not too long ago, she got a ten thousand soles loan to buy a spot of land and build a home and shop. her son stole the money and gave it to his girl friend, and when she was wondering about the money, he put her in the hospital. she was closed for a couple months recovering from that beating. Our laundry lady is a little different. her son is about fifteen. when he back talks her, she beats him. if he tries to fight her, she leaves him in a puddle of blood in the middle of the floor, as in other words, she does not stop beating him until she is too tired to continue. one day, he threatened to leave and never come back. she locked the door behind him. five minutes later, he was beating on the door saying how sorry he was and begging to come back in. our laundry lady says she will not have a son putting her in the hospital. her son is very well mannered, works in the laundry, goes to school, after school, goes home and cooks dinner for her and brings it to her in the laundry. Natalia was listing very carefully, Carola didn't care one tiny bit. I said, I don't care how much mama beats you two, how ever, the minute I see either of you beating on mama, I'll through you out and you will not come back in. Natalia's´ eyes got real big, carola wasn't paying attention, just playing at the table. then I said, I don't care how old you are, 16, 15, 14, or 13, if you are big enough to beat you mother, you are big enough to be on your own. Natalia was really paying attention, staring right at me, as for Carola, she was making bread crumbs.

Sun Jan 28, 2007

Why fix IT?

A night or two ago, on the news, the Lima Mayer was saying "its not hurting any thing, so, why fix it?" its a main water line that carries all the waste water from the largest part of the city of Lima. A news crew was there interviewing people swimming in the ocean right next to the major spillage. One woman stated she has known of the broken pipe for years, but she is not afraid of it because when she swims in the ocean, she keeps her mouth closed, and she tells her kids not to open their mouths in the water. The Lima Mayer states that the spillage is not causing any problems. No one is sick from it. The fishermen are bringing in lots of fish. So, what's there to fix? Its been broken for years, and no one has complained.

Sat Feb 3, 2007

On The Road Again well, any one who knows me, knows I love to travel any way. Faby is getting good at packing. I just stay out of the way and run Arron's for her. I mean the actual packing of the bags, some how she manages to pack at least twice as much as I can, and it looks neater too. We well be gone from home about a month. we will not be in Chile for a month, may be there for one or two weeks. we will be in Moquegua for about a week, the place we were married by law. I still can not get over the fact that every time we turn around, some one is telling us they need another original copy of our wedding certificate. we have handed out about a hundred so far. hopefully we will not need more than ten, that is all we are going after this time. those things can be pricey.—(PERU AIN'T BROKE!) Any way, from our calculations, we may be on a Plane by April or May at the latest! Faby is keeping very close eye on the process on line. Like every night almost. Not real sure when we will be on line again, or be able to be on family chat night. there are Internet cafe's all over Peru and Chile. this Sunday, we will be on a buss.

Sun Feb 4, 2007

count down its only hours away, and we will be on the buss again. we are about 90 percent packed. ok, Faby did the packing. about to eat breakfast, and unplug our tv, dvd and puter, so's not to forget. we'll stay in touch as much as we can

Wed Feb 14, 2007

Tacna here in Tacna, Faby sure is excited. tomorrow, she is going to be on the radio, and Friday, she is going to be on stage! its been a while sense I wrote last, but I got some time now, so lets see how far I get. we went to Erica Chile, last week, and after a few days, carola got us kicked out of the house we were renting. it was cheaper then the cheapest hotels around. we were paying 10 thousand pesos a night in the house, for the four of us, and the cheapest hotel was costing 20 thousand pesos per person per night. most houses, called "residential" don't like to rent to kids. after carola got us kicked out, we thought we would go to Argentina. come to find out, that was more than we expected, and wound up going back to Peru. here in Tacna, Peru, we are living in a house that is owned by a woman, who's husband have no idea if is alive or dead, I didn't ask, but has a daughter in Pueblo Libre, of whom we have helped out from time to time. any way, this woman is so happy that we have helped her daughter, that she is calling me her adopted son. she has two sons living with her, both work-I mean have good jobs, one is the director of a school and the other works at the local gym. She is not charging us rent to stay there, but we are not just free loading. Faby and I don't believe in that. we have bought some food for house and some cleaning supplies. the best part is the fact that Faby met up with some of her internet friends here and she is in. they want her on the radio, and on stage. so far she has three shows to do. one radio and two stage shows. these people don't want her going back to Lima.

Fri Feb 16, 2007

Curve Ball yesterday was some thing. Faby got on the radio, and I heard her telling a story. I took a few pictures. after words, she told me they tricked her in to telling the story. then she said she is a professional actress, and if put to the test, she will act. as in other words, they threw her a curve ball, and she not only swung, she knocked it clean out of the ball park!!! after the show, they talked a little, and she told me they were saying they want her on the radio starting two times a week for five minutes each, to see if any one is really listening. after words, depending on what the response is, and they were real sure it will be a good one, they said, her time will increase as her popularity increases, plus, there can be money in it for her. the more listeners she has, the more chance of a business would be willing to advertise, and that means money . . . not a lot, but its a start. after that, we were sent to the north American cultural center her in Tacna. they did not want us to leave.

we got there about four thirty, and did not leave until eight thirty, when the place closed. we were visiting a lot of classes. its real different from the north American cultural center in lima. they were asking us to teach there, and put on shows. today, Faby got on the radio again, this time it was the most important radio station in Tacna. I got a couple of pictures. and also today at six pm, we will be presenting a story tellers show. I have been telling my "Fish On!!!" story to several classes, and few other people. they really loved it. there are a few people here that can speak English, they are just hard to find. Tacna really does not want Faby to leave, we have told them we will be here till the end of the month, then we have to go back to lima for a while, but, we just might be back before you know it.

Tue Feb 20, 2007

A Couple of Things

First thing that happened, was, the woman-mama Chella as we call her, almost threw us out of the house. she is not happy with carola at all, and natilia does not make it any better. Mama Chella has dogs and cats, she also has dog and cat food. She really does not believe in feeding her dogs and chats plate and bowl full of people food. and the way Carola turns her nose up and to the side with the "humph" sound, really makes it worse. She does that with the food that mama Chella cooks, I mean spends hours cooking. Natalia does not make it better when she just sits at the table staring at the food for hours. as I said, Natalia takes a turn once in a while. The Food was the first thing Faby got yelled at about, or over. Second thing, was about how Carola was treating her pets . . . the same way as with the food, with the, "I'm better then you" attitude. one day, at the table, Faby and Mama Chella were talking, the girls were watching T.V., with their backs to the table. Chella's cat-George Bush, hopped on the table and was playing with her. he seen carola watching tv, and was keeping an eye on her. I'm sure you all know how cats play, any way, carola turned around and looked at the cat, when he seen carola looking at him, he left burn out marks on the table. Mama Chella firmly believes carola did some thing to her cat, because even though, he does not like strangers much, he does not run like that when some one looks at him. now for the KICKER Mama Chella does not want Faby to leave, she is so afraid Carola is going to kill Faby, if not a combination of both carola and natilia. ya, its a good one here. mama Chella is always screaming at Carola, only once in a while with Natalia.

Thu Feb 22, 2007

carola and the dog

Mama Chella has two dogs, one named peachy, she is seventeen years old. she can barely walk. the other one is named antenas, she is some where between seven and ten years old. well, I wrote about how carola treats and acts around the animals. mama tells the dogs to bite carola. peachy just lays down. one day, mama fixed dinner, which is usually a bowl of soup and a plate of food, carola finished the soup and went in to the kitchen. she had a real snobby attitude with antenas and mama told antenas to bite carola. antenas was some thing else. she at first has a real wimpy wine, then hopped up on her hind leg's and put her paws on mamas chair and was starring at mama eye to eye. Carola came back in, and the dog was really talking to mama. to the point of barely wolfing, not showing her teeth. then Carola rattled off something. the dog left.

Thu Feb 22, 2007

back on the Home Front our dear sweet laundry lady, Juanita, is really stirring up things around there. just how do you thank some one for doing things you dare not to? I mean, the land lord wanted to come in, and she slammed the door in his face. saying to him, this is her cousins house, and her cousins name is not Fabiolita, its Señora Fabiola. as for the second floor woman, well, she came in and was starring at Jaunitta while she was cooking, she screams, "did you loose some thing in here? just what do you think you doing?" that woman explained what she was doing, and Jaunitta told her that her business does not include looking in to her kitchen and slammed the door in her face. then to top it off, Jaunitta waxed the every thing out of the floor. the second floor woman and her mother came up to hang up clothes, and they had an accident.

Fri Feb 23, 2007

cut short

I ran out of time yesterday when writing the two stories, or was it day before, oh, well. about carola and the dog, I guess you can only imagine what the dog was saying. she was really arguing with mama Chella about biting Carola. when Carola looked at the dog, she rattled off some thing in Spanish. the dog just left the room, Faby screamed "CAROLA!" that was all Faby got out, when mama Chella tore in to Carola, verbally. I don't know what was being said, Faby never told me, but Faby was in tears trying to hold in the laughter. as for the home front. well the second floor woman and her mother hit a very slick waxed floor. they love waxing the every thing out of the stairs and making Faby fall down. well, it looks like they got a taste of their own medicine. best part of the whole thing is Faby and I are not there to take the blame for any thing. when we get back, I guess you all know we will get an ear full. oh well, we or Faby will just say, "its not my problem if you upset my cousin" our dear sweet laundry lady is shorter than Faby, and is a real ball of FIRE! I wrote about her before, I thing I titled it "role reversal" or some thing like that.

Fri Feb 23, 2007

Stand Up last night I did it. told a few short stories, of my life experiences. Bob, they love you in the "Fish On" story. told a few of my real life ghost stories, one in the audience wanted to know if I believed in ghosts, my reply was "do you want to hear some real life ghost stories of my past?" and of course they all did. what was bad about last night was, I did not get the crowd that Faby got when she did her stories. about Faby's stories, she really loves getting the crowd involved. at the end, I told my "Fish On" story, Faby translated. then I was at the door with my straw hat. we only asked two soles for the show. one guy dropped in 80 cents, then several just walked by with out putting in any thing. Willy, the culture center guy, who set this thing up for us was telling me in Spanish, and the girls translated to me, that I have to demand from every one two soles, or don't let them leave. I said, I can not do that. just then, one old woman walked up just grinning and dropped a ten soles bill in my hat, said thank you in Spanish and left before I could offer her change. after her, another old woman came up and dropped in a five soles coin, smiled and said thank you in Spanish and left. after every one left, and we counted it, I was telling Faby what happened at the door. then I said, looked like every one paid to me, how could I demand any more? we have been told over and over, that we have to come back to Tacna. the North American Peruvian Culture center is offering Faby a teaching degree, in teaching English. and it would only take four month to get! but the best part of the deal is the cost, it would only cost a couple of shows a month!!! we did a puppet show and a tell tails show for them a few days ago. they loved us and want us to join them! Tacna does not want us to leave! we told every one we would be back as soon as we could, how ever, if we get the visas approved, we are going to the U.S.

Sat Feb 24, 2007

Blind

We just found out why so many kids don't pass their classes. its a law here that kids 12 and under are not allowed to be tested for eye sight. That can be over turned, by paying a lawyer, and paying a judge to allow a child to be tested for sight, but if after the eye test, if the child does not need glasses, the parents get heavy fines, like in several hundred soles worth depending on how old the child is. As in other words, the Government of Peru does not care if their children are blind, they will not allow the children to go through the torecher of wearing glasses. after the child turns 13, then its ok to get them tested. can you imagine a thirteen year old in the second grade? I am talking about one of Natalia's class mates who has been in the second grade for four years now. I am beginning to believe its because he can not see. we found this out because some times the girls say they don't see things. small things. it was getting irritating, so we seen a cheep priced eye doctor and he told us what the law states.

Sat Feb 24, 2007

Carnival we were just at a party. they call it here a carnival. some people from Puno. and here is Faby with her magical way of speaking the language of the Puno people "aymia" which is very close to the Quechua, she got us invited in the party. I got pictures of her dancing with them . . . plus the fact that they also invited us to drink with them. mama was just asking me how the girls are doing, I told her I didn't really care, can you guess why??? I have said Faby knows eight languages, I was wrong, she knows nine, reads and rights five, but speaks nine that I know of so far. after a couple beers, we for got about the missing tooth aches we have. after a couple more we were taking pictures of one of them Puno women, the one who invited us. after a couple more I was telling Faby we need to leave before I loose every thing, so, what happens next, we had a couple more, and I really didn't care how much the girls wanted to fight.

Mon Feb 26, 2007

Happy Buss the trip down was ok, we did not take the buss from Lima to Tacna, nope, we went from Lima to Moquegua, so there was no baggage control checks nor was there any police inspection checks. when we went to Tacna we took a taxi. the taxi did not stop at the police check point and he did not stop at the baggage control check point. he did slow down just long enough to wave at some one and then hit the gas. the buss trip from Tacna to Lima was very different. we had a very happy stewardess. she sprayed scented spray about four times, or at least that is how many times I counted while I was awake. we were suppose to through two baggage control checks and two police checks. we got off the buss once at the first baggage control check point. after that, well, Faby said it smells bad in the buss. well, my nose was clogged, so I did not smell too good, ok, so that don't sound right, I'll rephrase that . . . your sniffer don't work right when it is full. any way, that was right after the first check point. the other three, well, Faby and I had our little camera-key chain camera with a fresh battery ready to be used. and the police were not allowed on the buss. the stewardess took up a fist full of I.D cards to show the police. and that was what happened. we had a Happy Buss Ride. so for those of you who were worried, we are letting you know we got home safe and sound.

Mon Feb 26, 2007

another Scary

Faby called mama Chella about a couple hours ago, good thing she did. Mama Chella was worried to death. Apparently just after we went through the first baggage control check point, terrorist took control of the place and were holding all busses leaving Tacna. these are not Humalas' people, those people don't care who they hurt. Humalas' people are doing other things. making problems for Garcia. they caught a Chile fishing boat in Peru waters. that in it self scored lots of points for humala. he is not trying to take the government by force, he is trying to get the people to put him in, by kicking Garcia out. Faby told me in Gracias' last government, there were terrorist attacks all the time. now that he is back in office, the terrorist are coming out of hiding. hopefully that is the last trip we had to make to Tacna. still, I wonder what is worse for Peru, Garcia or Humala. it is believed Humala will have the government by the end of July or the beginning of August. by then, if Garcia keeps messing up, congress will kick him out and Humala will automatically get the government. that is the law here. the vice president don't get it, its the runner up that gets it. that is how he wants to take the government. we really want to leave as soon as possible. right now we are safe, we are back home where the people know us. just letting every one know what we just found out.

Tue Feb 27, 2007

Superstitious

I don't mean to offend any one, how ever as superstitious as this country is, its unreal! Ok, what happened, while checking the girls into the school, Faby was wearing a surgical mask. here in Peru, if you are not a doctor and you are wearing one of those masks, you are close to death. Any one around you could be infected and will probably die soon as well. that is the belief on that here. they don't care to hear any excuses. they told Faby because she is wearing one of those masks, the girls need full medical exams-that costs around two hundred soles each-before they will be allowed to go to school. when Faby tried to explain to them it was because of her dentist, the school just said, "you are wearing a mask, you are close to death. if you want the girls to go to school, you will get them a full medical exam." that was all they had to say. where the biggest problem lies is the fact if the girls are not in school and the visas are approved, Peru may not let the girls leave, and yes, Faby has checked on that. Well, I told Faby to play a little head game. Go to the school Thursday with out the mask, and when they ask her about the medical checks or where the mask is, to reply with some thing like, what are you talking about? Mask? Medical checks? the spring the lice problem the school has, and how many kids there have lice. plus the fact our girls are going there with no lice at all, and the first time they come home with lice, she will have health inspectors all over the school . . . things like that if they keep insisting. well, you all know Faby is an actress, I'm sure she can be convincing. the best part is when uncle Roberto came over. yep, he came over complaining about how poor he is, amongst other things. he noticed Faby wearing the mask and asked her how bad she feels, if she was going to die soon. Faby laid it on thick to him. Uncle Roberto's response was "drink piss" he says every morning he has a glass, and he feels fine, for the most part. Faby asked what was wrong, he said his joints hurt him some times, his knees, elbows, shoulders and back. well, what Faby told him was this, "you should rub poo poo on your aching joints." he says really, she says yes really, I do all the time it works wonders. he said he will try it. she said to be sure to put it on while its fresh and worm. it acts like a moisturizing cream, and to leave it on until it dries out completely.

When she told me that, I said you have got to be kidding. she give me a wide eyed look, and I said, I know he is full of it, but you are covering him in it as well? and she said "if he wants to believe, it is his problem. I will don't drink piss." And while eating lunch, I couldn't help but to think of it, Inca cola is yellow, and I just started laughing, Faby asked, what was so funny, I said, uncle Roberto getting up in the morning going in to the restroom for his morning drink and moisturizing cream.

Fri Mar 2, 2007

3-2-2007,Friday

I am happy, I am mad, I don't know what to do say or think. Ok, to start out . . . We got the next step of papers, it was bills. The national visa center wants three hundred and eighty dollars each, that is a total of one thousand, one hundred and forty dollars. That is not including the mailing fees. Those three payments are to get the packages for Faby and the girls medical checks and U.S. Embassy appointments. The sooner we get the national visa center paid, the sooner we get to come home. Next . . . Carola . . . How can a ten year old have so much hatred for her mother? Some times Carola wants some thing different, and Faby knows this. Carola, today, was some thing else. We had to get up early to go to the post office to get the mail, before it got sent back to the States. We had to be there at 8:am. Which meant no breakfast. The post office is in town. So, we decided to have breakfast in town while looking at the mail we got, which was the papers from the national visa center. We seen a little restaurant, looked nice, prices were cheep enough, so we tried it. Natalia spoke up, she wanted the bowl of fruit with orange juice. Carola did not show any sign of emotion of any thing except the eggs with Turkey ham, in which she nodded a little. The silverware came out, Carola got a knife, spoon and fork, Natalia got a knife, spoon, and straw. Carola started laughing out loud and pointing. Natalia just sat there with a blank look on her face. You know Carola was laughing because Natalia did not get a fork. Then the food started coming out. Natalia received her bowl of fruit. Carola received her scrambled eggs and turkey ham, and I don't know how she did it, I don't know how to explain it fully. I will say this, she turned on the tears so strong she had three streams flowing from each eye. One on each corner and one right down the middle, and the balling out loud, so loud the other people there along with the waitress were all staring at us like we just beat the hell out of her. She put on such a show it was totally unbelievably to me. She was crying so hard and hanging on the back of her chair that Faby almost had another attack right there in the restaurant. Faby started speaking English to Carola, but after a few minutes, Faby was very desperate and started rattling off trying to figure out what was the matter with Carola. Carola said nothing, just was balling so hard she had tears flowing like water out of a faucet from her eyes. Faby in desperation told the waitress to get a bowl of fruit for Carola. As soon as it got there, Carola stopped crying, tears stopped flowing and she acted as if nothing at all happened. Faby's chest was pounding, I was afraid she was going to have an attack right there. As for Carola, she does not care. She keeps wishing for Faby to die so she can take all of Faby's things. I don't know what to do say or think Faby keeps telling me that Carola is trying to get me to yell at her in public to make me look bad in front of every one, and of course make her look like the abused child. I have not said one word to her after that. I may not speak to her for a while. She really tried to make her mother have a heart attack in that restaurant today. She tried saying "good night" to me a little while ago, I just stared at this screen. Where ever we go, please be ready for Carola. "JUST CLAP AND LAUGH" don't let her get to you. I'll hold Faby while the rest of us cheers Carola on in her little fantasy . . .

Sun Mar 4, 2007

little scare

Last night, carola did it again. Faby has medicine to take. At One A.M. was time for her pills. While I was up getting them, I heard voices. "uhhh, aaa, no kiddo" I told Faby, she immediately told me to check on the girls. Natalia's room was locked from the inside, no opening it. Carola's room was open. I looked in, didn't see her. Turned on the light, nope, she ain´t there. I told Faby. The look Faby gave me wasn't good, I said not to worry, I'll check. I went to Natalia's door and knocked. I do believe I woke up the second floor woman. Oh, well. Faby came out saying "what are you doing?" I told her the door is locked and the girl wasn't getting up. Well, I guess you know, they all woke up. I went back to my room. I heard Faby talking in English, Carola was answering in Spanish. Faby told me Carola said last night they heard noises, so she was comforting Natalia. Wrong. I did hear Faby yelling at Carola saying "you have your own rooms. You may have had to sleep together in the past because we had no choice, but we fought for this extra room so you can have you own rooms. You will sleep in your own bed." there was a lot more said than that. Carola does not ever say any thing. She has done this several times in the past. Once, there was some one in our living room. Some one who jumped down from the roof. when that person left, I check to see how the girls were, and Carola was missing, Faby was so scared she was in tears, and Natalia's door was locked and no one was answering. That is why this time I TRIED to wake up the Whole BUILDING! and if any one complains, I'll say, "noise, what noise?"

Sun Mar 11, 2007

Re-union

Last night, Faby was invited to a little reunion of her school class mates. It was suppose to start at 9pm. we got there around 10:30pm, and we were not the last ones to show. I am still trying to get use to the Peruvian ideas-but that too is another story. any how, Before we went to the reunion, we went to the Union Church, there was a movie being shown there, "The Ten Commandments" of course, I have seen it several times, but Faby and the girls have never seen it. Faby enjoyed it. The girls enjoyed the pillows on the floor and hot dogs at the intermission-its a three hour and thirty nine minute movie, and has two diskettes. On to the reunion, Faby sure did have fun there. yes, there was beer, and whiskey. a couple people even got drunk. How ever, these people are a little different than most, they be educated-highly educated and well mannered university graduates. Faby and I did drink a little, and no, we did not get drunk, we did not even try. the party at the house ended at 4:30 am, and was moved to a little restaurant, in which it continued until 6:30am. Faby and I got home around 7am. it was a long night. And we still went to church today. I added some pictures of Faby's class reunion, she may name them later, the pictures was taken with our little camera. A few of them took some pictures, and said they will e-mail to Faby later, so I may add more later for every one to enjoy. I am not real sure what time we got home today, I do know I woke up at 6pm, and its 7:15pm its taken me over an hour to write this. I am still waking up, Faby is still asleep

Sun Mar 11, 2007

Peruvian Ideas

Peruvian ideas are very different from the ideas that I grew up with. You tell a Peruvian one time, they show up at least an hour and a half later. You tell a Peruvian a better and easier way to do some thing, they scream at you about how you think you are better then they are, and continue to do things the hard way. Ya, well, I have come to the conclusion there are two kinds of Peruvians, Proud Peruvians, which Faby is, she likes new ideas, most of the time any way, so, please don't force her, and Real Peruvians, like Carola. Faby sure is scared Carola will some how mess up the meeting at the embassy just so she can hurt Faby. That is another Peruvian idea, to hurt others as much as possible to get what you want. I have not spoken to Carola ever since the restaurant incident. I am sorry, I just can not get over how she turned on the water like that. It was almost as if she tried to give Faby a heart attack right there in the restaurant, and when a bowl of fruit came for her, she did not say thank you, nope, it was as if we were her personal servants and we have to do her will at all times with out question, or hesitation, or there will be consequences. I can not go on. it looks like to me as if I am crying over things I can not change right now, I just read it my self. I'll see every one on chat tonight, or at least those who show up

Tue Mar 13, 2007

Rights

Faby keeps telling me that women have no rights here. In fact, congress, Peru congress has stated and passed a law saying a woman's word means nothing, be happy you can still vote. This is what Faby has told me. Apparently no one told our dear sweet aunt next door. The house on the corner was sold. Dear sweet aunt had made sure the inspectors were there. She sure does love a fight. Any way, the building was condemned. The new owners stated they don't care to live in it any way, they want to destroy it and build apartments. And the fight was on. Aunt says you'll be working early in the morning and late at night, I am an old woman and needs her rest. They came up with a plan of work hours, so not to disturb her while she was sleeping. That did not work. Then she asks what kind of people will be working there, rob guys, killers, or lots of other criminals. Again, she states she is an old defenseless woman. She is home alone most of the time. She is worried that one of the workers will steal some thing or hurt her in some way. So, she has stopped construction before it even started. Funny thing. She worked so hard to get it condemned, then she worked even harder to stop the new owners from destroying it and building a better building. The building in question, is on the corner of the street, and is attached to Faby's fathers house. The aunts house is behind Faby's fathers house. I do believe I told every one, dear sweet aunt already had Faby's fathers house condemned. Is every one getting a picture of Peruvian ideas and how mind boggling they are? They will do their best to get some thing changed, but when the change comes, they do every thing they can to stop the change. Personally, I don't get it.

Thu Mar 15, 2007

a little about Mama Chella

I for get if I wrote about her. I looked and could not find any thing. any way, she has one son and one daughter. both of which have degrees. the son, Carlos, is a director of a school. he went so far as to be on the government board of directors of education. he took a step down to be in charge of a school close to his mother. the daughter, Charo, is another story, all Peruvian type story. Charos' son is Lucho. To hear him talk sure is some thing according to Faby. she says we need a tape recorder. He told her stories that were some thing else. one was, Mama Chella bought a small microwave. Carlos bought her a bigger one. he tried talking her in to using the big one and getting rid of the little one. she said the little one is hers, and she will use it until it don't work any more. so, one day, he cut a few wires inside the little microwave. he then told mama that it don't work, she tried it and sure enough, it didn't, so she threw it out. he then repaired the wires and sold it. he had many little stories like that. another one was just before we left Tacna, mama had a motor cycle. ya, had. he told Faby he was going to sell it to get a bus ticket to Lima. Faby told Carlos what Lucho planned to do. guess it didn't work. First thing Lucho said when he got here was he sold the motor cycle. not surprising. Lucho tried to sell a plot of land that Carlos owned. Carlos bought the land through a school loan. when Lucho tried to sell it, the government education board called Carlos asking why he wanted to sell so soon after buying and still owning so much on it. Carlos was not happy. Carlos still has his land, the board would not allow the sale. Lucho was just here tonight, well, after this posts, it will be last night. any way, Carola tried putting on show for him. Faby told both the girls to wash dishes. they ignored her. she told them several times, they refused to obey. when dinner was ready, Faby told them both to go strait to bed. oh how they put on a show. mostly carola. trying to make Lucho believe she is so mistreated. Natalia straitened up a bit, convinced mama that she would be good, and get the sink cleaned up. as for carola, she was throwing things around in her room and rattling off real good. I was ready to throw a bucket of water on her. Faby stopped me, and sent Lucho in to talk with her. Faby said while she was laughing, "its the pan talking to the oven." I am sure there is a better saying, I can not think of it right now, its after midnight here. as for Charo, she said she will do her best to move to Tacna, and move in with mama. she will have her mother declared incompetent, so she can take over the home, then she will force Carlos to provide for her and her daughter and granddaughter to boot. as for what brought this on? was this, Mama Chella bought a house here in Lima. Charo took over the house. mama told Charo if she wants it, she has to pay all the bills. Charo refuses to pay the bills. right now she is with out power and water, plus she owes so much back taxes the city is planning on throwing her, her daughter and granddaughter out. as in other words, they are almost in the street and are desperate. you have any idea what mama said? "THEY COME HERE, I'LL BARRICADE THE DOOR!" Faby talked with mama Chella last week for a few minutes. and if your wondering, Charos daughter is not married. she changes boy friends regularly

Fri Mar 16, 2007

The Girls

To start out Carola's teacher yelled at us. In front of all the other parents. Carola's teacher had a parent teacher meeting today. and she was screaming mad at every one. Faby was translating to me. She said she has twenty kids, and nineteen of them are failures. The second highest score in the class was an eleven. She was asking what was she doing here with only one student. She was not happy, and demanding that every one buy the books for their kids education. the highest score any kid can get is 20, the highest score in the class was 19. Can any one give a guess as to who the kid with the 19 was? At first, after two days of school, she told Faby that we really need to buy the books because Carola was so slow. saying that Carola was never going to do very well in her class with out the books. Today was a little different. After all the other parents left, she told us that the books would only turn that 19 in to a 20. she also said that if Carola keeps up her good work, she would see to it that Carola gets a diploma this year, along with a medal and her picture and an inscription on the school wall of honor. about Natalia, she is number one in her class, I mean to say she gets 20's on her tests. in fact she was so good last year, that this year she was named school police. Faby tells me that means she walks around with the Flag crew at the start of the school week day. well, there are two starts, one in the morning and one in the afternoon, and she is in the afternoon time. that honor also comes with other advantages, like being first in the line, and have a sharper looking uniform. only one problem, they have practices on Saturdays at 8am, we usually don't start moving until after 10am

Fri Mar 16, 2007

Question

How do you praise some one who does not care? Plus the fact she is always doing things to upset you. She even went as far as to tell us, Faby and me, that she wants to get kid napped, and purposely stayed several blocks behind us in a town that was vary dangerous for the "white" looking little girls. And to please her is so difficult, she will go so far as to try to give her mother a hart attack in public places, while her mother is trying to please her. Today, while we were tilling her what her teacher told us, about how good she was, all she said was "I DON'T CARE!" in English so I could understand. I really don't know what to do. I have a real smart child here, I don't want to discourage her, but I really don't know how to encourage her. at least natilia cares. Natalia works so very hard, she is number one in her class, strait A student. but Carola is a strait A student, the difference is, Carola don't care. so, the question is, How do you say, "you did good" with out upsetting her? and possibly encourage her to be a better person in the process?

Sat Mar 17, 2007

School Police

What a bummer that turned out to be. The P.T.A. president was there. First thing she said was that Natalia has to have the complete school uniform. that in it self is one hundred soles. Plus, she needs to have a name tag, a plastic pin on flag of Peru, and a plastic pin on school patch, and the ropes that go on the shoulder. yes that costs extra. the girls have uniforms. only one problem, they are the government uniforms for the government school system. that school is a government school. but the P.T.A. decided the school needs their own uniform, its slightly different. Then the president went on to say that we might as well get carola a uniform, because it would not look right if only one of our girls had the uniform. Nice People. we got hit with a two hundred soles bill right off the bat. we are still arguing over the books they are trying to get us to buy, that is going to run almost four hundred soles it self. right now the exchange is about 3.15 soles to the 1.00 dollar. Faby and I were upset at first when we found out that Carola was beat out of being school police by one girl who got the 11 in her class. you see, each class chooses the best and smartest kid for the job. Carola is one of the smartest students in the school. after we found out what the bill was, we were not sure what to say. Natalia really wants to be school police, but there is no way we can afford it. As for Carola, well, you already know, she does not care. Faby and I are more worried about the process and leaving as soon as we get the approval.

Sat Mar 17, 2007

Land lords brother this sure was a funny one. we had our laundry lady living here for a month. just before we left, Faby intruded her as her cousin to the land lords brother. that was a good one. but what was real funny, was when Lucho came over. Lucho looks black, and Faby was telling me the land lords brother is racists Faby was telling me he don't like the black people at all. Lucho looks black, big nose, big lips, very low voice, only he is a little darker than Faby, is is not real dark. but Faby introduced him to the land lords brother by saying, "this is my brother" poor guy, his eyes got big, he was holding a set of phone books the phone company sent to

Faby and me. he looked at me, handed the phone books to me and said by and then ran. I told Faby its not nice to mess with people like that. she just looked at me. ya, I guess I should listen to my self. oh, well, it is fun though.

Fri Mar 23, 2007

Can't Believe Carola

To start out with, Titi, one of Faby's friends, whom she grew up with, lives in Miami, Florida. She speaks no English, only Spanish, and is a T.V. star on the Spanish channel. Titis' mother is sick, so she came back to Lima Peru. One of the directors, of plays, called Titi begging her to act on stage for him. Titi said only if Carola acts with her. Saying she has her Florida people with her to document the event. Her producers, writers, and photographers-picture takers, along with some news people—T.V. and News Papers. As in other words, she would have opened the door for Carola in the United States Television-Spanish channel. And carola threw her nose up at it. I wonder how many people would love a chance like that. Today, Faby talked with Carola's teacher. that sure was some thing. the teacher says carola is bright, intelligent, but is also very slow and refuses to finish her work. Mostly her home work. She has the highest grade in the class, but refuses to do her daily assignments. The teacher says, she would love to put Carola on the honor role, but the way carola is, the teacher says she can't. Nice ain't it. Carola didn't say a word while in school, but when we left, she turned on the water, just rattling off like mad. Faby started speaking in English, then in Spanish, and oh how the show went for a few minutes. Carola rattling and crying out loud, Faby rattling off. after a few minutes, Faby switched to English, saying how her mother made her stay up till three am doing her home work. and if a teacher asked a student a question, if the student got the wrong answer, the teacher would grab the student by the hair and drag the student around the class room screaming "why are you answering with stupidities, I am teaching, you need to be learning" things like that. What did carola do, she took off like a shot, didn't want to hear it in English. she would fight in Spanish, but to hear in English, she gets huffy and puffy and leaves. from what I caught was carola was saying she did not have any time to do any home work. I interrupted saying, "you have time to beat you sister, and be in you sisters room messing it up" and no, carola didn't like that. part of the reason she took off like a shot. I guess if probably should not have said that. oh, well. Still, you would not believe the opportunities Carola has and she refuses them.

Tue Mar 27, 2007

Banana Pie

Last night, I wined and cried a little bit. Faby got some bananas and told me as soon as we got home, half each to the girls. Waaaaaaaa!

Every time we would get bananas, the girls would eat them up before we got home. Any time I would say to try to save any for later, I would just get dirty looks from them. all three. last night I started crying. I told Faby I wanted banana shake and banana pie. so, last night, I did get the shake, but also last night the girls were in the kitchen, so I really didn't expect to much. By noon today, I finally ate, Faby surprised me with Banana Pie. It was soooo very gooood. Two kinds of bananas, a little bitty one about as long as you finger, and a great big one, that really has to be cooked, or it can hurt you. It was really tasty. sorry about the pictures, the pie only lasted for two shots, and I forgot how close I was with the little camera. But I think you can still get a good idea what it looked like.

Thu Mar 29, 2007

Light poll

A missing light poll. Faby has told me, if the city pays enough, the ones who stole it, will sell it back to the city. Most of the time, the light polls are cut up and sold by the kilo. They do leave the base intact, so the city can put up another one. The law here sure is different than back in the states.

Fri Apr 6, 2007

A Messianic Passover Haggadah

That is the title any way. The first one I ever went to. it was a Christen Passover celebration dinner. I had always thought the Passover was some thing only certain people did, you know the ones that are always knocking on your door-J.W., or the Jews. It was really interesting. The pastor of the church we attend, asked Faby to help set up every thing, because Faby has shown talent in arranging things to look good. Faby thought the pastor was testing her. She spent the whole week studying every thing she could find, even talking to the leader of the Messianic church her in Peru. She got pictures, instructions, and a mind full of knowledge of another religion.

Pastor told Faby, when we arrived, that he only wanted Faby to help his wife to set up the tables, because Faby is very neat. They both like Faby and they both like the way Faby does things. I told pastor that Faby studied so hard all week that it gave me a head ache. he just laughed. still don't know where the rabbit came from, but the egg now fits. the bread for the last supper fits in as well. instead of washing of feet, its washing of hands during this service. what I am getting at, is when Jesus was performing the last supper, he was also performing the Passover service as well. looks to me like a lot of churches have for gotten the whole service, and just remembered the very last one.

What I would challenge every one to do, or at least those who go to church is, ask your pastor about it. I would like a little more feed back on this one. and of course the whole traditional service did not happen, because there is no more sacrificial lamb, and that was because of Jesus. And I still want to know where that rodent, the rabbit comes in? the lamb is a use to be, the egg now fits in.

I'm tired and rambling.

Faby had a real good time. she met up with a few more Peruvians, all including her, are about to gang up on one Peruvian who hates being Peruvian and tries to chase all Peruvians out of the church. That one is the English teacher for the church school, and does not speak very good English. when Faby asked him, in front of me, if he was Peruvian, he said "no no no no, I am not Peruvian, I am Christian." that guy has tried to chase Faby out of the church several times, and has chased a lot of Peruvians who were married to foreigners out of the church. This guy is not nice. when he came in to the kitchen, Faby and the pastors wife were preparing the dishes, and talking in Spanish. they stopped talking when he came in, he and the rest of us all said "hi" and shook hands, after words, Faby and the pastors wife continued rattling off in Spanish. he put on a scowl and marched out. a little while later, she found one Peruvian who could talk the native language, I ain't going to even try to spell it, any way, her an him were rattling off real good in the native language and that one with the scowl walked in for some reason, realized what was going on and got real mad and marched right out again. with me there, he does not say any thing, its when I am not around Faby that he attacks. I also heard a couple other Peruvians saying the same thing. when their spouse is not around, he attacks. sounded like to me that Faby and them are planning their own attack. granted all I heard was a whole lot of rattling, but at the end of it, just before we left, Faby said in English, "see you all on Sunday." and they replied the same in English so I could understand.

Fri Apr 6, 2007

Dove

The girls and I were in here doing their home work and watching TV with me, and Faby was out running an arron. I heard some ruffling going on. I looked out side my door, and there was a dove out there throwing garbage every where. I told the bird to stop it. It just looked at me, and i continued watching TV. a few minutes later, it started again. I looked out and yelled "stop throwing garbage every where" the bird stopped and looked at me. so your probably wondering why I didn't chase it off, because it comes back as soon as you turn your back, so why waist your energy. so, I started watching TV again. a few minutes later, the bird was really starting to make a mess, so this time when I yelled at the bird I added, "if you don't stop, I'll start throwing things at you" this time when it stopped and looked at me, it turned its head to one side, then the other, then hopped on another bag of garbage and started pulling peaces out of it and tossing it across the living room. when Faby returned, I told her what happened, she shook her head and asked me why I didn't run off the bird, I told her because it just comes back . . . I miss my gun.

Mon Apr 9, 2007

Opportunities

Lets see, she, Carola, has had a countless number of minor opportunities, but as for the calls for major ones, that is a different number. Carola was called to be an on line tour guide for Peru. That would have taken at least a year, if not longer to produce. It would have been in Spanish of course, targeting all Spanish speaking countries first, then the Spanish speaking regions of other countries. It would have been her face and antamated body, and her voice on screen. you would have had to buy a program to install so you could get hooked up to the main program of the tour guide. That would have been a world wide promotion. I don't think there is any thing else that would have come even close to this one. what did carola do? she was demanding the lights get changed, then demanding a drink of water, she had the staff running around doing every thing she commanded, until they got tired of her and told her to leave, they were not going to put up with her any more. Natalia was begging for a chance. they told Natalia, they were not looking for a brownie, but they also told natilia, don't waste their time. I had to take carola several rooms away, because she started screaming her head off. Carola hated the fact that natilia was getting a chance at her spot. nearing the end of Natalia's casting, Faby found me and told carola they were willing to give her one more chance, if she does every thing correctly. when Carola's second chance came up, she turned her nose up at them.

A Second time, was for some kind of TV show. they called for carola again. Natalia was studding the casting very hard, this was after carola left for her test. one of the casting directors came out, and natilia was begging for a chance. the director told Natalia, they were not looking for a brownie, but, if she gave natilia a chance, natilia better not waist her time. Natalia agreed and understood. Carola came back out, Natalia left with one of the directors. there were two female casting directors. any way, carola was not happy. I could see that, as for the rest, it was all in Spanish. when natilia came out, she was bouncing, very happy. Faby did translate this time, saying the director was wishing Natalia has a lighter completion. and they would keep Natalia's casting on file just in case. of course you know, Carola was not happy.

A Third time, was a call just for Natalia, by the same people that had just called for Carola, the same two female directors met us. They said that one TV show was looking for a brownie, because the main star him self was a brownie. and he was about the same age as the girls. Carola was not happy and it showed. the casting directors told Carola she could do a casting as well, the show was looking for several kids. and Carola did do a casting right after Natalia. well, every one knows, Natalia got the part, and Carola didn't. carola was determined to ruin it for Natalia. sorry, it didn't work right away, Natalia did go in TV, but we missed it. lots of other people seen it.

Fourth and Fifth times, Faby and I did not even mention to carola. they were for commercials. both times we received at lest three phone calls, and Faby was telling them no, that Carola does not want act any more. Carola never knew about those times. how ever, just before I posted this poll, the other actor, the one Carola was suppose to act with in both commercials, came by to say "HI" to Faby. he is fifteen right now, he has been acting for ten years. he said twenty more years, and he can retire with full benefits, medical, dental, and retirement check to boot. as in other words, when he reaches 35 years old, he is fully retired with full benefits. he told Faby every time he gets a paying job, the first thing he does is go to the actors union and pay them, he wants to make sure he will be taken care of when he gets older. and he said he takes every opportunity he gets. he asked Faby how carola is, Faby said, Carola is right over there, he said, no, no, no, I just want to know how she is, I don't want to see her. you see, at the end of Carola's T.V. show, her long one several years ago, he was starting a new series, and wanted to invite Carola to his series. Carola threw her nose up at him in discuss. Faby could not believe it, and was saying how sorry she was. as a result, he never forgot how Carola treated him. as Faby and he talked, he told her about a couple commercials he was suppose to do recently. it was two different agencies, two different products. one major problem. he would have to work with Carola, he said to the production agencies "You can find another actor!" as he walked out the door. this kid has been acting sense he was five years old, and he is fifteen, he said he will not act with any one who might make him look bad or even feel bad. and then he said to Faby every time he gets a chance, he will say hi to her even try to find time to come by to visit for a few minutes from time to time. he said just before he left, "no disrespect to you, but the minute I see Carola, I leave with out notice."

Sixth time, an on stage director called for Carola to act in a new Cinderella play. now granted, this was not as big as being the on line Peruvian tour guide. But, it would get her started in acting again and put her name in the papers, and would get some promotional advertisement to boost her name again. this director is one of Faby's so called friends, his wife and Faby are close friends. Carola threw her nose up in the air saying "I don't want."

Seventh time, almost as big as Peruvian tour guide, Titi, a Peruvian woman, grew up with Faby, got her degree, went in to acting, went to Miami, Florida, became famous there, and the show she is on there shows here in Peru. She called Faby telling Faby she wants Carola to act with her. Faby and Titi were like the best of fiends growing up. Faby couldn't just say no, but Carola sure enough did. I don't know haw many times Titi called. but finally Faby was saying Carola don't want to. well, a week ago, it was Titi's birthday, and Faby had to go to the play, and carola was determined to ruin the day. you should have heard the fight. I hid, had my face in this poor screen playing solitary. Faby grabbed my belt, I heard it sing as it was going through the air a few times, and I heard it connect with something. both Faby and carola were screaming, natilia was in here watching TV. after a while, the shower came on, the shower lasted about one hour with both screaming and belt hitting some thing. Faby finally came out saying to me that Carola finally agreed to let her be with Titi on Titi's birthday. well, after a while longer, carola finally emerged, you wouldn't believe the shape the bathroom was in. I was surprised there wasn't standing water on the ceiling. just before we left, carola rattled of in Spanish, Faby took a deep breath, I grabbed Faby in a hug type hold and demanded what she said, Faby said "carola said ''when I am causing problems at the play, you don't say me anything, you have been wormed." I said, "not a problem, I am caring my camera, you have been wormed, and ill post every picture I take" the play went well, at the end, we were back stage, Titi and the director got a hold of Carola. then a couple of other actresses got in on it as well. Faby just stepped back, telling me they all know how carola really is, they can handle her. I don't know what all they told her, but what ever it was, its working. Carola went to a practice yesterday, and is going to one next week, and the week after that, she is going on stage. plus the fact she has been acting a little better after that. from what I seen, that night those people attacked carola, after a while, almost a half hour of them screaming at her, they had her raise her hand and recite some thing, in Spanish of course, Faby said she was just promising to be a good girl and do what mama says, sure she said only that, it seemed it was a long speech for only those words, any way, Carola has been acting better after it happened. personally, I thing Titi and the director were about to tear carola apart, do to the fact Titi had her Florida contacts there in the audience taking pictures and taking a video of the play, and they were expecting carola to be on stage with Titi, that would have not only boosted carola, but also boosted the director and his play, it would have done nothing for Titi, she has her spot, she was only wanting to help Carola and this director.

So, to answer the question, there were seven major opportunities, five that carola knew about, and two super major opportunities, that is why I didn't put in the number 2, I was afraid every one would only guess those two, how ever, I think I only mentioned the two commercials to my mom, so if you guessed 5, you were right with what you knew, I wrote about those. but the correct answer was seven, that is how many major opportunities carola has had sense I have been here in Peru.

Sun Apr 15, 2007

A few short stories

The Birds
Got more than just one dove that comes by and visits. There are at least four of them, and they do coo at me. Also have at least five pigeons a couple canaries and I don't know how many sparrows. Faby is amazed at how many birds come by. She has only had problems with one before I arrived.

House
The corner house, to our surprise, was bought by some one we know. And because of that, some one else is very upset at Faby. There is a woman, that Faby knows, she says she is very close to the Mayer's wife. Faby has complained about a few things at several times. This woman said the Mayer and his wife don't care. Guess who bought the house on the corner? Same person that tried to buy Faby's father house, and ran in to too many obstacles. The Mayer's wife. Faby was not overly excited, Faby yelled at her. The security guards just turned their backs, they all knew Faby. The Mayer's wife was very surprised, saying "she never told me any thing." A couple days ago, that other woman came up to Faby and screamed "The Mayer's wife screamed at me, and you know why!" then walked off. Faby was just laughing and told me "serves her right." I am guessing the street we live on is about to become "high society" and safer. Carola has been acting a little better here lately, next week providing she keeps doing ok, she will be going on stage again. Only one time she refused to eat. That

was on Monday, and she did not get to go to school, that was about the worst punishment you can do to her. She loves school. Other than that, she has not had Mommy screaming her head off at her this week. So, that is an improvement.

Tue May 1, 2007

Playing

Told mama that I would try to be on every night to say "HI" and all. then last night was another story. well, it started out a couple nights ago. that too was a different story as well. Then again, three nights ago was a good one as well, OK, I been a little busy? I was Playing in Yahoo answers. you would not believe some of the questions in there. one question was, "what would you do about all the illegal aliens?" at the end of my answer, I put "I just gave up and moved to Peru, South America. There is no difference between here and Texas. the language is the same,—Spanish—and the attitude is the same,—they all hate the North Americans—I tell my wife I feel right at home. She looks at me funny." I answered that one yesterday. Another one, "How to remove unwanted grout?" I put, "lots of water, soft brush, and a rag. its not easy, but it looks better then using lots of chemicals that will ruin you tile." other people were putting, "use this chemical or that." I got voted best answer. now I am rattling on about yahoo answers. sorry. last night was a birthday party of one of Faby's high school friends. our gift to him was one of the Cars Pins. other presents were beer, vodka, and other forms of whiskey. Faby and I do believe our gift will last a day or so longer. we didn't pitch in any money for the alcohol, then again, we don't drink enough to make hardly a dent in any of it. The girls spent the night with one of our church friends. they have five kids. so we were not too worried. they kept inviting us over, and didn't realize they meant for the girls to spend the night. that was a surprise, that is why Faby and I went to the party. its Peruvian labor day weekend here, no school until Wednesday. we were over there Sunday, they invited us back Monday. it was because their kids wanted our kids to spend the day with them. it worked out, they are good people. The play Carola is in is going good. we invited the Mayer of Pueblo Libre, the director gave us invitation cards to hand out for a promotional thing. carola does not get paid very much at all. only a few soles each play. she has one every Saturday and Sunday at 4:pm. it lasts an hour. last weekend, which was basically a rehearsal, she received eight soles.

this weekend-a couple days ago, she received six soles. that is total for the two days. almost not worth it. but it is good for the experience. The other day, Carola was asking me to get her some hair clips. her bangs were hitting her eyes. I told Carola a hair dresser would be easier, you know, a little snip here and there. you should have seen the look on her face. she got so mad at me. I told Faby. Faby just laughed. Carola already asked Faby, and guess what Faby's answer was? every time carola tries to play Faby and I against each other, we some how wind up with the same answers and that just ain't fair for Carola.

Wed May 2, 2007

Caffeine

Its kind of funny how some people don't know what they believe, or even why they believe some thing, other than some one told them. This little story has two parts to it. A long time ago, when Faby and I had the sandwich cart. There were a few arguments, over coffee. Our neighbor, in business, was Seven Day Adventist, and most of the students of the church would eat lunch at her place. Faby would have coffee once every three of four days, just one cup. she likes it, but it does not do her very good. The students would see her having a cup and yell at her, "you can't drink coffee!" Faby would ask "why" they would say, "because Ellen White said so." Faby asked me why they are yelling at her. I told her to think about it. What is in coffee? Faby is very smart. Didn't take her long to figure out "caffeine" then I asked, "what are those students drinking at lunch" she smiled, saying "one liter, or two and a half liter of Inka Cola" Faby is not dumb. She looked it up on the Internet. her little one cup of coffee has much less caffeine than the same cup of Inka cola. then she thought they thought she was stupid, that made her very upset. I told her its not that they think your stupid, they might not know why they believe what they believe. then she smiled, she has some thing to fight back with. The last argument she had with them went like this, them "you can't drink coffee" Faby, "why?" them, "because Ellen white says so." Faby, "why does Ellen white say you can't drink coffee?" them, "because its bad for you." Faby, "why is coffee bad for you?" them, "because Ellen white says its bad for you." Faby, "when you can tell me why Ellen white says coffee is bad for you, then I will consider giving up coffee, until then," she raised her cup and said "cheers" couple days ago, part two, took me a while to catch on, you know I am slow at times. one of our church friends. She and her daughter came to our house. we had a bottle of Inka cola to offer. She said "no, caffeine is bad, very bad, I will not have it in my house. I don't let my kids have any of it." I mean she made a very big deal out of it. we went to her house, on the way, because she was inviting the girls to spend the night, we stopped at a store, her daughter wanted ice cream. she asked the daughter what flavor she wanted, the little girl was saying she wanted about half the freezer full, mama said, no only two flavors, no more. the girl picked out her two flavors. Faby came over and said, "you will not have any caffeine in your house, what is the ingredient in ice cream? as she was pointing to the container. both flavors read "caffeine" the poor woman was saying "ah, ah, well, its ice cream." Faby just smiled. The moral of the story, before you tell any one some thing, be sure you know what you are saying. There are some people out there with enough intelligence to look it up. Then what are you going to say?

Thu May 10, 2007

Tarma trip

To start out with. May 6, Sunday. Carola was not happy. The first night, the party started in the catholic church. we have pictures of the start of the party. Faby did find out what sugar cane alcohol-whiskey tastes like, along with other things. Faby and I were told we have one bed. There were too many people there. There was three beds in the room. So, we were squeezed up tight, I was against the wall, Faby next to me, Natalia against Faby, and Carola was crying. There was room for her on the bed, but instead, she curled up on the floor. One of the women there came in, showing the beds to other guests, and seen Carola on the floor and started screaming at Faby. Faby translated to me later what was said. the woman was saying "how is possible, how could you put your daughter on the floor." Faby was saying, "she did that her self, I told her to come to bed." that woman was just screaming at Faby, while picking up Carola and putting her in to one of the other beds. What a first night that was. Come morning, Monday the 7th. Carola had to use the restroom. Faby took her, when they got back, Faby was laughing. she told me when Carola seen there restroom, she started crying. Those people have no idea what a toilet is. we have pictures of their restroom. I thought it was funny. After breakfast, we were sardined in to buses to take us to the main catholic church in down town Tarma,

where we were was the very out skirts, a real country side. when I got on
the bus, I seen one seat, I grabbed it and grabbed Faby, putting her on my
lap. Faby was worried for the girls, we seen two guys, who were friends
with hector-the god father of the party and the Internet owner-which was
the very Internet where Faby was when we met five years ago, grabbed the
girls, and were doing what they could to protect them from the crowd.
the guy that grabbed Carola was a big shock to her. Carola said out loud,
Faby heard and told me, "I want to know nothing about you!" the guy said
out loud back "good, I want to know nothing about you!" Carola's mouth
dropped in a surprised look, like she was saying or thinking (how could
you say some thing like that?). after the bus ride, Faby was saying how
sorry she was for Carola's attitude, and he said not to worry, he had to raise
his little sister, and she was just like Carola. then he told us to have fun, he
will keep an eye on her. and he did, during the dancing part of the party
that day and night and the next day and night, on the 8th, he kept a real
close eye on Carola, and would tell Faby and me to have fun not to worry.
we do have pictures of that. Carola sat out of most of the dances. she did
get up a few times, but the look was the same. Carola is "high society." and
could not stand to be there. Carola tried to get Faby in to more trouble, but
it back fired with that guy. he messed up her plans. I got pictures, wished
I had more film, oh well. Come the 9th the party was over and the time
to go home came. before we caught the bus, Faby wanted to eat lunch, we
found a restaurant, I really had to go, it was difficult for me to use the out
house, I did use it, but it was difficult. the first place i go, right to the toilet,
(boy that felt goooooood) when I got to the table, Faby said, the food
here was way to expensive, so she just ordered some egg sandwiches. there
was another place she seen where we could get combos for less then one
plate in there. combo was three plates versus one. I told Faby I was good
with the sandwich, but I guess she did not believe me. because over there
we went. what did carola do? give a wild guess. we ordered two combos.
first plate was the appetizer, noodles with some sauce and lettuce. I ate
most of the noodles, Faby had some noodles and lettuce, natilia had some
lettuce, Carola didn't even look at any of it. second was the soup. Faby
asked the girls if they wanted soup. Natalia said yes. carola started crying.
the restaurant was a big one, and about half full. the people in there started
looking. Faby put the bowl of soup in front of Carola, and she shook her
head almost to screaming saying "no!" and was really crying loud. I took
the bowl and started eating. Carola started rattling off, and I said, "rattle
rattle rattle, is that all you can do? I don't thing any one will believe you?

I did notice by then no one was looking. Faby looked around and said to Carola in English "no one believes you. you are putting on a show for nothing. look around." that really made Carola mad. Faby's plate came out. she asked Carola if she wanted it, it was rice and beans with a fried egg. Carola did not stop crying, I told Faby not to force her, just eat your lunch, no one in here believes Carola, they seen you put the soup in front of her. I was about half way done with my soup when my plate come out, spaghetti with chicken. Carola had not stopped crying yet. Faby asked her if she wanted that plate. I said if she is not eating it by the time I finish, then I will eat it. Faby put the plate in front of Carola saying "you better eat, he is serious." she did the (humph, with the head snapping thing) I said I don't care, I will eat that too when I finish this. when I was almost finished she did start eating. that girl does not miss any opportunity to get Faby or me in to trouble. at least this time the people there noticed, even the workers, what was going on and did not pay any attention to Carola. there was one more thing that happened. RAIN! I asked Natalia if she ever seen rain before. she said not like this. it does not do this in Lima. of course, Carola was not speaking to me, and Faby could not believe how much was coming down. that happened at night. it was cold at night and rainy. during the day it was hot and sunny. I mean they have the four seasons in a twenty four hour period. not only that, but this is the first time we were offered a free peace of land with the promise of help in building a house. other places, like were we got married, Faby's brother Gustavo, he offered to let us use his house. in Tacna, we were welcome in some ones home-mama Chella, and a couple of places offered us jobs with the promise of helping us buy an apt. this is the first place where we were offered a peace of land to call our own. and the people said they would help us build a home as well. I have pictures of a mud house built in 1873, and its still standing! I will be adding them shortly, I have to eat breakfast now. took those pictures with the little camera, the others will be added when the film gets developed.

Sat May 12, 2007

Happy Mothers Day

Today was some thing. The Mayer Rafael, came by and invited Faby to the Mothers Day Party he was throwing. it started at five pm. We showed up. We ran in to one of the women in Rafael's party. she asked Faby why she does not come to the ferias any more. Faby told her we can not afford the forty soles a day. that woman, who is very hard to please, Faby says she is live vinegar, almost nothing is good to her. she said, "No, you helps us win. you were there with us from the beginning. You will not pay any thing, I will have a talk with the one in charge of the ferias and get this settled." we will see. the people that were handing out the tickets were not being very nice. They came by Faby three times, looked at her and turned around and went the other way. she was not very happy, but she did not fight. finally one gave her a ticket and said only one raffle ticket and one bingo ticket per woman. We walked around. it was a Feria type party. lots of things being sold, we got a few refer. magnets. looked at all the gifts. Mostly chocolates were there. Only One Big Gift. the Stove. She just looked at it like she did ever time we went shopping. those things are so expensive. it was six o clock and was getting cold, so we went home to get coats. An hour later, we were back. they already started the drawing for the raffle. so close so many time. Faby just took a deep breath and said "I will win the big one" after a lot of music and people dancing, and us eating a few hot dogs on sticks-chicken dogs. the Bingo game started. After we got five across the top, I raised my arm, Faby said, "no, its a wipe out, total number on the card has to be called." OK, we kept going. we had one number left. I—22. and some one yelled "BINGO" and was running fast. the announcer was calling off the numbers. OOOPPPSS, one number off. she handed in the wrong card. she tried to give another one, sorry, she cheated, only one card per woman. she was ran off. the balls started tumbling as the announcer was chattering. finally the ball was grabbed. he held it high and said "I—22" FABY WAS RUNNING AND SCREAMING!!! the announcer was a man, there was a woman handling the numbers, she also had a microphone. she was saying "I can't believe it. Do You all know who this is? This woman (Faby) is one of the hardest workers around here. God must want you to have this. You deserve this." she took Faby's card and was reading off the numbers. during the reading, another woman came up screaming that she got bingo too. that was her prize. there was almost a fight, but Faby was well protected. the woman said the last number and screamed "WE HAVE A WINNER!" Faby was in tears, pictures were being taking all over the place. Thank you Heavenly Father above. this is one special gift for one special lady.

Sat May 12, 2007

another Mothers Day Party it happened again today. well, sort of. today while trying to get some business for Faby, I heard some loud speakers going.

Faby did have a couple nails to do. I went out check out what was all the commotion about. it was another mothers day party starting. nothing big, just some baskets of goodies. the way to get tickets was to buy some thing in one of the stores. tickets were free as long as you bought some thing. any way, I almost forced Faby to go. I was telling her its another party, lets go, see what happens. we got a little desert and got a few tickets to go with it. when the drawing started, the first ticket drawn, the woman was not there. some one ran in side to ask if the people had to be present or not to win. when that person came back out, the announcer said, no, you don't have to be present to win. OK, we will pass out tickets to all who is here, so at least we will have one person here that wins. one ticket per woman. and of course, there were women fighting for more tickets. after all the free tickets were passed out, the drawing started again. Faby was the first one to pick up a basket. she went so fast, I didn't even have time to get a picture. she was back sitting down before I could get my camera out, and she was looking sad. I did get a picture of her sitting there holding the basket. then she told me why she did that. a couple women sitting behind her was saying "that's not fair. last night she won the stove, now tonight she gets a basket. she works in the other gallery, she does not even belong over here. get rid of her, send her away." amongst other things. well the announcers and a few other people were trying to tell her not to listen, those women were just jealous. last year Faby did not win any thing, and we went to several of those parties. I am happy for her that she won. we went back to the gallery where they let her paint nails, and those people were doing their best to cheer her up. she was telling them what happened. And I got a better picture of her basket. with some of the people who encourage her to paint nails there. I guess you could call them "friends?" well, they are good enough.

Tue May 29, 2007

Natalia did it again

Carola only missed one week of school, didn't take her long to catch up, one day all caught up. no problem she was not worried. Natalia missed two weeks of school. Yesterday, Monday, she did all her assignments for the past two weeks plus Mondays assignment and still had time to play at break. no it didn't take her two hours like the teacher thought, took her two and a half hours to do two weeks and one day of assignments. not only that, but she also participated in the class room activities to boot. I added a picture of what her prize was today. in the Stickers folder. Her teacher bought stickers to give to the best students for the best grades. ya, right. the teacher decided not to just hand them all to Natalia one at a time, so she just gave them all to her today. one girl in the class got upset. she was number two in the class, not close behind Natalia, but was passing. so, the teacher cut off the bottom row to give to her, and she still made a fuss, so Natalia offered her one more. That is why Natalia is missing four stickers.

Mon Jun 4, 2007

those Girls

Its just hard to believe how much hate those girls have for their mother. Faby was called to a casting for a movie last week. The casting was for today. I don't know what the movie was about. Faby received an e-mail to go to the casting. She would have, more than likely, gotten a part. I really thought she was going, until this morning when I asked what time she was leaving. Faby said no, she could not, the girls need her here. The girls have tests they have to do in school and since they can not go, she will not go. I now know what all the crying was yesterday and two days ago. Oh, how clever they are. If I had known, they would have received a bucket of water, over their heads. Those girls can not stand the idea of their mother being happy. One more tiny little thing. Natalia was making such a fuss over what her teacher was saying that Faby called Natalia's teacher this morning to find out just what was going on. Boy did Faby get an ear full. I guess the starvation thing was not working too well. Now we don't know how to dress them. The girls were telling their teachers that we were not letting them wear their coats. For the past two weeks we, Faby and I, have been almost screaming at them to wear their coats. Both girls teachers know each other and keep a close eye on them because of the hunger scare they gave them. Faby was in tears when she hung up the phone. Why am I writing this? because I don't know what else to do. I can not touch them, not here any way. Even so, Carola will make it look like I beat her. In public, she will start crying, and cowering away from me like I was about to hit her. It is unreal how they, yes, both of them act. I am not asking for opinions, I am really just keeping a record. Today, as I was walking those girls home, Carola was really putting on a show. So, I left her about five or six blocks behind me. May have not been very smart, but what else could I do? I was not going to be close to her while she was putting on her act.

Mon Jul 2, 2007

Package

Just got the package today that mama sent. One of the post office people was yelling at Faby. Faby was yelling right back. It went on for several minutes. Faby told me just after, when we sat down, that the guy was telling her not to ever make any more copies of the notices they send out. Faby was telling that guy that she was told in the past to make copies. He kept telling her its a waste of time and money and not to do it any more. I mentioned to Faby that one possible reason for that guy to be so insistent was because so many packages come up missing, and if there are no extra copies, they can loose the original and say there was no package. She told me she was making several more copies for the next package. I am guessing the package that mama sent was too small and didn't look like it held any thing worth stealing. Yes we did get it, but we had to pay storage fees. The package arrived on the 19th of June, we received the notice on the 28th of June. We went strait to the post office and they told us to come back on Monday, today, 2 July. They said it was not their fault for us to come in so late and we were lucky to even get the package because it has been in there for so long. Thank you for the Fudge :) that sure is good ;) I don't know if the girls even like it. Never said any thing. Oh, well. I did give them a peace. They even turn their noses up at Faby's cooking. And she is a Very Good Cook. She has those linties down perfect. One day last week, she made a big pot of it, and the girls barley touched it. There was one bowl not even half eaten in the fridge. The other one, just over half eaten still on the table. I didn't get it, well, actually I did, sorta :). I got yelled at. Faby told me she made enough for lunch, dinner, and lunch again the next day. Hmm, the girls ate spaghetti that night. Boy those things sure were good. I still don't understand those two girls.

Thu Jul 5, 2007

Package

A thank you note to Charce the package arrived yesterday, sorta. we got it today. the notice stated it arrived on the 27th of June, but it went to the wrong city. No, you addressed it correctly, but some one in the post office sent it to the wrong place. They were going to charge is late fees—storage fees, but this time Faby was fighting mad! They were happy to get her out of there, no charge this time :) and Thank YOU for the Chocolate ;)

Sat Jul 14, 2007

Driving?

I sure am glad I did not get an international drivers license. If I had, I would have been in so much trouble. You all know or heard the joke "any stop sign out lined in white is optional", they take it seriously here, or maybe they can't read. Red light? What's that? and by all means, if some one steps in front of you "DON'T STOP!" Step on the gas! If a cop is following you with the lights flashing, don't pull over, if you do, just start forking out the doe. If you run, they call in reinforcements, just continue on your way, they will get tired of trying to spook you and follow some one else. I just seen some thing a few days ago, wasn't right at all. Some one on a bicycle got ran over, the bike rider was OK, just shaken up a bit, the bike was mangled, and the front tire of the car was flat. The person driving the car, ran a stop sign, and ran over a kid riding a bike crossing the street in the safety zone of the cross walk. Get this, its the kids fault for being in front of the car and the kids parents have to buy a new tire for the car. The law here is some thing. Say the tire costs 30 dollars, which in fact it does cost about that here, new. If the kids parents don't buy a new tire with in 30 days, the price of the new tire is added again, making it now 60 dollars. They now have 30 days to pay the owner of the car 60 dollars, if in 30 days the full 60 is not paid, another 30 dollars is added. Nice law here ain't it? I have very very rarely seen any one stop at a stop sign, and I have seen lots of people run red lights. When the light turns green, "Wait a minute, look both ways then proceed" if you just punch the gas pedal when the light turns green, your going to get hit, then again, if you don't go fast enough at the moment the light turns green, you could get pushed from behind. Yep, seen that too, and a few times ridding in a buss, the buss got hit from behind.

Wed Aug 22, 2007

Earth Quake???

I don't know if Mama or Connie remember, but, when I was 11 years old, Connie had a horse stabled in a place on Red Bluff rd, some where around

Pasadena, TX. I think it was. Well, the horse got loose and was playing with me, I was of course playing with her as well. there was a stallion that did not like me running around behind him. I was goofing off and the stallion kicked me three times in the right knee. he did not break my knee, but it swelled up bigger then my leg, and I had to walk with a Cain for about three weeks after. The day of the earth quake, my knee was not feeling too good all day. the buss ride was not helping, the quick turns and stops, and the people who kept kicking my foot-twisting the lower half of my leg, putting more pressure and pain on my knee was not helping one bit. We did not feel the initial hit of the earth quake because of the buss ride, thankfully he was as fast as he was or we would have been in lots of trouble. We did feel the after shock and hour later when we got off the buss. When we got off the buss, my knee was hurting so bad I could not even stand. I stepped off the buss and fell, not because the side walk was moving, but because I could not put any weight on my knee. I did not even know the earth quake was happening until I felt the shaking of the side walk under me, then I looked down the walk and seen it doing the "wave" like at the beach? rolling waves. I could not believe my eyes. that happened around 7:30pm, the initial quake happened 6:30pm. So, I think Faby miss understood, I did not trip, stumble, or fall because of what was going on. I fell because of my trick knee, it gave out again. I can't even blame it on Carola, she was sitting on my leg, but she sits on that leg a lot and nothing happens, some times my knee don't want to work.

Sun Sep 2, 2007

Peruvian ways

Weather I am "winning and crying", "chanting a curse", or "casting a spell", I don't know, don't care, you decide for your self. I just have been debating for days now on weather or not to say any thing, but this is just too disturbing. So, at the end of this note, you can decide what you will do in response. You can pray about it. You can say it three times. Or you just can read, laugh and forget about it . . . its in the past and there is really nothing much that can be done about it any way. I do believe this happened on Monday. How ever on Tuesday, Faby almost went to jail. That was not funny. On Monday, when having to pay fees for this process, this one bank, the National Bank of Peru, gave Faby a fake 20 soles bill. Come Tuesday, we were in the External Relations Building and they deal with a different bank, Interbank. Faby had to pay another fee there and tried paying with that 20 soles bill, which she had no idea was fake. To pass a fake bill to a Bank or any High class business is an automatic jail sentence. They were ready to arrest her on the spot. Thankfully, Faby had the receipts, and the papers we were doing on Monday, to prove what we were doing, and that the 20 came from that other bank . . . the receipt was with the money. They had Faby in tears. Finally the manager told Faby that he believes her, but she needs to be more careful in the future. They destroyed the bill and Faby had to pay with another bill . . . no, she did not get reimbursed. They said they have heard complaints about that bank, but there is nothing they can do about it because its the National Bank of Peru (I am sorry, I don't know the real name of it in Spanish, but that is the name translated in to English). That bank passes fake bills to people all the time. It was on the news, where there was a lot of people protesting, but bank security forced the people out of the building. The police did nothing but stand outside and force the people back. Why? Because its the Bank of Peru. I know, enough of the Winning and Crying, I am just upset because they almost sent Faby to jail. So with that in mind . . . . "May the person who passed the fake 20 to Faby have a hole burned in "his or her" pocket, and may the Whole chain of banks fall for what they do to their customers"

Mon Sep 10, 2007

Opportunities

As most of you know, Faby is working at a school. What most of you don't know is what kind of school it is. That I am not real sure of, how ever, this school is registered with a lot of Embassies, and with the Union Church of Lima, the church is also with lots of Embassies. The primary benefactor is the wife of an Ambassador, the Holland Ambassador. She is called the "Owner" of the school. She may vary well be, who knows? Any way, Faby got the job due to the fact that Ada, the wife of the Holland Ambassador, and Faby are pretty good friends at the Union Church. We have been going there for the past two years. Usually, the Peruvians that go there are always begging for money and talking about how bad of a situation they are in. Not Faby, nope. Faby was doing lots to help out her and there. It took a while, but some of the people noticed that Faby was not acting like the usual Peruvians, and started asking her to do a few extra's, like the Passover dinner. Any way, some where between eight or ten months ago, some time last year, Faby seen a museum with a for hire sign visible for the tourists. The requirements included a knowledge of English, and at least a seven grade certificate in the university. Faby thinking she has finished the Ninth grade it would be easy to get the seven grade certificate. Well, her uncle said "NO" he would give her a third grade certificate, but first she had to start going back and start in the third grade, after a few weeks he would give her a test and if she passed the test, then she would get the third grade certificate. Of course, Faby was not happy. A few months later, Faby and Ada were becoming good friends in the Church. Talking "b.s." you know. Any way, during one of their B.S. sessions, Ada mentioned she has a school in a very remote area, about a three hour trip from the Church. Faby said she finished the ninth grade, but not sure if she could get the certificate. Ada told Faby to see if she could get a Seven Grade Certificate, and they would go from there. I am not going in to detail on that one, but to sum it up, Faby's uncle told her, she would never be a teacher, and he would do every thing he could to make her records disappear. She did get her Seven Grade Certificate. But, just after she got it, Ada said she got the replacement she needed, so, several more months passed, and Faby was just crushed, thinking her uncle was right, that she would never be a teacher. Well, the new pastor, his wife became the head of the children's church not too long ago, I think I wrote about that, and she asked Faby to be her aid. At first, Faby didn't know what to think, maybe they were making fun of her, or testing her to see what she would do. The first thing she said to me about it was this, "I will don't get paid any thing, but I get to teach the children's church next week" after words, she was wondering what was going on. Well, the first theme was the Noah's Ark, that lasted four or five Sundays, Faby thought it was over, until two weeks ago, when the pastors wife said they will have another theme to do, not sure what that one is yet. Any how, it was the day of Faby's first Sunday school class, I believe, when Ada came to Faby and asked if she could go to her school to sub for a week. But to call first because they might have found a sub, so not to make a wasted trip. We didn't call, we went. Thinking to show a face would be much better then a phone call :) and it was, she was put right to work. They are trying to make her the permanent English teacher. But, that is not likely to happen, because she does not have a degree. There are several people in the school who don't like Faby and want her out. Even though that school is registered in so many places, it is also a Peruvian school. It only teaches Peruvian kids. So, that means it also falls under the Peruvian government education system, which means teachers must have degrees. If they find out Faby is working full time as a permanent teacher with out a degree, they will force her out, by heavily fining the school until they comply. And of course if her uncle finds out, he would do every thing he can to get her removed. So, no, she is not wrote up as full time permanent teacher, its part time, temp, sub, some thing like that for now. But who knows how long that will last. Ada says till December, some of the other staff members are wanting to oust her sooner because she is not playing ball with them, (milking the kids for as much money as possible) is a major problem. Faby will not do it and some of the other staff members are very upset about it. Bringing me to the point of this story of "OPPORTUNITIES" We started out with a little restaurant, a small space with a sandwich cart. Some of the people thought it was a joke. But we made some very good food. So good that some of our competitors were stealing our cooking utensils, turn our back for a minute and things would disappear. Cheep things too, like our spaghetti scooper, spatula, serving spoon. Well, I guess they had a right to be upset with us, we made in one night around 80 soles once, usually between 30 and 60 soles, but that was during only a few hours at night, between 6pm and 9pm. It almost killed Faby. Her legs were swollen up so bad it wasn't funny, and she couldn't walk for about three days once. We decided the restaurant was not a good idea. We started selling icy pops and gelatin sticks, along with a few sandwiches at times. We found some very good tamales at a cheep price. I also found out Faby could make them just as good, but you really have to buy in large quantity to sell so cheep. One day I told Faby she should just relax and get her nails done professionally. After the session, Faby told me she could do a better job then that woman did on her nails. At first I thought she was kidding. But she kept insisting that she could do a better job, so, I said to her, "lets go to town and see what kind of things they have for this business." in the process, of going to town, Faby was telling me she could also paint faces. I am thinking "sure you can" well, we get some items for both, brushes mostly, real cheep, along with a few colors. And wouldn't you know it, the start of a small Feria. Rafael Santos for Mayer, his Feria. They said, "come and join" Faby was proving over and over how good she was. I mean the fact that her customers, the nail ones, were talking very good about her, and bringing in their friends. After the Feria was over, we found a gallery that let her set up in front of them. Kind of funny, the restaurant we had, we did not need a license, but the owner had to have one, so we worked under his, same in the gallery, the owners asked for our I.D.'s, saying it was for the business license. There was times at that gallery when Faby was busy all day. She had about 8 or 10 clients that followed her from the Feria, and has told her where ever she goes, they will follow her, as long as they all live in the same town, or area. Well, there was some problems at that gallery, number one was the video guy, who also owned the hair saloon. He hated any one else making any sales and did every thing he could to prevent any one from making any sales. He had the first stand and if a customer was not interested in a hair cut or video, he would chase them off. He and a couple others in that gallery would constantly tell the women looking for Faby that she is out of business. Some times they would do that on a daily bases. It was some thing. Well, Faby also has a "Cheese may" group there, you know "B.S." :), and the owner of the gallery is, or was, or some thing, any way, some times she would be part of the group. Well, enough of that one

On to the next :

Yesterday, while walking home, from the buss stop, after church. We seen a new gallery being built. It is so new, the stands in side don't have any doors yet. In fact, most of the windows are not in, they only have the roll down bay or garage door type things. We were only looking. The first stand will cost 150 dollars a month, plus a security deposit, so the first month would be around 300 dollars, yes dollars, not soles. But its on the main street of Pueblo Libre with a big window facing the street. From what we have seen, if the first stand does not impress the public, then the people in the back of the galleries don't do any business. the stands in the back cost 120 dollars a month, but are small and way out of site. And if some one at the front says, there is nothing in the back, then the people in the back are "S.O.L.." I am sure you get the picture. Faby said at first, no. I told her I just wanted to look. So, we went in, and were asking about it. They are not real sure when they will open, they are still working on it and letting people look. Well, it would be nice. I do believe as good as Faby is, she could no doubt make enough to pay the rent on the store, and maybe even pay the rent here, that combined with K.F.C. just might do real well. I was telling Faby this, because of what is going on at the school, and what some of the people might do to get her kicked out. Then she tells me, "what about this process?" Well, I say "its been going on for a year now, just the process it self, and every time we turn around, there is another paper we need to pay for and we are running out of ways to get the money, this might be a sign, so we don't always have to ask." she said, "maybe, we will see" The school and KFC don't pay very much, but they do pay some. enough for the buss tickets and some food, and also paid for some of the paper work for this process, which I wrote about the last time, when the national bank of Peru gave Faby a fake 20 soles bill which almost got Faby arrested by another bank because of another fee . . . . that was not funny. Faby told me not to say any thing. She said she does not want to ask for some thing, or make it look like she is asking for some thing that will wind up being a failure. I really don't see her failing. Working at that school is a very good thing, because it is registered in so many Embassies. But, also working for KFC, that is a U.S. based company, and she can transfer her employment to the U.S. with permission of course. One more thing that would look good at the U.S. Embassy is your own business, a profit making business would also look very good. Faby and I were talking about this, and again she just said "maybe, we will see what happens." I know, I have written a book this time, I wonder how many will read all of this one :) I just had to tell you what was going on, and not to scream at Faby, or say any thing, because then she will be screaming at me for opening my mouth.

Fri Sep 14, 2007

The Girls

This an interesting subject. They have not been in school most of the year so far, for various reasons. Mostly the paper work we have to do for this process. any way I got Natalia's report card, all "A's" even though she has not been there, her teacher would give her the assignments she missed and the tests, and guess what? She did every thing, and passed the tests the same day. Some times she was gone for weeks at a time. Carola, is a different story. Her teacher told her she was going to repeat the year. She missed too much school and there was no way she could pass the grade. Well, for this past week, carola was upset over hearing the news. Some how she convinced the teacher to give her some tests today. One test, she didn't think she would do very good on was the religion test. Its all catholic, and we are not catholic. Guess who got every question right on the test, only one kid in the class got all questions right on that test. One kid, little girl named Beth, one of Carola's friends, thought she would do very well, she was raised catholic, and knows all about the catholic church. She got a 14 or 16 on it. 20 is the highest you can get on the test. Carola was worried . . . she got the only 20 in the class on that test. Carola had a few more tests then the rest of the kids because she was attending for so long and missed a few. She passed all of them. Her teacher told her this, if she remains in school the rest of the year, she will do her best to get Carola put on the "Honor Board" a big plaque in the school that has the names of all the Strait "A" students. That was some good news for Carola. I am surprised that Natalia has not gotten on that "Honor Board" she was the first student in the second grade to receive an honorary diploma. The only one ever so far to receive one. Well, any way, both girls are happy about what they did and got today in school. Thought I would share it with every one

Mon Sep 17, 2007

a little funny

This happened last Friday, a few days ago. but first: Starbucks is a high society coffee shop. They tend to refuse to serve people from time to time. Some Starbucks have separate lines for different category of people, like 1. English, 2. Spanish, and 3. Peruvian. and if you don't fit the look, you could get kicked out. About a year ago, Faby and I were going to the Embassy, quite a bit. In fact, in one week alone, we went four times, Monday through Thursday. That was some thing. The only place we could sit down and relax was in Starbucks. (probably because of me) Faby has told me if I was not with her, they would have probably asked her to leave. Any way, on one of our trips, Faby lost her travel mug, (more then likely, my fault) and we were looking for another one. Some of those Starbucks mugs really cost a lot here, seen one for almost 200 dollars, yes dollars. One that Faby liked cost 35 dollars, only one problem, all plastic, thin plastic, but it fit her hand. The people in the Starbucks had gotten use to us coming in by then, we had been in that place about a dozen times by then. Yes, lots of Embassy trips. Most of them not fun. any way, One of the people there showed Faby a flier on some new mugs Starbucks is coming out with. Showing their anniversary special, limited time offer, and not every store was going to get them either, and those chosen to receive would get a limited supply. No more were ever to be made. We were only looking, average price for all these cups was around a hundred dollars. There was no prices on the fliers for the new cups. I do not remember if it was the Tuesday or Wednesday, any way, we went in, and they had been chosen to receive the special cups. They were just opening the box they had received, only about a dozen. That Thursday we went in, they were out. I do remember that. Those special limited cups, were made of the stainless steal and had Starbucks embedded on them, with a lid of course. The price was cheep enough, only 55 dollars. When they pulled it out, I was telling Faby to get it, that is not going to hurt us that much, just get it and enjoy it. She finally said OK and got it. and Yes, its a Needed item . . . she carries it with her to many places, and uses it. one woman, the director of the school she is teaching at, said "you can leave that cup in my office, nothing will happen to it." sure nothing will happen to it. Faby told her no, its going with her, she don't want to loose it, and the director said, "that old thing, you can find in any black market any where," and Faby interrupted her saying, "this is a Starbucks anniversary special cup, limited offer, only a few of the best customers got one of these, and as good as the Peruvians are at coping, they will not get this one right, you can look all you want, but you will not get my cup."

On to the best of the story:

Friday, a few days ago, Faby had a couple parties, and some time to spare in the middle. it was in an area where there was a Starbucks. She wanted to relax and went in. She told me there was the three different lines. She went to the English line and right away, the woman told her in Spanish, you have to go to the other end where the Peruvians are. Faby told her in English, "I want a cappuccino with milk" and I for get what else she always orders, in her coffee, any way, again the woman said, "you have to go to the last line way over there where you belong. Faby said, "that line does not have my order, I want this order" and repeated her order. The woman was getting irritated and repeating her self again, and Faby said, "wait a second" and pulled out her "STARBUCKS" mug. That woman's eyes opened wide, and she said in English being very polite this time "sorry senora, had I known you were at this level I would not have been so rude, your order will be ready in three minutes." And of course, she sat at the English section, and relaxed while she enjoyed her coffee. And no one bothered her with that cup in her possession. you know, when they seen her with that cup, they knew they made a mistake, only the best customers got one of those special cups. those cups did not last long. Faby told me its like a ticket to comfort, a better place, and best of all, its not that expensive to have a coffee, they just pick their customers. They have certain look and they want to keep their look.

Tue Sep 18, 2007

Peruvian Thinking

I don't get it. This morning was some thing. On the news. The Government here has put a stop to the free food going to the earth quake victims. Why? Because they are selling them "food packages" the total package cost 4 soles, which includes, two packages of cookies-50 cents each, one fruit juice, 1 soles, and one tuna can, 2 soles. Total cost is 4 soles. How much is the government charging the victims? 34 soles each package. UNBELIEVABLE? try this: a cheep house, manufactured house, four walls, floor, and roof, costs about 500 to 800 dollars. Depending on materials used. up to four bedroom could cost up to 1500 dollars. Each bedroom would cost 200 to 400 dollars. There was several Peruvian organizations building houses for these people for free, from donations of course. Plus a lot of out side organizations coming in to help. Last week, the Government put a stop to that, saying if these people want houses, they have to pay for them. Remember the prices I told you, I know Faby and I were checking. The Government is using the same houses, and the cheep one is 15,000, yes 15,000 dollars each, on up to 30,000 thousand dollars each, or more if you want more rooms. and if they refuse to pay, because they have no money, no way to make any money for what, a hundred miles? or so? so what, they can live with out. Same with the food. Does not matter if there is no businesses, no paying work of any kind, every one is homeless, nope, if they don't pay the 34 soles for the food package, they can go with out eating as well. Well, Faby is doing her best to get her self fired. She refuses to play ball. I mean play like the usual teachers. In other words, she refuses to "rip off the students" as much as possible. Faby was asking her students to get a dictionary. Just a cheep 8 or 10 soles dictionary. In the process, the school was making deals with the local book store. Each book sold the teacher gets 15 soles, the director gets 10 or 15 soles each as well. I for get, any way, Faby was saying "no" don't need any of your books, go away. They were trying to tell her their English books were the best, and for 100 soles, to 130 soles each, she would get 15 soles for each book sold. She chased them off. What did the school do? Had a meeting with out Faby. How did she know this? One of her students mothers came in pleading with Faby saying she did not have the 130 soles for the dictionary at this time, and please don't fail her child, she would get the dictionary as soon as she could. Faby almost blew a blood vessel. Faby was telling that woman, "I never gave that order! Don't pay for that book! If you get that book, I will refuse it! I will not teach out of that book!" oh, she was upset. She went on to say, "get a cheep 8 or 10 soles dictionary. my dictionary cost me 12 soles. It should not cost you any more than that. Don't pay any more. Those other books are no good!" You see, Peruvian thinking yet? The school talked Ada in to getting English books at the beginning of the year for the last English teacher. The cost was around 100 soles each. Ada bought the books, and with out Ada´s knowledge, the teacher got her commission. after that, she was selling the books to the kids for 80 soles each. If the kid could not afford the book, she rented the book for 20 soles, but the book could not be written in and had to be returned undamaged. When Faby found out about this, she blew a fuse. It was after that, when the Book store tried to get her to sell more books to her students. She was ready to fight.

Tue Sep 25, 2007

Just in

The second floor whore is making demands. Telling the land lord to order me to build a roof so her laundry don't get wet in the "so, called, rain" here" what would you do? I water tightened Carola's´ roof, the living room has no kind of roofing now . . . but then again, I was never using it any way, so why do I care? I don't. Carola is more important to me then that woman's clothes. its bad enough I don't get to use my living room, and she comes and goes like she owns the place. She don't clean the floor, I or Faby do that, and she is saying we never clean the floor . . . some thing else the land lord was saying to us, why we never clean our floor for her. remember the close line that got in my way :), he mentioned that to us as well, "what close line? last we looked, they are doing fine ;-)" he was telling us, she wanted to hire some one to come and work on it, and guess who will pay the bill? sorry, I ain´t paying for that "B..S.." as for the floor, she can clean it once in a while her self. Land Lord said he will move his china closet some time this week . . . sure he will. he has been saying that line for some time now . . . . how many months has it been? I lost count. its 10 pm here, late and time for bed.

Fri Sep 28, 2007

Faby

Faby its 6:30 am here, in the morning. Faby just took the bus about 30 minutes ago to her school. She is carrying the Big Back Pack. after school she is going to the Union Church. for the Women's retreat. I am asking to all, as soon as you see this, to say a prayer, or blessing, or what ever you believe in for "good luck" :) please? this is a dangerous place. What i did not tell you earlier, that has me worried, and I don't want any one to worry, that is why i am asking every one this favor, is this . . . Faby was attacked and robbed two days ago. the attack was light, she told me two guys grabbed her and tried to take her away from one of the buss stops, but luckily her bus arrived just in time and the ticked taker of the buss knew her and she was able to get away, how ever before she could get away, those guys took all her money, I mean every thing we had left, about fifty soles. with Gods grace, she did have a few items—pens—that we try to sell in her school bags, which she was able to sell for her buss tickets on the rest of the way to school and home again. Yes, Faby is firm believer in our Heavenly Father above. He does look after us. But a few more prayers, or Good Luck wishes won't hurt :) The other thing is this, The school director—Principle—is very jealous of Faby, taking Faby's ideas and making them like her own. also stopping Faby from doing things, for example, (Faby found an English course for teachers who know English but don't have the teaching degree in English. This course was a 6 hour course, once you prove you know the English language and pass the course, you get a teaching degree in English, but you have to have a contract for teaching in a good school before you can take the course.) What did this director do? told Faby, "come back tomorrow" over and over again. Until, the last day when she said, "I have no time for you right now" come to find out that woman took the course her self, knowing nothing about English, just to get the paper to show Ada, the Owner of the school, that she was interested in all sorts of things. "nice ain't it" When Faby told the director that she can not stay late Friday, she said to Faby, "you have to cook the chicken for the pulyada—the chicken sale the school puts on and forces all the teacher to buy for different things, and the teachers have to force the students to buy the tickets from them because the money comes out of their checks. Faby has to buy 10 tickets, but she refuses to sell to the students, so the director told Faby she has to stay until 5 pm for the sale and she has to cook the chicken. The director feels she should go on this retreat, and not Faby, even though she knows no English, and most of the women on this retreat know no Spanish. Still she feels she has more right to go and because she can't, she will try to make Faby miss this opportunity . . . so, once again, I am asking for prayers or wishes of good luck for Faby today on that matter. She has to be at the Union Church by no later then 4pm today, which means she has to leave the school by no later then 1pm today. She was invited by several women of the church to go, when she said we have no money, no way we can afford it, they said they will sponsor her, pay for the buss tickets, and room and meals, she only needs to bring some snacks and clothes, along with her self. I know she will have fun there. She has been going to that church for about three years now, and this is a real big step up for her, she has made some good friends there, and this is the first real nice thing they have done for her. In the past different people would ask her to help out in different things, like the thanks giving dinner last year, and the pass over supper celebration, just to name a couple, there have been several others. This time she was invited and sponsored to be part of the group, not a helper but to be part of the group. I am missing her already.

Fri Sep 28, 2007

After 10 pm yes, here its after 10 pm, same time as most of the U.S., I know, but still :) Thank you for your prayers and or thoughts and wishes. Faby called me said she was still at the school when it was 2pm. which meant she had 2 hours to make a 3 hour trip. I was worried for a while, wondering if she was going to make it or not. so far no calls, and she is not here. she did say she would try to find a way to go on line to let me know she is ok. on of the women said she would take her lap top, it has wireless internet connection. That school director is some thing else. most of the teachers and of course Ada the owner of the school want Faby to be permanent, but you know the problems. it just can't happen, but that director is so jealous, because Faby was chosen by Ada, she can not make Faby do any thing, like selling dogs on a stick, pulyada tickets, books, cakes, yes cakes and many other things she has going on. its just not right, Faby tries to leave, but the kids keep her coming back, she loves teaching so much, even though she is not getting hardly any thing for it. i do believe Faby told me the administrator, the one just over the director, gave the order that Faby did not have to buy any of those tickets, so, what did the director do? made Faby go class by class taking names of the students and putting the pulyada ticket number by the name of the student or an "x" by the ones who did not buy. well, the paper already had the names, Faby had to find all the kids, or she would get wrote up for insubordination, I think is the term in English, don't ask me what she said in Spanish, I already forgot :(sorry. a funny :) Natalia went with Faby yesterday to the school. both girls are out of school for vacations for a week. and in her class in Ada's school, the teacher gave a math test. do I have to tell you what Natalia scored? I mean really, if she misses one problem or question on a test, you can not punish her worse then she punishes her self. She was telling me she had problems with a few problems, but would not give up on them, finally figured them out, and of course, she received a 20. one other kid in that class got a 20, she said, also most of the kids got 18 and 19, very few, like 2 or 3 failed the test. nothing like her school where there is no competition for her. most of the time she is the only one passing the tests, in fact she is also the first one done. which tells me, even though Faby's school may be in the stone age, some what, they are trying to teach :) . . . but that is also a private school, the girls school is a public school . . . baby sitting place. the funny part was, the teacher told Natalia, that she does not have to take the test because she was not here for the lessons. Natalia was demanding the test. it surprised the teacher.

Mon Oct 1, 2007

Faby's trip first things first, The Cup . . . that unbelievable cup. sorry, not a good picture of it, took it this morning real quick before Faby left. it has become a ticket to comfort. with Faby holding it, it looks real big, but its about 700 mills, witch is smaller than one liter, but bigger then a half liter. Its not that big, but it sure has a BIG impact. I was wrong about my story before on how she got the cup, you know, I don't know Spanish, just catching a few words here and there, and guessing at the rest :) That cup, a collectors item, only a dozen came to Peru. Four Starbucks stores only received three of them. One of the stores was right across the street from the U.S. Embassy. What I seen was the cup coming out of the box, what I did not realize was it was the last one they had, and they chose Faby to show it to. Starbucks was given the Order to sell those cups to their Best clients. With all the trips to the U.S. Embassy, we went to that store quite a bit, and they did get to know us. Faby told me last night she got the last one that Starbucks had. I had to correct that mistake. Can you imagine the looks Faby received when she pulled out her cup in that retreat . . . eyes popping out, words like "how did you get that?, where did you find that? do you know that is a special anniversary limited time offer cup?" oh, ya, she was excepted right in once she pulled out her cup. here is the story on that one, with embassy workers . . . Faby said there was three of them at her table, from U.S and other countries as well, and the first thing they were talking about was their love for Coffee and showing off their Starbucks mugs, all plastic, real nice ones too, but plastic cups. well, it came to Faby's turn, and of course, the looks on their faces was "another Peruvian looking for money, we'll just humor her for a while" Faby said she loves coffee too, the reply was "sure you do" and she went on saying different types and her favorite, but it has to be made a certain way. and they are just nodding . . . . until she said, "and here is my cup" pulls it out . . . . eyes popping and mouths dropping . . . like I said, one was U.S. Embassy worker, looking for that cup and could not find one. They were expecting a long, drawn out sad story of how bad life was here and how desperate she is to get a visa to another country, any country, just to leave Peru, and what did Faby do? She slaps them silly with just a "and this is my cup." She was "IN" I do believe she told me that was the first group she was in. Well, Faby was having problems. Two of them to be exact . . . Two other Peruvian women managed to wine and cry and beg until finally they were allowed to go, of course they needed some one to pay for their trip. Faby was saying she could not go because we had no money, no way to afford it. Faby did not ask to go, three other women in the church stated they will sponsor her trip. Well, when the other Peruvian women seen Faby at the sign up table, they were hurt, and they were making a scene. and well, they were finally allowed to go. Well, what they did was complain about way too many things, both could not speak very good English at all, and one who is married to a South African (white South African) her English was so bad it was unreal, and he speaks no Spanish, only English . . . . I'll get back to that later, any how, Faby said they were showing a movie, and was about to make pop corn, well, the one married to the South African, "Vanessa" stated she was allergic to pop corn, and they were not allowed to make any because it would make her very sick. Faby was furious. But what could she say? They had to skip the popcorn. Not only that, but those two kept bothering the others, telling their sad stories on how bad life is here and how bad they need a visa to another county, and of course, asking for any thing mainly money, to help them out in their terrible situation. Are you getting the picture? There was about 30 or so women there, and only three Peruvians, most of the women were Embassy workers, or married to Embassy workers or married to Ambassadors, I think

Faby said two were married to Ambassadors, may have been three. well, most of the women there were looking at Faby saying, out loud or to them selves or thinking "another Peruvian just looking for money or a visa" that is what Faby was fighting and with the other two Peruvian women there, it was not easy with what they were doing. But Faby did not give up, and she did make some very good friends, and had a great time in the process. One of the women who sponsored Faby had a broom and was starting to clean, Faby right away stated she was here to help. That woman said, "no, you have done enough. Its time you relaxed. You have done wonders with my child. Changed him so much to the better, how could I ever repay you. You owe me nothing. My child use to never want to go to church, and was running wild all the time at home. Because of you, he is being have and wanting to go to Sunday school. Its time I served you." That was some thing. Faby could not believe what she just heard. There was a black woman there, that was very distant. Faby thought she came just to make a statement, (I am here and you can't move me) some thing like that. when she introduced her self, she said her name and said she works at the embassy, and sat down wrapped in a blanket with a stone cold face type stare. Didn't say what Embassy she worked at just worked at an Embassy. Well, as time went by, Faby wound up being sat next to this woman. Turns out she has a daughter that goes to Sunday school, one of Faby's kids. Just arrived two weeks ago. Faby was saying how great her daughter was in class, she just nodded, and said, she tries to raise her daughter right. This was a tough one for Faby. This woman didn't shake any hands, didn't hug any one, didn't even hardly speak to any one. What a challenge. She asked Faby who she was, and why she came to the retreat. Well, you know, how some blacks are, looking for racism. I am sorry for the way it may sound, but still, this one was. From what Faby told me, she was the only Black Woman there. And of course, Faby sitting next to her, Faby looked white, here is this story: OK, she asked Faby why she was at the retreat. Well, Faby says she is married to me, a North American, the woman nods, and says she is member of the Union Church and she teaches Sunday School. The woman says, "really, I was there last week with my daughter." Faby asked "how old is your daughter?" sorry, I for got, 8 or 10, some thing like that. and he name was Ashly. That was when Faby said "Ashly is your daughter, she is such a great child" and went on for a while. any way, on to the rest . . . the woman asked what Faby's plans were, does she plan on going to the U.S.? Faby says, "if it was just me, no, I would not go, but for my mother and father in law, I will try." she nods, Faby continues, "I have two jobs here, so I don't plan on living there very long, just want to visit for a couple month. Its because my husbands parents are getting old and they wish to meet me and my girls, their grand daughters before they die." The woman's head bowed, she took a deep breath and a couple minutes later regained her composer. Faby continued saying how much she loves Peru, and how much she does here, teaching, acting, the K.F.C. parties. Just threw that woman a serious curve ball. Come to find out, that woman is one of the people who has the last say in weather or not a Peruvian gets a visa. (there are a lot of people who have the last say in weather or not a Peruvian gets a visa in the U.S. Embassy, she was one of them, Faby did not know that right away.) Good thing, she found out later, when the woman came over to Faby and gave her a hug. Would not touch any one else, but have Faby a hug, and said "maybe we can share a coffee some time in the future" Faby believes she has a fifty percent chance in getting the visa with this woman, if she has the last appointment with her. Of course this woman already met the other two Peruvian women and was not impressed, and at first wanted nothing to do with Faby. As much as you might hate Peruvians, its hard to hate Faby once you meet her. During one of the fun time activities, Faby was making balloon flowers. just having fun. I mentioned this one on mIRC. any way, One woman, who was a U.S. Embassy worker, works in the Education department, and giving out donations to many different schools, Adasa the one Faby works at is one of the schools she donates to in the name of the United States Embassy. she collects money and decides who gets what. She may have some thing to do with Education Visa's, Faby was not clear on that. Any way, she wanted a butterfly balloon figure. Well, Faby is thinking she has never did a butterfly, how could she possible do this?, while blowing up the balloons, the woman asked Faby why such a small air pump? Faby says its all she could afford, when she gets enough money she will get a better one, and continued trying to make a butterfly. Well, Faby pulled it off and made one, a good one. That woman was going around showing off her butterfly, saying "Faby made it for me, look!" The woman did come back asking "how much would a good air pump cost?" Faby said "about 20 soles, but when I make enough money, I will get one, until then, I will have fun with this one." and continued making balloon figures, mostly flowers. when every one had one that wanted one and Faby was done, the one with the butterfly came back, bumped in to Faby saying "I need to talk to you" grabbed her arm and shoved a 20 soles bill in it. then said, "now you have the money, get your self a good air pump." Faby said, "I can't except this, I am doing this for the fun of, I don't want to get paid for this, some one else may need this more than I do.", and the woman stopped Faby saying, "look, I work at the U.S. Embassy, dealing with Embassy sponsored school. I am the one who collects the money for the donations, and I am the one who donates to these schools in the name of the United States Embassy. I hear people begging for money all the time, giving me all kinds of sad stories, some to the point I tell them to go cry on some one else's shoulders, you are getting me all wet. I don't give to just any one. I see you. I see how you work. I see how you are. You deserve this, now get your self a good air pump." Keep in mind, there are two other Peruvian women there, begging and pleading for money or visa, or any thing else you might throw their way. Faby was not asking for any thing. But she was making impressions on some of the people there, and making friends. She would say from time to time, "I am Peruvian" they came to the conclusion, 'nope, she was born in the wrong country' some told Faby that if they did not know any better, they would guess Faby was from some where in the South West part of the United States, like Arizona, maybe Texas, because of her ideas, attitude, and the way she talks. I may have taught her how to speak English, but I did not teach her how to act, or give her, her ideas, that was all her. When she told me this, I asked her, if she is finally understanding what it is to be an American, to be called an American. its not just a place to live, its our ideas, and you have the same, ideas. Its with in us all, and it can not be learned, you are or you are not. I think I said that right, any way, she was excepted. Even by the toughest one in the whole group. by the way, the school that Faby works at, may loose all their donations. for number one reason, trying to make Faby miss out on this retreat. That was just not right As well as a few other reasons, like the books that the director refuses to use, because she is making money with the book stores by forcing the kids to buy books they don't need. Oh, yes, thousands of books locked up and not used because there is more money in forcing the kids to buy new books from the book stores, the director and teachers get commissions for each book sold. Ada has bought books, several other embassies besides the U.S. Embassy has bought books amongst other things for the kids and the kids don't seem to get any thing but a bill for a new book at the book store. Faby will not lie, she was asked a direct question and gave a direct answer. by then, when this conversation was going on, Faby had proved at what level she was and was excepted in the group as part of the group. Faby was told by a lot of the women, mostly Embassy workers, to keep going to these little get to gathers', it will look better when she starts the Embassy appointment's, and if by chance, she might get her last appointment with some one she knows, and that could be a great big help. Yes, the Embassy workers were telling her this. Saying they tend to go easier with the Peruvians who they know, from special get to gethers like this, the Peruvians who are not constantly begging for some thing, that is. Also, some thing else she was told, that is this, it doesn't matter who fills out the sponsorship forms, the more the better, even if you don't qualify, fill them out because it shows you care and are willing to take a chance. That shows you really care. It goes on the files. it helps. Last thing Faby was told was this, if I leave, yes, me, if I leave, then Faby and the girls will not get a visa. For as long as I have been here, if I leave now, it might suggest we had a fight, and they will use that as an excuse to cancel the process. Saying Faby only married me for a visa. In fact the best thing if did was come here to live. That in it self is proof I love Faby, and staying for as long as I have builds the proof of love, and not marriage for a contract. They were telling her this, because she has proved she was part of their group. not just another Peruvian begging, but part of the group. any way, they told her there would be plenty of people at the Embassy saying that it would be best if I go back and get a job and sponsor her and the girls my self, and don't listen to them. why, its because they have been given the order to stop as many Peruvians as possible that want to go to the U.S. because of the problems with Peruvians in the U.S. most of the Peruvians in the U.S. married for contract. some were caught, and escaped, and are still there illegal. that is a big problem in it self. they are cutting down on the traffic.

Mon Oct 1, 2007

Carola well, Carola just threw a fit, for no good reason. She is always going in to Natalia's room, but got very upset when Natilia went in her room and expected me to punish Natalia, sorry, couldn't do that, I said if you don't want Natalia going in your room, then you have to stay out of her room. She stomped out crying her eyes out. So, I flooded the floor, I lost count how many mop buckets of water I threw on the floor, but her room was flooded, every thing on her floor was floating. there is about 2 inches of water covering her floor, no, this third floor is not even. Natalia's room is lower then Carola's. I did put a towel in front of her door before I started throwing water out. But that is no guarantee. Oh, Well, I thought by now, she would have learned that I will not put up with all this nonsense. But, I keep forgetting where I am. Peruvian way of thinking is very very different. I really flooded her room, but she better not start crying, or I will just start throwing more water out.

Tue Oct 2, 2007

Vanessa

I just remembered, I said I would talk about her later, and for got, oh, well. She is married to a South African. A White South African. He speaks real good English, but no Spanish at all, not a word. Last time i seen him, about three weeks ago, he said he still don't know any Spanish, only a few words like I do, nothing more. She goes to church every week, to beg for any kind of hand out any one will give her. He goes to church once a month, if he is lucky. His little story, from what I know is, He came from South Africa, selling every thing he had. He has no family there, that he is in contact with any way. When he got here he was loaded, lots of money. He and Vanessa opened up a chicken restaurant. Right away, her family, (such good Peruvians) showed up. Ate him and her right out of business. He came here six months after I came. I came in January, he came in June. her family broke him in about four months, took every thing he had. Then they kicked him out of his house, well the one he bought for Vanessa. She, being such a good Peruvian, got him a job, as night security guard, watching a street all night. Nice woman she is, he speaks no Spanish. Her idea is, and what she says, "he must provide me, no mater what." He makes about 400 soles a month, and she takes most of it leaving me with barley enough to pay the rent where he is staying. Why he does not leave? He says he has nothing to go back to in South Africa. He thought about taking Vanessa to the U.S. until he visited the U.S. embassy . . . . he thought his embassy was bad, that was sad. He thought about Australia, nope, well, he made some friends in New Zeland, and was in the process of making paper work for Vanessa to go, saying it was easier to go there then any were else. Last I heard any way, not sure what is going on now, I barley see him. He works 8 to 10 days a week 12 hours a day for just 400 soles a month. Faby asked me what I would have done if her family did to me what Vanessa's Family did to the South African, I am sorry, I for got his name. I reminded her of what I said when I first arrived and what I told her on line. that I was not going to deal with in-laws any more. if they come around I would drive them away one way or another. well, come to find out, I did not need to do any of that, she don't like her family more than I don't to begin with. And well, you know the story about her family. Vanessa tried begging money from us, saying "your husband is North American, he is rich, you have to help me, I am poor." Faby told her to come over and she will teach her to paint nails, real nice designs, and give her a few nail polishes and brushes so she can make some money, instead of begging. That really upset Vanessa. Faby says things to her like, "why do you send you husband out to work, he does not know Spanish, what if he gets in to trouble, you know he is not Peruvian, and he can not touch a Peruvian, or he will go to prison or get kicked out of Peru, then what will you do?" she says, "he must provide me no mater what." then she adds, "he does not make enough money and we need help." At the retreat, some of the women there seen how worried Faby was, and just so happened, poor Vanessa was close by to hear, it was upsetting what she heard . . . Faby was asked what the problem was, Faby answered "I am worried for my husband and my daughters. will they be OK with out me? will they be able to get to the church. he does not speak any Spanish. do they have enough to eat?" Vanessa was getting upset over that, just huffing and puffing, while Faby was being comforted by a couple of the other women saying, "not to worry, they are in good hands, Gods hands, they will be just fine, you need time to relax." Oh, and Faby was ready to beat Vanessa, because it was Vanessa who canceled the popcorn for the movie saying she was allergic, even the smell would make her vomit. Faby says, "I may not have any teeth, but I love my popcorn with the movies!" she is missing almost all her molars, mainly has her front teeth for biting. Faby told me that Vanessa, mainly Vanessa, as well as the other Peruvian woman were trying every thing they could to ruin the retreat. But most of the women didn't pay any attention to those two and their games. And every time Faby mentioned she was Peruvian, they, most of the women there, would say, "no, you are not Peruvian, those two over there are, but you are not. your problem is, you were born in the wrong country, you are North American. You are one of us." its good that others told her that. I have told her that her ideas are just like ours, but she would not believe me. I think she is finally understanding, that I was not just trying to make her feel good, I was being truthful when I would tell her, "you are not Peruvian" at first. then I would reword it saying, "you are proud Peruvian, not real Peruvian."

Mon Oct 15, 2007

Upsetting

I'll start with Saturday morning, at five am, I was asking Faby for one soles. well, we tend to wake up a five am now, any way, she was just ignoring me. I was asking until 9 am for one soles. why, because the only place I can get air in the girls bike is in the bike shop and they charge one soles, the tires have a very strange thingy, needs a special clamp. any way, I cooked breakfast, Faby don't eat breakfast, just drinks a coffee with milk in it. told the girls breakfast was ready, several times, of course, they can not hear me even though I am knocking on their doors saying "breakfast is ready, time to eat" this was about 8 am, Faby was in here checking her email and writing to Ada the owner of the school she works at. I told her breakfast was ready, and I have been telling the girls its ready, but they just can't seem to hear me. She says, "girls, time to eat" does not scream and says it in English and they go and eat. I am still asking for one soles. to get air in the tires. to get new tires would cost ten soles each, twenty soles for new tires, its a small bicycle. well, Faby is not about to get new tires for the bike, and is always asking me "why do you want to take them to the park to ride the bike any way, with the way they treat you?" she has also told me to throw the bike away, more times than I care to remember. Well, come 9 am, I noticed one of our plastic chairs was broken. they are stool type chairs, very tough, and the seat was broken. I asked them "what happened?" its not the first time one of these chairs got broke, its the second time. I got the same response, both just gave me a dumb founded look as if they had no idea what I was saying. yes, I was getting mad, I stated that I stand on these chairs and they don't break, how could this one break, what happened, then they got mad at me and started crying, like I was beating them, I went to Faby showing her, then all the rattling started. maybe I am just trying to justify what I did, I don't know. well, the second floor woman came in, and she was not happy, I had started doing my laundry, and her clothes were in my way, so, I scrunched them up so I could get to my lines. a few days ago when she hung them, she hung them right in front of my bedroom door, when I came out, I ran right in to them, clothes went every where . . . Faby re-hung them saying I should not have done that. well, she went right to the land lord, we were all in here for a bout an hour, while he and her were out here rattling off, and then her by her self doing what ever she wanted. he came back and knocked on our door telling us he needs to speak with us. That is when I took the bike down stairs, the girls did not see me take the bike, they were in here watching T.V. Land lord told us, that the second floor woman is very upset with us, and is looking for another place to live. She said she wants to report me to the police for sexual harassment and demand money from me. The Land Lord told is also a lawyer, he told her it would never work, for one thing Faby is High class, and High society, she does not come from a straw house, from the middle of no where, she has had very expensive education, private schools and collages. not only that but the second floor woman is a hooker, so, who do you thing the judge would listen to :) we were told we can not play with her clothes, and she said she will be out of here in a few months, so, try to keep the peace. rent was due on the 12Th, Saturday was the 13, he did not mention any thing about being late. we came back out and the bike was gone. we live on a street where the Mayer lives on one side of us and a congressman lives on the other side, not side by side, but on the same street. not much happens on our street, but that bike did not last long, it was gone fast. Yesterday I was feeling a little bad at first about what I did. until church. But first, breakfast, of course they could not hear me again, and Faby had to tell them to eat. Then came church, right from the start. its an English speaking church, and they are rattling off like mad, fighting and crying, I looked and got very dirty looks from both of them, as if I had no right at all to even bother with stopping them from embarrassing me in church. OK, well, we go with Mac, a friend of ours, 81 years old. I had finished reading the bulletin and folded it and put it in my pocket. Then remembered Faby wanted me to go to the children's church with her, it might be her last class with them and she wanted me to take pictures, lots of pictures . . . they tend to change up the children's church teachers to give the teachers a break and let them enjoy the regular service, and to give others a chance. well, I also tend to mark the Bible for Mac, its hard for him to read what they have on the screen, yes we have a big screen in our church. Well, I seen another bulletin in the book rack took it and looked up the versus. Natalia started crying out loud, well, I was not paying any attention at that time, I was flipping threw the bible to mark the pages for Mac, because I would not be there. Not only that, but both girls had been fighting and crying for a while any how. Then Faby says, "that one belongs to Natalia, and she wants it back." By this time the church was about half full almost ready to start, and people were starring at us, she was getting loud . . . I could not believe it, I just gave it to Faby. right after the song service, the children's church begins and that is when the kids and the children's church teacher is excused. Faby just loves it, she was almost in tears, but she is a professional and kept her composure Right after church, in the chase hall, Faby was talking with Ada, the owner of the school. Maybe, Faby will finish out the year, but only if the director does not say a word to her, I don't know, after that, Faby had two parties to go to. The girls and I went home. I came in here and turned on the TV, and they started rattling off, I screamed, "if you want to watch TV, then kept your moths shut, I have heard enough of you!" on chat when you guys asked how the girls were doing, I was not lying when I said "they are being quiet" :) Faby told me yesterday they are just "Peruvian" I screamed back, not just at her, but to make sure they could hear and understand that I was not happy "That's not being Peruvian, that's just plain and simply Hatred! Nothing More, Nothing Less then Pure Hatred!" I guess you could say, they were not trying to upset me too much more yesterday. I wonder what I will tell them when they ask to go riding their bike. in the past when I made it disappear, I just put it on the roof over the kitchen, it ain´t there now, its gone. Oh, well, at least I won't hear Faby telling me to throw it away any more.

Fri Oct 19, 2007

today :(

I believe owe mama and papa an apology. I'll show you later why, but for now this: Yesterday, I went with Faby to her "party" office. Where her supervisors are to get her schedule. while in the building, but out of the office, Faby was looking at her schedule, she asked, "what day is today", I answered "Thursday" she then asked, "when is 20, I have two parties on 20, what is today'" I said, "today is Thursday, and the 20 is Saturday", not that quickly, but after I looked at the watch, and her paper. she then looked at the watch saying, "today is 18" my reply "do you want the day or date?" she said "today is 18" by then we were at the main door of the building, and there was a lot more said then just that, not getting in to it. After we left, she said, "you were yelling at me and making me look bad in front of my bosses." me, "sorry, I was just answer you question" you have no right yelling at me like that, you make me look bad" me, "sorry" her, "don't say a word", me, "I was just trying to give you an answer" her, "don't say any more" me, I took a breath, her, "don't say any thing." we got on a buss, and she would not stop talking to me trying to get me to answer. then she was saying I was mad at her . . . she told me not to say any thing, now I am mad at her? I don't get it, first she asked a question, then I am yelling at her, she tells me not to talk, now I am mad at her . . . OK. that was yesterday all week was not real good . . . today I was playing in yahoo answers. getting real board, I asked a few questions our of boredom, I was seeing lots of weird questions, the answers I was getting was very strange, so, I looked at the time, thinking, maybe mama or papa might be on line, I logged on to yahoo messenger. mama popped up right away, well, I was not sure at first, but it was her. asking how I was, I told her a little about the day, girls are in school, Faby is at work and has two parties tonight and won't be home until real late and that I was playing in yahoo answers. after a few minutes I get an answer saying, she can't wait very long for me to answer her, she is real busy and for me to email her. so I said later and logged off. then I wrote this :

From: *farmerpeck@hotmail.com*
To: *rootsdown2002@yahoo.com*; *littlewalkswithwolves@hotmail.com*
Subject: Sorry
Date: Fri, 19 Oct 2007 15:20:45—0500

I don't know who I was talking with . . . sorry for upsetting you. after I logged off, I did the dishes, ate a sandwich, and check my email. the whole time wondering who I was saying "HI" to?

I signed off because here recently, I have done nothing but upset every one around me in one way or another. of course the girls are always mad at me, they can't even hear me when I am right in front of them . . . they just give me real dumb looks as if they have no idea what I am saying. Yesterday, I was with Faby when she picked up her "parties" schedule, and she was asking out loud, "what day is today and what day is the 20th?" I answered her, saying "its Thursday and the 20th is Saturday" and an argument started, she seen the date on the watch and said "18" looking at me. I have no idea what I said or did, but when we left the building, she told me I was yelling at her and making her look bad. then she added several times saying "don't say a word" I was just trying to answer her, and I got yelled at for it. so, to who ever I upset, sorry for disturbing you, I'm going to take a nap now love ya

Cecil and Faby
Have a Good Day
http://graphics.GlitterMaker.com/1/417/115868280133151.gif

Only in America . . . . do we use the word 'politics' to describe the process so well: 'Poli' in Latin meaning 'many' and 'tics' meaning 'bloodsucking creatures'. papa answered me, From: *littlewalkswithwolves@hotmail.com*

To: *farmerpeck@hotmail.com*
Subject: RE: Sorry

Date: Fri, 19 Oct 2007 12:34:26—0800 sorry to get you upset, but you know you have the habit of waiting 15 to 40 minutes to answer things because your playing games, and we have things to do besides wait an wait for you to say something. papa and if you think you would know its me because mother is in Texas and she uses yahoo not msn I guess it can be true at times . . . six of one, half dozen of the other. but that ain′t all, I also wrote this later :

RE: RE: Sorry?
From: Cecil Peck (*farmerpeck@hotmail.com*)
Sent: Friday, October 19, 2007 5:32:26 PM

To: Robert Leininger (*littlewalkswithwolves@hotmail.com*); Charlene leininger (*rootsdown2002@yahoo.com*) well, I was logged in on yahoo messenger, and some times papa, has talked with me yahoo, I answered on msn, well sent out the mail on msn to both, because I was not real sure who I was talking with . . . any how . . . update on today about 3:30, 3:45, some where in there, right after i was laying down and napping, the door bell was ringing . . . who would be at the door . . . Faby is always telling me not to answer the door when I am here alone, when will I ever listen to her? hopefully not too soon . . . it was natilia with the school door guard. she is real good at not having any idea of what I am saying or making it look like she can not even hear me, but when she has no choice, she can speak and understand English very well. telling me Carola was hurt and that I had to go get her right away, and that she may need a doctor.

Carola has a hernia, as well as a medical condition almost like Faby. she can not over do in P.T. it will hurt her. she has had her teacher yelling at me and Faby several times now because she has over done her self and was hurting, in the past. Today, she was almost completely out of it. way over done her self and she knows what is wrong with her and she does not care. her teacher was screaming at me, natilia was translating . . . "you need to take her to the hospital right away, you need a cab." amongst other things, Natalia was giving me funny looks. cab? hospital? right, who would listen to me any way, even if I had any money . . . that's right, Faby don't even let me hold any money for any reason. you see, I am in a forging country, I have no business going out any way, the people here will only hurt me, rob me, or do what ever they want to and I can not do any thing about it. so, here I am no money and having to carry Carola all the way home . . . its a 30 minute walk as it is, my arms are killing me, its 5:30 now and I have to go back to the school to get Natalia, I don't feel very well my self now, cool breeze and sun out bright as ever, throat hurts and sweating like a pig. time to go love ya

Cecil and Faby
Have a Good Day
http://graphics.GlitterMaker.com/1/417/115868280133151.gif

Only in America . . . . do we use the word 'politics' to describe the process so well: 'Poli' in Latin meaning 'many' and 'tics' meaning 'bloodsucking creatures'. and my legs don't feel too good either, I think I need a shower, but its very cool out there, and it could make me very sick. I am sorry for offending you, I just wanted to say "hi" and got yelled at. I guess I should be use to it by now.

Carola is fine, she just loves putting on a show. I mean she loves putting on a show. More then once she was carrying her sister, who is just as big as she is, knowing she has a hernia and is not suppose to pick up any thing or any one that is heavy, while walking in the middle of down town with lots of people. Both Faby and I have told her not to, but of course, she don't hear me and is screaming in Spanish at Faby and continues carrying her sister. Then complains about her hurting belly, in full view of the public. you can tell if some one is in pain, and she loves getting us yelled at. she is fine. one more thing that happened today . . . Deer Sweet Uncle Roberto came over . . . one of these days I may listen to Faby and not answer the door. He was yelling at me, almost screaming, popping the back of one hand in to the palm of the other yelling "Fabiola, Diez, Manyana" repeating several times and popping his hands together. meaning "10 AM., tomorrow" so, how was your day? mine was fine :)

Mon Oct 22, 2007 foolish

I feel foolish . . .

Faby surprised Carola today :)

Faby was with me picking up the girls, and Natalia was right at the door, 5:50 pm, the school bell rings at 5:45. Natalia is always one of the first ones out the door. Well, Faby and I just walked right in. Natalia was there waiting for us. Carola's back pack was at the door, but not Carola. She was with her teacher. In her class room. Second floor, fifth room down the hall, her back pack was right by the door . . . nice place for it considering how much stuff comes up missing all the time :) Why do I feel foolish? Faby caught Carola's teacher, I bet that was interesting. Carola has told her teacher so many stories, she thinks of Faby and me as some kind of monsters. We are always mistreating poor Carola. Faby pushed Carola out of the class room and told me to take her down stairs, Carola got real mad, almost didn't go, until I told her some one may take her back pack and we can not afford to get her any thing more . . . she did not even look at me for a couple hours, oh how mad she was. Come to find out, Carola did not do any P.T. last Friday, instead, she was just putting on a show for the school. Having every one believing she was going in for surgery, and she would be lucky if she was able to go back to school Monday. Now do you know why I feel FOOLISH . . . I carried her home. of course she had no sympathy for me, and how much pain my arms and legs were in for carrying her all the way home. I remember when I told Faby, Friday night, she was working late, she did not buy Carola's story, nope not one bit. Carola was so mad, she cried half the night. Saturday and Sunday, she was just fine, bouncing around with Natalia. I should have known. Remember when I said/wrote "just clap and laugh" if I had done that in the school, I would have probably been in lots of trouble. Oh, Well, nothing much I can do about it now, except cry about it on here and let every one who reads, know just how Carola, and Natalia are, because some times Natalia has to put in her two cents worth in. Just be prepared. They will do what ever they can to make you look like monsters and gain sympathy from total strangers . . . more Carola then Natalia . . . my arms are still shaky . . . I must be getting weak. its after 10pm and the second floor woman is in my living room . . . ya, still complaining, I know, it don't do much good, but still, there should be a law :(

Sat Oct 27, 2007

Geography its the first time I heard Carola talking any thing about geography. and all she said was, "see, I got an A" like it was nothing. two maps, one of South America, and one of Peru, forty questions-lines, with coloring as well. coloring the bordering countries of Peru. well, I have been so negative about Carola, I had to say some thing good, that ain't easy. any way, she was the only one to get all answers right, she said one other girl got an A, but got two answers wrong. I asked her where the other girl was, she said the girl was sitting right be side her. I asked, was the other girl coping your answers, she said, she was until she noticed and covered her answerer's. Carola said she was the first one done and the other girl got mad . . . oh, well. but the way Carola said, "I got an A" like it was nothing, in geography? I know she is real good in math and language skills. if I could only get it through her thick head, how intelligent she is. any one remember "Valentina Lines" an Argentina actress? that Faby has talked about. she was worth millions, but her attitude drove every one away from her, and with old age, her only son, sold every thing she had and just blew the money . . . right now she is in an old age home, badly mistreated. she is over 90 years old. well, I keep thinking, if we can get Carola out of this environment, in to a better one, she just might change, or at least have a better chance at life, because here, with her attitude, she is not going to do much more then be a robber :(Natalia could excel here, she wants to be a doctor, and her attitude is much better. but Carola, she wants to be an actress and or a teacher, here, there is too many of both, and her attitude, she won't last. I wonder how many people could say, "I got an A" and not make a big deal of it . . . I can see some in math, or language, but in geography as well? just had to write some thing nice about Carola

Sun Nov 4, 2007

Rooms

Faby has been telling me since the first I arrived, she wanted the room I gave to Carola. it was not her idea to separate the girls. she wanted a "work" room. Ever since I got the extra room and gave the girls each one to them selves . . . its been a hassle . . . in keeping them separated. I mean we hear a strange noise, and then we can't find Carola, where is he, with Natalia. Its happened way too many times. Yes, they fight, and fight a lot. but they also fight to be together, as mean as Carola is to Natalia, Natalia still fights to be with Carola. Last night was the last straw, I finally agreed with Faby and now, after church, Faby and the girls are on a "day out" together, while I change rooms around. Church was some thing else. Faby, being the professional she is, did not shed a tear, but I heard the sadness in her voice when she said, "there they go and with new teachers" talking about the kids for the children's church. I know Faby was happy she got to hear the sermon for the first time in a long time, but sad because she was not teaching the children's church, so this outing is going to do some more good . . . for her, to relax.

Sun Nov 4, 2007

Last night what happened last night? well, for the most part, the girls were ok all day, Faby had two parties yesterday, and was gone most of the day. last night, a right after Faby got home, around 9pm, they started fighting again, it didn't last long. but come 10 pm, I said "10 pm, bed time", and of course, they speak Spanish, I heard Faby reply, in Spanish, and the girls got upset stomping and almost yelling, each one going in to their rooms. I asked Faby what just happened, she said they are demanding to sleep together again and she said no. why, because they live to fight, or fight to live, not real sure which any how. when they went to bed, Natalia locked her door, I know I heard it lock, I know the sound. and she turned her light off. come 4:30 or so in the morning, because when I finally seen the clock it was almost 5 am, I got a strange feeling, woke up, started looking around, seen a light on. Natalia's light. went out and her door was wide open. and there was Carola in her bed right beside Natalia. I picked up Carola and put her in her own room. when Faby woke up, around 9am, I told her what happened. she told me again, "I want that room for my work shop area" then she also added, "I don't get to teach today the children's church" that is when I said, "why don't you and the girls have a day together, you know do what ever you three do, right after church, I will go home, move all of Carola's things in to Natalia's room, and put some of your work things in 'your work shop' and when you come home you can finish what I started and be a little relaxed . . . besides, you have not spent very much time with your girls ever since you started working in the school and at K.F.C. you three need some time together any why." she agreed, and I have no idea where they are, and I am now waiting for the floor to dry, it should be dry by now, so I will start putting some of her things in there and get dinner started. I'll tell every one later what happens when they get back . . . I am sure its going to be good . . . Natalia was always wanting her own room, but she is the one who is letting Carola move in . . . if that is what they want, that's what they are going to get

Sun Nov 4, 2007

update . . . rooms yep, it all hit the fan first Natalia started throwing a fit, Carola was just silent, then they switched, it was Carola who started balling.

it was all in Spanish, I wasn't looking. I was too busy in here uploading pictures in mama and papa's group and laughing . . . didn't want to get caught, or in trouble but I did hear, and still hear. Carola is really making a big deal of it now, first Natalia was carrying, then Carola started in. she is refusing to eat and demanding her room back . . . sorry, it ain't hers, its Faby's now. Natalia did settle down and ate some dinner. Faby is trying to calm Carola down, and to see if she will eat, I think. not sure, its still all in Spanish. I am wishing I was playing the slots right now . . . if any one of the girls come in here, I'll be in so much trouble . . . its so hard not to laugh out loud . . . but they asked for it. all three of them. Well, at least Faby is happy

Sun Nov 4, 2007

Girls Day Out

They all three had a Good Day together. Went "shopping" so to speak. went to a few stores looking around, Faby did say she got cold and got a sweater and a light jacket, didn't cost much, she is a good shopper. found a little place giving free painting classes and her and the girls participated, then they went to the theater, the one where her friends are acting and Carola acted in last. I for get what they seen, but they had a real good time today.

Wed Nov 7, 2007

last night . . .

Once again, a long night, or sort of. yesterday, in the morning, of course, the girls refuse to speak any English, only Spanish, and just loud enough to annoyed me, doing it on purpose. After I told them to speak English or leave the room . . . my room, they started playing in the living room. Kicking their only remaining ball around. about a half hour, it stopped, and lots of Spanish, like arguing. I finally came out asking what was going on, of course, they could not answer me, I was looking around and asked where the ball was. still nothing like they could not understand a word I was saying. I finally said, "you know, this area here is for you two to play in, I am not going to bite your head off for playing, so, can one of you please tell me what happened, where the ball went?" Natalia finally pointed to the roof. OK, I got a chair and a stool and took a look, sure enough it was there. I got it down for them, and said, "have fun, play away." Carola said, very sarcastically "thank you" as she was looking at the floor and turning away from me . . . nice after school, Faby had a party, so I had to get the girls alone. Carola was almost crying, saying in a couple weeks or so, may be in the first week in December, they have their final tests, and she said her teacher said if she gets a "B" she may have to repeat the year, because she missed so much school, if she gets a "C" she will repeat, the only sure way to pass on to the next grade is if she gets an "A". Carola was sooo upset over that, saying she can not repeat, hates the idea of repeating. I asked her how many times she got lower then an "A" on her tests. she said "a couple times, and once I got a "C" and I am really worried because this is the final test" I tried to tell her not to worry, she is so very smart. still she cried half the way home, at least it was getting too dark for other people to notice her crying. well, later on, they completely stopped speaking any English at all again . . . that wasn't much later, any way, Faby finally got in around 8:30 at night. she was talking to the girls in English, they replied in Spanish, that lasted for about a half hour, until Faby went completely Spanish . . . those two just flat refuse English, any way, it turned in to almost a heated argument, which lasted almost an hour, it was 9:30 before they stopped, and they were almost at a yelling match, at that point it was all Spanish. and no, got no idea what was said. I went to the kitchen. come 10:30, is when Faby said she was going to bed and the girls went to their room, Faby was out quick. the girls how ever, started in again, getting louder and louder, come 11:00 pm i was afraid they were going to wake up Faby, and she was so tired, I was not going to let that happen, so I went to their room, I didn't make a noise, I got to about three feet away and the door opened, there they were, balling their eyes out and speaking in Spanish. I said "English, speak English or don't say a thing because I don't want to hear it." they kept crying, I told them their mother was very tired, and they were not going to bother her. that did not go over well with them. they tried crying louder, I interrupted, saying, "you three got what you wanted. Mommy always wanted that room for her work room, ever since I arrived she has been begging me for that room. But, no, I would not let her have it, because I wanted you two to have rooms for your selves, your own space, privacy. Did you two want that? no, why, because it was probably my idea, right? mommy is always telling me how wrong I am for what I do or say, and you two eat that up don't you." by then they started getting mad at me, but their crying was slowing down, Carola had stopped crying and was glaring at me. and I went on, "I may be wrong again, but I will not let you come out and bother mommy right now because she needs her rest. you all three got just what you wanted." I looked at Natalia and said, "that other night was the last straw, you had shut your door and locked it. you had to unlock and open your door to let Carola in, you keep inviting her in." and then looked at Carola, and said, "you keep trying to move in, bringing you clothes, and toys in there all the time. not just a few items, but the whole basket of cloths, clean clothes." looking at both of them I said, "you two wanted to be together, and mommy wanted that room, I am tired of fighting all three of you, I gave you all what you wanted. now deal with it." by then it was 11:30pm yes I was very tired and natilia was so mad at me she even stopped crying as well. neither of them would say a word in English, both so mad at me they could not even cry any more. I finally said, "I am too tired to stand here any longer, I am going to bed." with that I shut and locked their door . . . from the outside. they stared talking in Spanish, and I said, "now I do not want to hear any thing more, if I do, you two will be up all night scrubbing floors, if you don't believe me, then think back to the last time you stayed up all night, I will do it again." I didn't hear another word, the rest of the night. they got up about a half hour ago, just before nine, well more like 45 minutes ago now, they have yet to speak any English, I guess they are still mad at me, I don't know why, they all got what they wanted, oh well, at least mommy is happy. that is what counts the most any way

Wed Nov 7, 2007

Balls

Just a note, because I don't remember if I mentioned it before. The girls had four balls. Two of which were given to them about four years ago. One problem, those two balls were made here, from Peru. They did not like those. Shortly there after, Mama Birtha sent two balls from the U.S. These, all four, were about the size of soccer balls, but they were not soccer balls, a little smaller, plastic balls. The two from Peru that they rejected, last year, we went to one of the natives communities, to the French community with in, that helps the needy and gave those balls to them. The girls tried to make a scene, with no effect. Faby said, "you two don't want them, now they belong to these people, at least they will appreciate them." Well, there went two. One, Carola's ball, well, Carola purposely destroyed some thing of Faby's, I for get what, but Faby was very upset, and since Carola has a bad habit of just leaving her things laying around and not putting any thing up, there was her ball laying out in the open. Faby grabbed a stake knife and well, Carola lost her ball. Do you know how protective Natalia is with her ball? Especially when I or mainly Faby gets angry? Those girls do play with that last remaining ball, but Natalia is quick to remind Carola, that, that ball is hers and she is not going to loose it for her . . . she keeps a close eye on it.

Fri Nov 9, 2007

Fired

Tee Hee, I'll get back to the title in a few . . . Yesterday, well more like two nights ago, almost yesterday, Faby got a call, real late at night. KFC called her. Boy oh Boy was she worried, she forgot her cell phone and they called several times, while she was teaching at her school . . . she nearly hit the roof after hanging up. I have been debating all day weather or not to mention any of this . . . don't want to jinks it. But I can't hold it any longer . . . so, please, no negative waves . . . its not locked in yet. To the Title . . . The director of Faby's school has fired her twice so far . . . yes, two times Faby was FIRED. Both times Ada, the owner has put Faby back, making the director look powerless, not only that, but last week, the director fired another teacher, who just happened to be an assistant director at an University at nights, just as Ada made a surprise visit . . . he took her to one side and locked her in a room with him for a hour or so, so no one could bother him as he told Ada what was going on . . . he told Faby already . . . he is still working there, that poor director, loosing and loosing. Well, she has fired several other teachers that Ada sent out there, and they never came back. she fired Faby twice, and that sure did look "dumb" and it didn't help when she fired the other teacher . . . when Ada showed up . . . OK, what happened? KFC is looking to expand a little. Just thinking about it. Having "princess" parties, with like a mini saloon for the girls parties, some thing like that. and they want Faby to be in charge of it . . . she would be "training" manager, in charge of the princess parties. low level management, not permanently locked in, but it would be a start in the right direction. Faby is no dummy. she got all her things together, we went to town and got a few extras, for her to show and tell, plus the fact, we went our favorite telephone place, and had them print up a real nice paper, sure wish I could have scanned it, sure did look sharp . . . all Faby's idea. Yesterday was the meeting, at 4pm. and I was crossing my fingers, hoping all goes well. she did not get home till late last night, and she could not stop talking. still, its not locked in, they are just thinking about doing it. Well, there was a problem. School, KFC, School, KFC. what was the problem, training today at 12 noon. She loves teaching, training, teaching, all night. I could not tell her what to do. she was awake before the TV came on, I know we were talking. It had to be her decision. Finally she said, "I can't pass this opportunity up" come 8am, she called the school to say she was not feeling well. then she told me she felt bad for lying. what would any one of you tell her, and no, I am not asking for responses, just think about it. I told her she did fine, if they new the truth, she would be in so much trouble. I left it at that. I don't think she is worried about being fired . . . lol, I keep laughing about that one . . . poor director . . . ROFLMAO!!! Even if they decide not to do it, I do believe it is still a good mark on her record with KFC. She sure is excited, I just hope I didn't jinks it by talking about it too soon.

Sat Nov 10, 2007

Breaking News!!!

The Girls just Took a Shower!!!
Its only been five weeks. Natalia was crying, and Carola, well, she just looks like Carola. Not sure if she is Mad, or Upset, looks the same. A little cleaner, they both look as well. I guess Faby got tired of something, and well, she forced them in, one at a time . . . I just had to mention it, I wonder how long before the next one?

Sat Nov 10, 2007

New member just got a new member of the house, this time not a doll, got a couple photos. Under the name, New Member. Faby would not let me get a bird . . . we have too many already, and they can be real demanding at times. Dogs and cats are out, land lord would not allow them any way. Fish would probably die in the heat, we have no A/C here and it gets real hot when the sun comes out. Soooooo, Faby let me get a turtle, any ideas on how to take care of one? We have been told lettuce and bread to feed them, so far, there are three bites in the lettuce leaf I gave her.

Thu Nov 15, 2007

Lisa

One thing about Lisa, We have been informed several times, that baby turtles tend to die. most don't survive the first year, some only a few days. So far, so good. She likes straw berries. Faby was feeding her a peace of straw berry tonight. She did not like her "turtle" food, not even the peace of banana. She did eat the straw berry right out of Faby's hand.

We have also been told, if she does live, she would only get to be about 8 to 10 inches long. None like her has ever been found any bigger. Plus the fact, that if she does get to travel, most air lines let turtles travel in the passenger section of the plane, do to the fact that almost all turtles will die in transport if in the pet or luggage section. they have done studies, when the turtle travels in the passenger section, chances of living are greatly increased, most all live in transport. But, they have to be in a certified pet carrier.

Fri Nov 16, 2007

Sad Story

Yesterday was Carola's birthday. She turned 11. Faby and I got her a real nice cake, sorry, no pictures. In fact, Faby and I were not even invited to her party. The girls go to school from 1 pm to 6 pm. Faby teaches from 7 am to 1 pm, and gets home around 3 or 4 pm, depending on traffic. Faby told Carola she would take the cake to school when she got back from work. Faby also had planed on taking Carola's gifts and some refreshment as well. Carola had other plans. At noon, her ride came and she took her cake, along with a knife and the little plastic plates we had, she took just them, didn't even ask. When Faby called, saying she was leaving, to have the cake and presents ready, and we would get the refreshment on the way, I had to tell her, Carola already took the cake. Faby just said, "Carola does not want us at her party, that's OK, we will not go." So, sorry, no pictures. We were not invited. Carola did not even mention her party or how it went. Faby was hurt last night, Carola did not even offer us any cake, of what was left . . . I am guessing, come next year, she may have to make her own or buy it her self. As for the presents, we got her an Rubix Cube—comes two, one little, a key chain, and one big. Faby thought it would keep her busy for a while, and a bottle of bubbles that comes with a little fan. Both girls go nuts over those bubble blowing things . . . she may get them for Christmas. not real sure yet.

Sun Nov 18, 2007

Lisa she was eating from a spoon. I couldn't believe it, Faby got her a jar of baby food and with a spoon, she fed Lisa.

Thu Nov 22, 2007

2 weeks?

The girls surprised me!!! they are taking a shower!!!! its amazing!!! Well, this morning, Faby woke them up, and almost screamed at them, talking in Spanish, not real sure what she said, but she told me, that the girls better be showered and wearing clean clothes, because today is "Thanks Giving" and we are going to the Union Church. oh, ya, HAPPY THANKS GIVING EVERY ONE !!! I was certain it would be about 4 or 5 weeks until the next one, considering how hard it is for them to shower, and the fact, they wind up having very bad, I mean BAD days when they shower . . . I wonder how tonight will go . . . I am worried . . . just a little, nothing I can do, if they try to embarrass me, I will do again like I did in the translators office . . . I'll Clap and Laugh . . . and get yelled at by Faby again . . . I don't like upsetting Faby, but those girls are some thing . . . they act so happy when they believe they have hurt me, so tonight, it ain´t going to happen, I will "CLAP AND LAUGH!!!"

Thu Nov 22, 2007

Happy Burrr, after Thanks Giving :)

Yep, it was GOOD!!! Almost could not walk out of the place, it was the "pecan pie" that did it. The service was nice, preached about Psalms 67. Then the Dinner came, oh, it was good. I was doing great :) my first three plates . . . some of you my remember how much I use to be able to eat . . . I have made restaurants sweat, and there has been people, probably management, saying, "we are closed, please leave." some thing like that.

Then the pies, they were all cut, in to eighth slices, the first four were fine, but the last one, they kept the best for last, out came the pecan pies . . . oh it was good, half way through it Faby looked at me and said, "you are going to make your self sick, you don't have to finish it." Pecans here cost 100 soles per kilo here, that is 10 soles per 100 grams. 100 grams is almost a half cup, if that much. the dollar ratio is roughly 3 soles to 1 dollar, still its expensive. Those pecan pies would have to have cost at least 100 soles to make, especially that one I grabbed, full of pecans, oh how good it was. I was fighting that last bite, and Faby said, "you are going to brake your tummy, you don't look well." But it was gooooood. Now before you all think I was the only one making a "pig" of my self, just wanted to point out, I did take my time, and there was "thirds" being served before i got sat down with my second plate. There was plenty of "pigs" in there, more so than me :) OK, the girls I guess they did fine, Faby did start yelling at Carola for some reason, she did not say why, and it was all in Spanish, so, no clue . . . Natalia at one point came walking up to me just rattling off like mad, I said, "you know I don't understand that, would you tell me in English?" she gave me that "duh, what?" look. The table would have been all "Peruvian" table, but I was there, so, there was very little English at all at our table, yes, its an "English Church" lots of Peruvians love going there. and we had sing a longs :) at the end. was lots of fun . . . a traditional "Turkey" dinner, every thing there I could eat . . . very rare for me, but this time, it was Good! food that is. well, its after midnight here, and my belly is finally settled down, burped a few times, don't feel so bloated any more. Faby and the girls are asleep, I better be heading that way my self, so, love you all, hope you all had a Good Thanks Giving Day ☺

Mon Nov 26, 2007

Puzzled

The past four days, Carola has been taking a shower. Each day. Makes me wonder if she has been reading over my shoulder or not. She does know how to read, write and speak English, and I don't always hide what I write when I am writing. Natalia how ever, hasn't been. Don't know what is up with her. As usual, every time Carola takes a shower, she has a bad day. At least she is clean. Have no idea what she says, but she has been fighting, by words with Faby, and both words and hits with her sister, and I of course, can't do any thing about it. She took her shower today, and next thing, she had Natalia on the floor, both girls screaming, not just yelling, I mean screaming. I walked by them several times, and they both acted like I was not even there. As in other words, I am only here to feed them and escort them to and from school, nothing else. That is the hint I get from both girls any way.

Tue Nov 27, 2007

a Few things To start out with, the girls school; The presidents of the PTA. has announce she is going in to a "partner ship" with the Mayer. She is either very stupid or is planning on destroying the school. about 20 years ago, the communist government, of Peru, took that place. it was not a school then, it was some ones house, and had rooms for rent, from what it looks like, or could have been a plantation of some kind. any how, it was taken, but the government never laid claim to the property. So, the school has no owner, and the Mayer, Rafael and his wife Francesca, knows this :) One corner of the school, the Auditorium, is right close to city hall, and is just across the street of the city park. Very Good Location. yes, they have a very sharp eye, or close eye, on the place, and the fact it has no owner is a plus in their favor. the president of the PTA. has already started making deals with the Mayer, the side and the end of the building, the auditorium, is already painted real nice, with adds, from city hall and a tourist company the city deals with. what dies the Board of Education have to say about it, one rep. came and said, he don't like it and the board will probably reject it. saying "you are doing things that are not legal, you may loose your school" she repeats, "we are going to make a lot of money, these adds on the building are giving us 3,000 dollars a month, yes dollars, not soles. Personally, I like Rafael, and Francesca, if they do take the school, more power to them, I would be cheering them, so would Faby. Why, because the City has more right to the place then the Board of Education. and all the Mayer has to do is get a contract letting him inside, and he can take over from there. City Hall has taken lots of building, most of the buildings around the City Hall, and the City park are owned by City Hall, because they started out with a little contract to let them in. We got part of this info. from the PTA meeting we went to, then Faby told one of the teachers, Natalia's teacher, she has been teaching at the school for the past 20 years and knows the real history, that is how we got the other part, she was there from the start. Faby's school is some thing else. Friday the director demanded all teachers stay for a meeting because Ada, the owner would be there. Faby laughed, why, she did not tell most of the people there, only a few "trustworthy" ones, that Ada is in the hospital . . . stomach problems, probably from eating "Peruvian" food that they, the school was feeding her from her last visit. any how, the director demanded that Faby stay late because Ada was coming to the meeting. Faby just laughed a little, signed out saying, "I will see Ada at church" sorry, she was not at Church, still sick, we are wishing her well, she has a big heart, and is too trusting. Also, the notes, grades for the students. Faby has turned in the notes four times so far, then some how, the computer blew up . . . all files lost. not just the main one, but the sign in one as well, and its not connected to the Internet or any other computer at all, just plugged in to the power, turn it on and sign in and out, and some how it blew when the other computers blew . . . right after Ada did a surprise visit, and Faby was the first one to see Ada and show Ada all the notes she turned in, three times before, and was signed for, by several people . . . she is not the "home room" teacher for any of the classes except one, the "4th high school" grade. so her notes must be signed for by the "home room" teachers as well as the main "grades" coordinator, as well as the director-of which she will not sign, and showed Ada. what does the director do, or rather say? "she is lying" calling Faby a liar saying Faby never turned in any notes at all. over and over again, and Ada was with the proof in her hands. and the director says, "I am your school director, how can you believe this English teacher over me? she is lying." over and over again. to end that meeting, Faby called me just before taking the bus, and in the process, she said, "here comes the director, and she is getting in to Ada's car, telling the driver to take her some where. She is getting in to the back of the car. Here comes Ada, she is getting in to the front seat, there they go. The car stopped, and Ada is screaming and waving her arms, the director is out and the car leaves. Now the car is backing up, the director is saying, "she is changing her mind and will take me after all" the driver is saying some thing to me, I got to go, bye" After Faby got home, she told me the driver said "get in" Faby says, "me" Ada says "no, me!" the driver says "get in before the director reaches us" and they were off, and the director was standing there with a dumb look on her face . . . some how that night, all the computers blew, all grades were lost, come Monday morning, Faby go the news, that she was going to have to stay until 8 or 10pm redoing all the notes for all her students . . . FABY BLEW!!! Yes that was last Friday, and all the puters are still down, all the teachers are showing up late and leaving early, because now they only have a "sign in sheet" only about thirty minutes either way any how but that's not even the half of it . . . some of the kids . . . Faby says its unreal . . . yesterday, there was a girl, one of her students, walked in to the class room and left the door open. Faby tells her to shut the door, she says, she did shut it. can you imagine the argument? she does this with colors as well, you say its blue, she says green, you say white she says black, and she winds up crying her eyes out, and does so with all her other teachers until she gets her way . . . Faby has lots of experience with carola, didn't faze her a bit. Faby says home is one thing, school is another thing and will not put up with "stupidity" in her class room. says, "if you want to cry, take it out side, I don't want to hear it, and the rest of us have work to do." that's about it for now, and by the way . . . Natalia is 9 and Carola just turned 11

Wed Nov 28, 2007

Faby's School

Well, Faby did ask me to start writing things down. At first she was saying, no, why would any one care, its no ones business, and so on and so on . . . well, I do tend to write about the most interesting things any how. Plus the fact I don't shut her out, when she wants on the computer, I don't just log out, some times I have my group open and she is looking, I'm not hiding any thing. Here a couple days ago, she did ask me to start writing every thing down . . . you know, to keep a log of what is going on, and told me its OK to put it on the group, just maybe the family would like to know, who knows. The Director is or was up to it again. The kids don't like her at all. The director was a "grade school" teacher not high school. to start out this story . . . during the "Olympic" games, the director kicked the high school kids out of the high school, and put them in an abandoned field so sandy, you could not run, it was very hard to walk, the sand so loose some places you sank up to your knees. Why did she do that, because she wanted her teacher friends, and the "grade school" kids in the high school. both schools even though are of the same name, are separate buildings separated by about eight city blocks, not an easy walk, and Faby has to teach in both buildings, she is primarily the high school teacher and the Home Room teacher of the 4th grade high school. Plus two different awards that was tainted by her, one of which came from KFC, because Faby signed the school up for the contest, "mad science", the director was very upset over that, because a student won, and refused to share the winnings with her. it was not Faby's student, one of her class rooms yes, but the student demanded that Faby be part of the celebration along with her own teacher. So, the director squashed it, no school party, celebration or even an Honorable mention from the school. and two some kind of fair, from one of the University's, a teacher at the school also is an assistant director of an University and signed up the school for the fair, and one of his kids won . . . great! except the director stated he could not go to the celebration and went in his name, and took his and the child's prize in her name saying it was all her idea. Now, with all that in mind, you can imagine how much these high school kids don't like her . . . To the top . . . she is at it again Faby and the University teacher, who is also the 5th grade home room teacher, just found out yesterday, That the director is organizing a "farewell party for the 5th grade in the name of the 4th grade. She was telling the students that she was doing this because their teachers don't want them. The students them selves didn't want the party because they don't want to pay the director rent for the school . . . they already have other plans that don't involve the director and she knows nothing about it. oh, ya, at that school, 5th grade is the highest grade, and if they graduate on time, they are at the ripe old age of 16 and are ready for the University . . . in the girls school, of course, its a grade school, grades 1 through 6 there are 16 and 18 year old in the 6th grade, they have not even started high school . . . any how, can you imagine how the students reacted? they basically said, "you can have your party, we won't show" to sum it up :) Faby told me a little of what they were planning, a trip to Cuzco to see some ruins and stuff, the students are demanding that Faby go, but she keeps telling them she can't, its not that she don't want to go or be with them, she has no time, she has another job, plus a family she will miss, but she is also encouraging them to go, to save as much as they can to make what they can, and not to let any of it slip to the director. there are a few other teachers in on it as well, keeping every thing as quiet as possible. Faby one day finally told them, if there was any way possible that she could go, she would, to encourage them to keep trying.

Fri Nov 30, 2007

Carola

The past three days now, Carola has been sick, yesterday, two days, and three days ago, she has not been feeling very good. Last night, she finally told Faby she has not used the bathroom in about a week. of course it was in Spanish, Faby told me and I said, "well, if she would eat, maybe she will be able to go" that didn't go over too well . . . sorry, I just have no more sympathy for Carola. Faby tells me to make sure the girls eat . . . I have gotten tired of trying to force them to eat and then finding food rotting in hidden away places. Another idea I had with her feeling bad was fungus. Yesterday, I seen a plastic bowl in the garbage, it was full of fungus, and it was broke, which is why it was in the garbage, I guess. But, it came from the girls room, so another thought was, maybe they are hiding food in their room and the spores from the fungus is hurting Carola. I just got funny looks from Faby. I tried to explain to Faby about the fungus, and Faby told me not to worry about the bowl, it don't cost that much. ya, OK. Well, yesterday, I fixed four cups of rice, along with about the equivalent of about three chicken patties of ground chicken in the rice. Both girls turned their noses up at it, I had two bowls. I thought they might have some last night, I had fixed it about noon yesterday, well, more like 10 am. This morning Faby told me to throw it away. That should make the girls real happy when they see all that food in the garbage. For some reason, they just love throwing food away. Neither one of them likes Quinoa, and Faby told me to make some up today and to make sure they both eat, especially Carola. That will go over about as well as a turd in a punch bowl. you know, this kinda reminds me of when Faby was called to do a movie, she was so excited . . . up until the day of the casting, when she said she will not go because the girls will not let her. Any one remember me saying some thing about that? I am thinking they are not liking the fact that Faby, their mother, is working and is away a lot of the time. Last night, while Carola was in so much pain, belly ache, Faby started asking out loud, where the matches are. You see, you rap hair around the match, in several different places on you head, and chew on a couple, and your pain goes away . . . sure it does, I just don't believe it. To me, it was just a way for Carola to get some attention from her mother. Me, I said, "that ain´t going to do a bit of good, just a waist of matches" I got dirty looks from both of them. I still say, if Carola eats some thing, she might be able to go to the bathroom. Although, I have mentioned the condition Faby has. it has made it very hard for her to go. Faby needs special medicine to go to the bathroom, some thing like ex-lax, but more powerful, because of her condition, her system does not work as normal as every one else's does, Faby is afraid Carola may have the same thing. Charce mentioned that Carola might be coming "in", Faby says the normal age is 12 to 13 here for girls to "come in" Carola is 11. so that is doubtful. And I know, Faby maybe reading this so, I will say it again, If Carola starts eating, she may start going to the bathroom. I believe she is having stomach aches because her stomach is empty . . . put some thing in there, and it will stop hurting . . . and maybe she will wind up going to the bathroom as well :)

Fri Nov 30, 2007

Adesa

Adesa is the name of the School Faby teaches at . . . Two days ago, Faby called for a teachers meeting for yesterday. The director was upset over it, and tore up the sheep Faby put up calling for the meeting. Then Faby said she seen the director with tape putting the sheet of paper back together talking to her self about writing another memorandum to Faby . . . OK Well, yesterday, two things happened. First was the director telling the kids she has organized the party, the farewell party from the fourth grade to the fifth grade. the kids did not like it were very upset, both the fifth grade teacher and Faby were sitting back watching the show. no, the kids were not happy, and want nothing to do with the director. Second, was the meeting Faby called. Talking about Christmas, and exchanging gifts amongst the teachers and such . . . The director was not happy with any thing Faby had to say, saying, "how can they participate in this nonsense, they have to pay ten soles to the chocolate day celebration, plus they have to pay ten soles for my Christmas gift, and another ten soles for the school party, they will have nothing left for you." plus adding that the fifth grade "grade school" Sept. grades have not been turned in yet . . . again . . . Faby just told the director, she was not invited and not to worry about the "gift exchange" the director cut in on Faby while Faby was talking, so, Faby returned the favor, and cut the director off as well. So, this morning, Faby took the fifth grade "grade school" Sept. test papers back to the school to show again they have been graded . . . I keep telling Faby she will do much better with out the school, but I can not just make her quit, she loves teaching.

Sat Dec 1, 2007

Adesa

Well, Faby told me this, The director is none too happy with her right now. During sign out or break time, not sure which, all the teachers were in the teachers room, and the director was asking about having a Christmas and gift exchange party, completely ignoring the fact that Faby was in there talking. Only a few people in there was paying attention to her, the assistant director, the dance teacher, the religion teacher and the accountant, the rest were talking with Faby. Finally the director, was so upset she said loudly, "those who want a party with me make a file in front of me, those who want a party with Faby, make a file in front of Faby." The director got only those four, the rest lined up in front of Faby, then three of the directors four, said they were in the wrong line and went to Faby's line, leaving the director with the assistant director. The director was so mad, that she repeated all the discounts she stated the day before, and adding that the computer programmer is coming and all the teachers will be discounted for his pay, plus some how all the mouse's for all the computers came up missing, so, that is another discount for all the teachers. The director stated, with all these discounts, you will not have any money left for any party or gift exchange with Faby. Most of the teachers have other jobs, and didn't faze them a bit . . . the director left steaming mad.

Tue Dec 4, 2007

Adessa

The director is at it again . . . Now the director says all the students that have not been there all year need passing grades, the ones who's parents finally paid the fees up to date, so they will not cause any problems. Faby put, as well as all the other teachers, "N. P." I for get the Spanish word, but translated, means not present. There are a lot of kids that the director had kicked out because their parents were not caught up on paying the fees. This is a private school, with monthly payments, or yearly payments, depending on how much you can pay. Any how, there is a big number of parents that finally got caught up on paying the fees, and are demanding their kids get passing grades or they will cause problems, so the director has demanded that all the teachers pass those kids. Faby handed in her grade sheet saying, "you can put what ever grade you want, I put "N.P."" Also, The director is very upset at Faby about the book sales and rentals, Faby has not been demanding money from these students . . . Faby does not know which students owe money in the first place, so how can she be demanding any money from them plus the fact, she is against the book sales in the first place. The director along with the accountant and the last English teacher talked Ada in to buying I for get how many books, in which the director and the last English teacher were selling to the students or renting, some students still owe money for the books they bought, some owe money for renting the books, and if the rented books are damaged in any way, Faby has to pay for the books, but the director says Faby has to pay all the back due money that is owed. And get this, the director will not say how much money Faby owes, just that she will not get her November or December pay check, you know she does not get that much any way, enough for buss fair and a few snacks, but that is not all, there is more . . . The director is so upset, that she stopped the pay checks for all the teachers, for one reason or another. the mice that came up missing from all the computers, late turning in grades, the computer programmer needs paid-that money is coming from the teachers pay checks, along with all the other fees as well that I mentioned before, the director stated yesterday that no teacher will get their November or December pay checks because of all the money they owe. Faby is scared to tell Ada any thing because Ada is not well, just got out of the hospital. Faby believes that the director along with a few of the teachers there, gave Ada some real Peruvian food, not good for foreigners, it can kill us if we are not careful. Ada was in the hospital for two weeks, may have been a little longer. Nice people they are. I keep telling Faby she does not need to go back, but she loves to teach, she loves her students, and there are a few teachers as well as a few other employees that she is friends with and she tries to encourage, plus she has adopted a couple of orphaned kittens there that she is trying to take care of, she may be bringing one of them home one of these days, I did tell her that would be just fine :) with me.

Tue Dec 4, 2007

Natalia

I never would have guessed. Ok, well, Faby loves going in to the shoe and purse stores, there are a lot of them around . . . can't figure out why, but she loves going and looking. Last night Faby tells me Natalia is always making problems, always saying she needs new shoes. Faby does not go in buying all the time, she just goes in to look and dream about. This is what happened yesterday, some how, one of Natalia's shoes, fell apart. The soul just fell right off. It is a "hiking" type shoe, brand name "Buster Brown" a give from her grandma Birtha, from the U.S. for last Christmas, which she got I think was last March, so she has not had them for a full year. About 20 minutes to leave for school, Natalia came to me just crying, saying she can not go to school because her shoe just fell apart. She don't know how it fell apart, it just fell apart. I tell her, that I see lots of shoes in here, find a pair and wear them. I barley get turned around and the girls are arguing and screaming, and start crying. I come back to the room to see Natalia on the floor and Carola on top of her. I ask what is going on, and right away, tears start flowing down Carola's face, then Natalia says, "my sister won't let me wear any shoes" Now Carola is really balling good, the water is on full blast again. I blew up, screaming, saying you have fifteen minutes, be ready, and to stop crying. I added again no more Spanish, if I can't understand it, don't speak it. because most of the time here, they are fighting, with words mostly, and of course, there is nothing I can do about it. so, what are they doing this morning? rattling off like mad . . . what can I do . . . i told Faby about the shoe and showed her, she agrees, it did not just fall apart. that is when she also told me what Natilia is doing in the shoe and purse stores. Now Natilia has better reason for demanding a new pair of shoes. To top that off, when we went to get the girls, both were demanding money for parties at the school, the chocolate day celebration and Christmas party . . . Faby already knew about the shoe. and I did catch the part where the girls were demanding money, I broke in saying, "where is all the money you two had? where did it all go? now you are demanding more?" well, Faby cut me off, she was polite about it, and stated more of how hard she is working, just to feed us all. how did the girls react? well, they did not walk slow this time, they speed up quite a bit, leaving Faby and me behind, they did not want to hear any of it. its 10:20 here now and they are fighting . . . as usual, over nothing, this time fighting over who found some thing first in their room, and it was getting loud . . . but what can I do?

Tue Dec 4, 2007

Adessa

This just in, Faby just got home, and told me what she did today, it was funny. Faby got a couple red ribbons with bells on them for the kittens. Today she gave the kittens their presents, and what a show they put on. Right after Faby put their ribbons on, they came out of the kitchen, where they have been living, and right in front of the director, just showing off like saying, "see what I got"

Tue Dec 4, 2007

Good news, Bad news

Usually people say "hit me with the bad first" I guess because they are hoping the good news will off set the bad and they will be left feeling "OK" :) so, Bad News: I Broke the Washer, the rinse side :(Good News: its all covered under the warranty :) I had no idea it was not for rinsing, the repair guy was just here and said not to worry, won't cost us a thing to fix, but from now on, to remember, its only the "spin" cycle, not rinse. He said to rinse in the same side you wash in . . . that's going to take time, to drain and refill over and over. Oh, well, at least I know better now. Its been six months, and I still have the same bag of laundry soap, its a 4.5 kilo bag, and its got about one tenth of soap left. still enough for a few more washings.

Thu Dec 6, 2007

Adessa

I don't remember if I ever told any one about Faby's dreams, or visions. Some times she has them, they come at any time any where, and are very intense. When she has them, she tells me and so far, they have come true. I have mentioned to her about how to make money with this, but she just says, no. any way, while at school, while at school, she had a vision of a big fat woman, long black hair, she gave details, to the door guard, Funny, Funny is the name of the woman who watches the door and cleans the school. Funny asked how she knew this woman, Faby would not tell her she just had a vision, how superstitious these people are, she just said she seen her some where. Faby told me she seen in her vision that this woman was in a position of power in the school next year, not sure what position. Any way, Funny said that was the directors sister, who worked there last year, and was constantly making problems for one thing or the other, plus was beating the kids, not paddling, but beating. She was finally fired when too many kids and parents were reporting her to the police. Faby did not tell Funny any thing of her vision. Faby feels sorry for the school. One more thing. Faby said she ran in to one big guy with lots of papers. He asked her if she worked there, she said no, sorta, just a sub, that's all. and handed him a chocolate, she put little chocolates in all the lockers, including her own locker . . . teachers lockers. At the end of the day, she was sad, because the other teachers got chocolates and hers was missing, the thinks the director probably took it just to hurt her, well, just before that happened, she was in her "home room" class room, talking with one of the other teachers, the university assistant director, about different things, and Funny came right up to her, saying there is problems down stairs. Any way, this teacher Faby was talking with, is the fifth grade teacher, and he got an agreement with the university, along with some sponsors, to sponsor some of the best students, but they would have to take a test. The testers of the university was not aloud in the school, the Adessa director would not allow those testers to come in. That university is a very expensive one, and sponsorships are very hard to come by and so rare, you don't hardly ever hear of them. He could not give the test, because they are his students. And the best part of this conversation, was the fact it went on in front of Faby's students, the fourth grade class, which is the biggest rebellious class in the school. I mean when some very high up's of the Adessa program sponsorship people came to visit the school, (Adessa is more then just a school, they have help programs all over Peru) as an example : one of Faby's students told the rep. "we know how to make pullyada's" when the rep asked "what are you learning here?" she was kicked out for two weeks . . . of course you know, she has a passing grade :) that was not the conversation to have in front of those students, and both of them knew it, and both were not hiding their voices . . . Funny was saying, Big problems. The Government board of education is here, the Government Labor rep. is here and the Police is here. They have the director, the assistant director and the accountant in the accountants office. There was more to that, lots of teachers, high school teachers, making big problems because they did not get paid yet, all the grade school teachers got paid, but none of the high school teachers. so, yes, big problems, which Faby and the university assistant director were no part of. Well, as she was feeling sad, in front of her locker, the accountant was calling her, desperately calling her, saying to come here. Faby just saying, give me minute, ill be there in a minute. Finally she came, and just before she seen all those people, including the big guy she handed a chocolate to, she was saying, what is the problem? the accountant says here is your check, we had to discount you four soles, for various reasons. Faby says she don't care, she will not make any problems, she has not made any problems in the past, why start now, the accountant was trying to give her the check, and that is when she noticed all those people in there, that little office was full. i wonder how much of that will be blamed on Faby, when she had nothing to do with it. She was not even there, neither was the University Assistant Director, which the director has fired, and the same day, Ada rehired, due to her unexpected visit :) Faby was a little scared to go to school this morning, she left real late this time. She knows the director is up to no good, but the director never shows up before 8am, Faby will show up around that time, probably before the director. The director is still trying to force Faby to put passing grades to students who have not been there all year, Faby has stated, "you can put what ever grade you want, I put ¨N.P.´ I just can not lie I will not pass a student who does not know any thing," well, the director, the students-ones who haven not been going-and the parents of those students, finally talked Faby in to giving one last test, but Faby says, she will not run behind looking for the students, they have to find her, and she does not have the same classes every day. in that school, the students have one classroom all day, its the teachers who move to class room to class room, and the teachers don't have the same class rooms every day, they have a schedule, a weekly plan, some classes they see two times a week, some classes they see three times a week, some they only see once a week, except for their home room class, which they tend to see ever day, for about an hour at least. I don't know if I would have liked that or not, sitting in one room all day watching the teachers come and go with all their books and papers. I remember my teachers having desks full of stuff, and I see how much Faby has here, and some times she is caring so much, its hard for me to carry it to the buss stop for her, and she has to carry it all over the school and through about five or eight bocks of sand to the next "grade school" for her little ones classes. Well, Faby did loose all that extra weight she was complaining about, and she fits in her jeans she could wear when we first met, again. I guess that was one of the good parts of going there :)

Sun Dec 9, 2007

a few short stories

This Morning:

Just after waking up, Faby decided to wrap up the gifts for the gift exchange she has going at her school. Some of these gifts did not cost a thing, you buy so much and get freebies :) here, real nice items as well, like water jugs bicyclists use all the time . . . got eight of them. any way, as she was wrapping these gifts, she found out, she was two boxes of cookies short. Yes, cookies, she had fifteen of them, and was only coming up with thirteen. little boxes. Natalia started running a fever and feeling sick, while Faby and I were running all over the house looking for those missing boxes. Well, also, yesterday, something else happened as well, you know the one thousand mills, of shampoo? its the "family size" bottles, almost half of it and the conditioner came up missing in just four days time . . . these girls don't shower enough to have used that much. Finally, Natalia could not take it any longer, with tears, she told what happened. Carola took the boxes to school and made Natalia promise not to say any thing and she would share the boxes with her. when Faby confronted Carola, she just said that we never do any thing for her, or give her any thing. She said the only way she can get any thing is to take it. as for the shampoo, well, give a wild guess, Carola only wants to make us spend as much as possible. I think she is only screaming for attention, plus the fact she hates the idea of her mother working and gone all the time. but still, I don't know what to do. Both girls refused to go to church today, but Faby and I went . . . good thing too.

Christmas Party:

At the Union Church, Santa was a big hit . . . not only did the kids get to see Santa, but the adults as well, got to say "HI" and have their pictures taken with Santa :) nice guy, don't you think ;) (it was me playing Santa.) well, Carola put on a real good show as well, had the pastor running, trying to please her, I had to catch the pastor and apologize to him and explain to him. That Carola is an actress, and when she sees other people getting more attention then she is getting, she will put on a show . . . also the fact, that at one time she was a very good and famous actress, and when she snapped her fingers, she had a dozen people around her offering her items, so she could pick and choose what she wanted, she never had to say any thing, you see, Carola refused to say any thing to the pastor, he kept offering her items, but would not get them, saying she had to talk to him, tell him what she wanted, but instead, she just let the water flow, making puddles in the grass, I would not have believed it my self if some one told me, but I seen it, making puddles in the grass with all the tears that was flowing . . . she put on a show. That did not break Faby or me. In return, with Faby's hard work in pleasing the kids, several people were offering her meals, nothing there was free, but Faby and I did not have to buy any thing, until the end, in which, the pastor gave us about ten or fifteen soles worth of food for only one soles. that was nice, Faby told the pastor, she felt guilty for taking all the food and not paying for any thing . . . . so, any way,

The last one:

About a year and a half ago, this couple came to church. Real friendly too, he is black, she is white, and I really thought, and still think, he may have been looking for a reaction . . . you know, "racist" in which he did not get from me. I was being just as friendly to him as he was to me, I don't care about the color, as long as you don't treat me like dirt . . . any how . . . it was about a year ago when we seen him in the external affairs building, because Faby was having some problems, and had to talk with some of the "higher ups" and was called to the back offices. he seen us and said hi, but he had nothing else to do with us, he was busy doing other things. Later on, we find out he was working at the U.S. Embassy, and went to the external affairs building once in a while because of his job . . . foreign affairs . . . we find out, a few months ago, that these people are million airs, and he only works at the Embassy as a hobby, but has very important friends. This couple are High Class people. And yesterday, I can not say for sure, that Santa greeted this couple, but he sure did try to great every one, I think Santa did, there were so many, and Santa did his best to go stand by stand to greet every one. Today, She went out of her way. Yesterday, Faby painted snowmen on some of the children, and today, this woman was asking Faby about the snowman, if she could really do as good a job with the snowman on fingernails. Faby told her she could, but you know, she probably already asked around first, then asked Faby to her house. These people don't just ask any one to their house, they are nice to every one, but they don't just invite any one to their house. And as rich as they are, she asked Faby to do her nails. Faby does not want to mess this up. While she was inviting Faby to her house, he was buying some peanut brittle, he came back with two bags, saying he just loves this stuff. He was banging the bags together, saying he hates the big peaces, wants smaller ones, well one bag broke, and a peace hit the floor, he says, "i hate it when that happens" knelt down picked it up, blew on it, "much better now" and popped it in his mouth, "mmmmm, mmmm, good" he says. well, then they all started speaking Spanish, Faby translated to me, she was saying she invited Faby to their house, he asked if Faby knew the way, Faby said no, and he gave her directions, saying, if my wife invited you, you are invited. You know,

Faby is not about to charge these people a thing. She wants friends, very important friends. And these two are two of the top around, she feels, this is another very important test, and it will all pay off when the embassy appointments start. Good thing the girls didn't go today, but really no one even asked about them, Mac asked, but only because we ride with him to church every week, and one other woman ask how they were doing, but did not ask were they were. I am guessing, they ones who knew them were counting their blessings in the fact they did not bother them, and afraid to ask because they might show up, some thing like that, my guess. that was the last little story, but one more thing to say, or add: which is this, Ada was there, and you know, the director of her school has been doing her best to break the friendship between Ada and Faby, it has not worked, Ada was buying Faby drinks and sandwiches, talking real good about her and hugging her, Ada her self is very rich, not sure how rich, but she is rich and is high class as well. That was some party that those girls, mainly Carola tried to break for us. didn't happen, in fact, it got Faby an opportunity to impress some real important people with her talents.

Wed Dec 12, 2007

The Girls

They are at it again . . . They don't know, or don't care how serious it can be. Refusing to eat at home, and saying they are starving. I caught them at school, their school, with a dinner plate, full of rice and a couple eggs each, with a cup of coco. This school does not give out "freebies" every thing has a price. But, Natalia said the cafeteria lady invited her and Carola. Yesterday, they refused breakfast and lunch, went to school on an empty stomach, like they do from time to time. But this time, I caught them eating there. Funny thing, Natalia is getting sicker and sicker, just not feeling well, makes me wonder what she is eating. The serious part is, if the cafeteria lady decides to make a police report, on how we, Faby and I, are treating the girls, I could wind up in jail or kicked out of the country. We have told them over and over again how serious this is, and they seem to not care, because they keep doing it. I just watched as they ate more food in one sitting, just five minutes, then they eat all day at home, those were big plates, full of rice and eggs. And they were happy as can be. House full of food they refuse to touch, and they are eating else where, making up stories on how hungry they are, and how mistreated they are . . . some times I really believe they are doing their best to get rid of me, one report to the police, and I could be in jail until some one pays the fines and buys me a plane ticket . . . that is a scary thought. I had to tell Faby what I seen, because this is scary. Faby was not happy. She told the girls they are not going to school today. Both cried half the night. This morning, Faby took Natalia with her to her school. When they come back, Faby will go to the girls school to see what the story is. Right now the girls are taking their final tests, and Acing them. Just two days left before summer vacation for them. And they have to pull this stunt. I don't know what they have to do today or tomorrow, but, it looks like they may not go back, not after yesterdays episode.

Wed Dec 12, 2007

Disturbing

This is really more on the last one I sent, About the school cafeteria. You see, its a public school. Which means this, the fees to go to this school are very much cheaper. Which brings me to this, the homeless kids go there, or rather the kids who are fortunate enough to be in a home for the homeless. At least those kids have a roof over their heads. Not much else, because they are also given a bag of candies to sell at ten cents each, and when they bring home five soles, they get to eat . . . some times it takes them a week to make five soles, some kids only eat once a week. (takes ten dimes to make one soles . . . they get 50 candies and are sent out to sell before and after school) Get the picture? What is that cafeteria woman doing feeding Natalia and Carola, when she will not feed those kids who are really hungry. Who are really feeling lucky if they eat twice a week. There is no Charity at that school, no free lunch program, if you don't have the money, you go with out. the difference between the above and me, is I am a U.S. Citizen. According to Peru, all U.S. Citizens are million airs. And if a U.S. Citizen is caught mistreating a Peruvian, they are fined and kicked out of Peru. If they can not or do not pay the fine, or buy a plane ticket, they are put in jail until the fine is paid and a plane ticket is bought. as for the above, they have been doing this for hundreds of years, they are not going to change. Faby hopes to set every thing strait, again, before it gets out of hand . . . it almost did one this year, not its happening again. its almost as if those two really want me gone. I am wondering, as is Faby, just how those girls talked the cafeteria lady in to giving them meals, when she will not feed the homeless kids who are really starving. She will find out today.

Thu Dec 13, 2007

Carola

She is an A+ student. Her test papers say "A D" which is the highest grade here, there it would say "A+". She is some thing. Even after showing the pictures, during the parent teacher meeting that one time, she still has convinced the whole school she is starving, more so then the homeless kids who are selling little hard candies for 10 cents each, and don't get to eat until they bring 5 soles back to the home they are staying in. That is selling 50 candies. Some times it takes them a week before they earn enough to eat one meal. Carola is even begging them for some thing to eat. Begging her whole classroom, her teacher, every day. Even the cafeteria lady, every day begging, saying she is starving, that we never feed her. They don't feed her every day, but they have feed her quite a bit. The poor one. They say, they can't stand to see her standing there looking so pitiful, begging, so thin, not eating. She is real good. Faby blew up. Carola will not go back to school again this year. I thought today, Thursday, was the last day, no, its 28 of December is the last day of school. Natalia is going back, some how the teacher convinced Faby to let Natilia to return, and Natalia's teacher was Carola old teacher for the first of the year last year, she was the one who demanded us to feed Carola quinoa, because she failed the health test last year. She said next year, she will get the fifth grade, Carola's class. She said if Carola refuses to eat, put the food, mainly quinoa, in a tupper and bring it to her, and if she has to she said she will feed Carola like a baby in front of the whole class. This teacher goes to other countries. Has a daughter in the U.S. and has been there several times, as well as other countries. Been teaching for about twenty years, been teaching at that school for most of those years, if not all of them, i for got. Any way, She told Faby how Carola was begging even her for some thing to eat, and watching Carola begging her students as well as lots of other students when out on break, and watching Carola in front of the cafeteria begging. Faby won't let me bring any pictures to school, because she says it will only enforce their beliefs of how monstrous we are . . . here in Peru, you can fake any thing and make it look so real its almost impossible to tell the difference . . . even pictures, so, they won't work. Funny, how Carola puts on real big scenes in real nice restaurants, refusing to eat, throwing away food left and right, goes to school telling stories on how mistreated she is, and how we never take her any where or feed her at all. Those back packs they have are

"McDonald's" back packs, and you can not find them in just any black market. You have to have gone to a special party at McDonald's or where McDonald's is throwing a special party, not every kid has an opportunity to get a McDonald's back pack. I don't know what story they are telling on how they got those, but they sure are doing their best to destroy them, Carola's back pack is in worse shape then Natalia's. Yesterday, while Natalia was with Faby in her school, Carola was here all day, she refused to eat all day, she was upset, I had food out, and she refused to come out of her room. Up until I told her its time to wait for mommy and Natalia at the bus stop, then it took her ten minutes to come out, her door was open she was mopping, going very slow, from the bus stop we went right to the girls school, oh how both girls were not happy. After hearing all those stories, Faby Blew up at Carola's teacher, because even her teacher was feeding her. Faby flat out told Carola's teacher that Carola was not coming back again this year, you can pass or fail her, its your choice, she is not coming back to continue to embarrass us like this. The teacher was saying, "the poor one, she looks so pitiful, she gets such good grades, she is the best student in the school, you can't do this to her" and so on and so on.

Fri Dec 14, 2007

Adessa

Sorry it took so long, but the girls had us so upset, I just couldn't remember to keep writing about it. starting out on the 10th: The gift exchange was good. A lot of the people she was giving gifts to gave her gifts back, mostly cheaper then what she gave them, which wasn't much. Any how, a couple of the gifts were real nice, and I could not find any Internet picture of them, I tried to find them, couldn't, and it will be at least a month to develop the pictures . . . sorry. One gift was a ballerina dancer, real nice, porcelain doll with a music box and twirls around, stands about 10 inches, the other one, looks like it may have cost at least two or more paychecks, Faby could not believe she could have received such a gift. Its about a 12 inch tall statue of a soldier, could be Spanish, or Italian, not sure, with a gray hat, looks like a night, but with out the helmet, and has a sword. Looks expensive. The guy who gave it to her is one of the very very few people in Adessa who looks and acts like "upper class" and can actually talk with Faby respectfully. He just said to Faby that she was the only one in the school who could appreciate this type of gift. There have been others through out the week who have been giving Faby gifts and saying, "where is mine, you owe me, where is mine" any way, Yesterday was really good, birthday parties, several of them had birthday they were celebrating in one shot, and Faby was invited, no doubt because they wanted her to bring gifts . . . sorry, no gifts this time, but did create problems :) First of all, the director chased out the cafeteria woman, the door guard and the cleaning lady, three people whom all the teachers like and get along with, but the director says they are way too beneath her and ran them out of the cafeteria. That did not set well with Faby. She has a kitten there, and demanded a chair for the kitten. they were refusing, so, she got the kitten a plate and sat it on the table, it went prancing up and down the table, when it got its cake, it sat at its plate and ate. Of course you know, that did not set too well with the director, some of the other teachers thought it was funny. Faby was serious, saying the kitten has feelings, and a tummy. Ada sent two of her people there in her car, she was not there, plans to come today. Faby, talked the two people Ada sent out of their cakes, as well as the military guy to give to the three ladies who the director chased out. Then she asked for her peace of cake, and guess what she did with it . . . went to Ada's driver, who was not even invited in side the school, he was sitting in the car. She was saying these people are people, and they have feelings and a tummy too. Faby did not get a peace of cake for her self, she is not too much in to sweets, but, some one did give her a box of chocolates, which she carried around all day, nibbling on. She was satisfied with that. Final exams: yesterday, was the final tests, and of course, the director was kicking out all the students who's parents did not pay the December month, but Faby was not about to go running around trying to give tests after school lets out because they paid late. She was threatening to call me, at home to call Ada. Last time she called me crying, I did call Ada . . . All her students were present to take their tests, weather or not they were paid up in their fees. All the grades have to be turned in on Monday on the official government document for the schools grades thingy migigy . . . (I can't remember what she said, sorry) she was saying the kids will take their tests on time or Ada will hear about it through her husband. I can only remember the high lights, and that is about it for this week, not sure what is going to happen today, Ada is suppose to come today, this could be fun. The director is doing her best to break Ada and Faby's friendship, and its not working, I wonder what she will say, if any thing, about yesterday and what Faby did to spoil her birthday, yes, her birthday as well as a few others, party :) oh, well, I am sure Ada will understand Faby, they have known each other for a few years now.

Sun Dec 16, 2007

The Girls

Well, no showers today, none last week, that makes two weeks of no showers. As you already know, they did not go to church last week. Faby I am trying to make it laughable, because Faby does not need any stress of any kind. She had another attack yesterday, I may have helped in causing it, I feel real bad about it, not going to get in to it, I should have known better. The attack happened in one of the K.F.C. stores, where she was having a paint faces party. A doctor was checking her out and told her, she is lucky to be alive. Really, how many times we keep hearing that. Any way, he said one of her arteries is stretched so thin, its ready to blow, break, pop, some thing like that. its one right on her heart, how he knows this, I am not sure, but she sure can do with out any stress. So, I am posting these things trying to relieve my stress and to laugh about it, so I don't blow and upset Faby . . . So, please, help me laugh about, and Please, Please, Have Faby in your thoughts, prayers, or what ever you do for "Good" I really can't stand the idea of loosing her, she is such a good person, you would love her if and or when you meet her in person. She will not stop, she has two parties today, plus she has one more week at her school, I'll write about it later, I am doing laundry right now, but I had to get this off my chest and wrote down.

Faby

First of all, I want to send a special "Thanks" to Aunt Linda. Thank you for your help. Faby is not one to just sit around and beg. She will say what she needs, and let it go at that. When her mother cut her off, there went the rent, her mother was giving her a hundred dollars a month, that paid the rent. That was rough, then her father cut her off, but he was only giving her 200 soles a month, from Uncle Roberto, he is the one who gets her fathers retirement check, both her mother and father live in the U.S. When that happened, we were hurting. Thanks to Aunt Linda, our rent and Internet is paid. Well, President Garcia has reduced the retirement paychecks, and reduced the dollar, as well as upped the cost of living. One good thing is the rent and phone and Internet, has not gone up. Due to the fact Garcia has introduced a few more phone companies, for competition, and the owners of this building live in New York, and that is where all the rent goes, or so says the land lord, they have not raised the rent yet, thankfully.

OK, as I said, Faby is not one to just sit around and beg. We still have this process we are working on, and every time we turn around there is some thing more to pay for. This last bit we did, cost us some where between 4 and 6 hundred soles to translate and legalize and one hundred soles to mail out. That money came from her job, she was saving as much as she could for it. Right now, she is saving for the next step. Plus her job is also feeding us. Yesterday, was payday for the doctors, her fathers retirement check, and once again, Uncle Roberto cut her share saying he was in more need than she was. Yes, I blew a little. Not only that but a couple weeks ago, her fathers house sold, the one that she is part owner of the third floor, and guess what, she got screwed out of her share of the money. That did not help. They were saying she is married to a North American, she is a million air now, she don't need any thing. She should be helping the rest of the family. Yesterday she had two parties, she had an attack during the first party, I wrote a bit about it earlier. She called me, I went to meet her, and go with her to her second party, and be with her the rest of the day. Trying to keep her calm and relaxed. Special, Special Thanks to Aunt Linda for your help, as well as a Special Thanks to Mama. You two will have your very own beautician when we get up there. Faby knows hair, face, hands and finger nails. She is real good. Faby has told me as soon as she gets up there, you two will have your very own personal beautician, free of charge. With as much as you two keep doing, Faby says she has no idea how she will ever repay you. She is afraid if I start working here, it would only cause problems with the Embassy and immigrations office, with the tax for both countries and other things. Besides, she is making more then I could ever make here mainly because I would not be able to do much more then teach English or be a night street guard. Either way, I would not be able to make much more then two hundred soles a month, and out of that, I would have to pay taxes to two countries. So, its easier for her to work and me take care of the kids. She has told me not to say much about this to the family because she is afraid it would just get her in to trouble with my family. But right now, I am asking you to keep her in your thoughts, prayers, or what ever you do for good, because I just can not stand the thought of loosing her.

On a good note:

The woman she went to see last Monday, was very happy. Showing off her "snowmen". I heard some of the other women saying "that looks like Faby's handy work" my thoughts were, "who else does this around here" a week later, and her nails still shine like they were just done. Faby is real good. Thank you Mama, the U.S. stuff is ten times better then the Peruvian stuff.

Adessa

This is a good one. Yesterday, was a graduation for the elementary, grade school. Ada was there, Ada was telling Faby about it in Church today, Faby told me a little, here is what she said. The graduation was at six pm. At seven thirty Ada called the director asking why she was not there yet. And why there was so much disorder at the school. Apparently the director did not expect Ada to show up. Ada was there before six pm. When the director finally got there, she was asking what Ada was doing there so early . . . Ada was not happy, finally told the director to shut up, she did not want to hear any more out of her. Well, Faby started telling Ada what the director is doing with all the rest of the teachers. As well as coming to school late, school starts at 7:30, or 7:45 am, I forget, any how, the director does not show up till around 8:30 or 9 am., as well as causing lots of problems, and most of the teachers are afraid of saying any thing bad because the director has a history of firing people. Granted two of which are still there :) one of which has been fired twice . . . wonder who that was any how, Faby has a list of teachers and their phone numbers for Ada to call. We'll see what happens now. Ada was not happy with the way the director treated her yesterday. Friday, Ada showed up, late. There was a talent contest, and Faby was one of the first to go on, Ada showed up after Faby's kids were done. The director was doing her best not to let the "English" version go on. They did a song in English, Faby called me and let me hear them, they sounded good. Well, after the talent show, Ada said she wanted to hear Faby's kids, the director stated, the talent show was over, no more time, other things have to be done. Well, Faby went to her kids and told them the director was not going to allow them to sing to Ada. After a bit, a few of them caught Ada and told her they really wanted to present their song, they wanted her to hear them. Then Faby was called in, and they started. The director noticed and went in screaming for Ada, Ada was blowing the director off, telling her she wanted to hear these kids. The director then ordered the band to start playing to drown out the kids singing . . . that did not set too well with Ada, she went out and set them strait, that she was the owner of the school, and they were to be quiet while she listened to the song that was for her. After the song, she asked Faby why her piano was not used and a toy that belonged to one of the kids, Faby told her that the director was not allowing the kids to touch her piano. actually its the school piano, still its hers, the school is hers. That was a late late day, because there was awards being given out, and I think a graduation, I am not real sure as to what was going on, but they were all there till 7 or 8pm Friday night, Faby did not get home till 10pm. Any how, during the ceremony, the director expected to be the one handing out some kind of ribbon or certificate or some thing. The kids refused and Ada told the director to go stand some where, and told Faby this was her place, the kids wanted Faby, the director was not happy. At the close of the day, the director went out of the school to wait for Ada, Ada was calling Faby to leave. The director tried to catch Ada, well, Ada's driver seen Faby and opened the door saying to her to get in quickly. I am guessing the director was wanting a ride some where, well, Ada left the director standing at the school and she got in her car and they left. Ada did not take Faby all the way home, but she did take her to a bus stop, on the way to her home. Once again, Ada was showing her strong friendship with Faby . . . leaving the director not very happy. I guess we will see what happens next.

Thu Dec 20, 2007

Mad Science

The company Mad Science, the one who hires "paint faces" as well as other party types, like dancers, singers, magic and or science experiment shows, had a Christmas Party last night. Faby had to bring one gift for some one she did not know, a female, so, we went looking around, and found a raggedy ann looking type doll, its red and pink, brightly colored. wasn't sure what else to do. Any how, the party was at 9pm, we didn't leave until 1:30 in the morning, got home at 2am. the party was good. I am guessing, very upper class. all in Spanish, oh, well. Gift exchange, there were lots of neat items, most of which were purses . . . most of the employees in both party and paint faces are female. funny thing was, the guys were getting shirts, of the same color they were wearing, one guy got a back pack, red one, same color of his shirt and coat. a few guys got liquor bottles. there were lots of cheers during the gift exchange, and speeches and such, but nothing like the cheers when Faby was called. I could not believe it, she was the second to last one, and when she was called, they all were screaming and chanting. all the party people want Faby in their parties, because she gets the kids in to the party and dances or does what ever she can to help make the party a success. most of the paint faces girls like Faby as well, only a couple don't, but they don't cause any problems for Faby. any how, three times they raised the roof while Faby was standing, and after the party, she was saying bye for an hour and a half. What she got was a . . . you probable already know . . . purse, little brown and tan one, will go nicely with her brown and tan outfits :)

Mon Dec 24, 2007

Nellie

Our surviving chick. Faby named her Nellie. She helped decorate the tree, and this afternoon, she was trying to help get the chicken ready to cook. We got a chicken, our favorite little corner store gave us just over three quarters of a chicken, minus one leg :(oh, well, we go there most of the time to get things, and they tend to give us items they have not or have hard time to sell. We ain't complaining :) I almost got a picture of Nellie on the chicken in our oven, but Faby knocked her off . . . those two get in to some real good arguments. This morning, to my surprise, Nellie was right on my chest. Some how she got on the bed, her feathers on her wings are growing good. We don't let her out of the house much, she sure can be a hand full, always trying to get on the ground, and with all the cats and dogs running around, that wouldn't be safe for her, because of her size. She really hates being left behind. She gets really excited when I insert the key in the lock, she knows what that sound means.

Mon Dec 24, 2007

Christmas

Christmas drawing. Yesterday was a drawing for Christmas baskets. Faby was working. The drawing was at the gallery that Faby likes to go to. She sure did have plenty of tickets in there. Any how, While Faby was working, I and the girls went. Faby's party was from 4 to 6pm. The party at the gallery was from 4 to 8pm, the drawing was at 5. They had small, big, one large Christmas baskets, and several turkeys to give out. All the small baskets went first, half the big ones went, then Faby's name was called, they said if the person was not here, they missed . . . I went up, and the owners of the gallery said it was OK for me to get her basket . . . It just happened to be the large one . . . the difference was two bottles of wine and one bottle of champagne, where as the others were one bottle of wine and one bottle of champagne. I didn't realize this at the time, even though I had the girls with me, they didn't say a word to me about what was going on. Faby told me later, that her basket was the biggest one, she heard from her "cheese may" group inside the gallery, that she got the biggest basket. The story on that basket was, the owners, were arguing, yes arguing over the bottles of wine, which one, one or two, the wife was saying put only one, the husband was saying put both and the bottle of champagne, finally he won the argument, by saying, "You know, Faby is going to get this basket, so, both bottles of wine and the bottle of champagne are going in" any how, he was right, and I do remember how he as laughing, clapping, and shaking his head up and down, she was doing much the same except shaking her head from side to side, like in "I don't believe it" type way. That was kinda neat, we got pictures of it after we got home. That was some thing, even though she had to work, she still got the basket intended for her, made just for her.

Mon Dec 24, 2007

Graduation

Two days ago, Saturday night, was 5th grade high school graduation party. The director did not show up, she wanted the party in the school to bill the kids for every thing she could. Any how, the kids rejected her offer and had their party else where, and the director refused to show up, as well as refused to sign one of their documents, class picture and graduation book. That was OK, because there were two other former directors present, one of them was asked to have the honor of presenting the ceremony, and handing out the awards and graduation book. It was really nice. Those kids had Faby running all over the place, wanting pictures of her with them. They had one meal, cake and one drink for free, but you know, I keep saying this is Peru, there was also vender's present, selling chips, drinks, sandwiches, and many others items. At the beginning, the girls had to start fighting, I said to stop the fighting, and both filled their eyes with tears, and I said loudly stop the crying, then Faby broke in telling me not to say any thing because what ever it is, I would only make it worse, so, I just ignored them the rest of the night, now, I do believe Carola is mad at me because she left her ring there, she made the ring her self from the beads that Connie or Charce gave her. I really think she believes I was drinking her drink, when in fact, she was out side one of the servers took both the girls drinks, they were at another table, I was drinking mine, and Carola looked at me and tears started flowing, luckily, the people we were traveling with said its time to go, I left quickly. That is when she left her ring at the table she was sitting at. I didn't even thing to check, I was trying to get away. The party it self was from 9pm to 4am. Faby actually got me up to dance a few times, like four or five times. The average age of the graduating students was 15, if they graduate collage on time, they will be 20, still too young to drink legally, yes legal age is 21 here. some students were as old as 18, i think only a couple of them were. There was 15 total graduating. They were real happy. Probably more so that the director did not show up, even though she was suppose to.

Tue Dec 25, 2007

Christmas Eve

We had a nice Christmas Eve service. Talking about the birth of Jesus. There were nine different lessons, nine different people came up to read different chapters and verses of the bible, each time there was at least one song, some had two songs, where the choir would stand up and sing one, then we all would sing. There was lots of singing. Of course, you know the girls, they had to do some thing to be noticed, I don't know what it was, but Faby separated them, by sending Natalia to set by me. They were not happy with that. When we got home, we Finished our Christmas dinner. That chicken I cooked sure was good. Faby told me next time we get a free chicken, then I can cook it. Here, the cheapest raw chicken is about fifteen soles. you can buy the same size or bigger one already cooked for 9 soles, for 12 soles, you get a 1 and 1&2 liter of Inca Cola with it. Why buy a raw one? Any how, we broke in to one bottle of wine. The girls wanted a taste, they did not like it, or so they say. Nellie was tricked. I offered her a taste, but she didn't want any. She is constantly biting Faby's nails, Faby put a drop of wine on her nail, Nellie got a beak full. I am not sure if she was a happy birdie or an unhappy birdie, she was running round in circles for the longest time shaking her head. This morning, when Faby called Nellie, she ran in the other direction. I got her on my finger, Faby came over for a kiss, some times she would give Faby a kiss, not this time, she was sitting, she stood up, turned around and sat down. Makes me believe she was not happy with that beak full of wine she got.

Tue Dec 25, 2007

Christmas Day

Those girls. You can't get any thing expensive for them, they will destroy it. If you get any thing cheap, no matter how nice it looks, they will refuse it. Remember Carola's gifts? We added a few more and put around our little tree, both girls refused them. Oh, well. So, Faby and I went for a little walk. That lasted a good part of the day. During which, we were almost attacked. The guy did not say any thing to me, but Faby was almost in tears, he did say in English three times "give me your right hand" where she wears her rings, one is worth a car, and one is worth a house here. Family heirlooms. I am not sure what that guy thought or was doing. That was when Faby started to cry, I had about a three quarter bottle of soda in my left hand covered with Faby's hat, it was chest high, I brought my right hand up beside Faby's face, not in a tight fist, but ready, I was locked cocked and ready to fire when he took Faby's hand. I was thinking, there goes the rings, but not with out a fight! I was watching hard, my left foot was in front of my right foot by about two hand a half feet, get the picture? I was ready to break ribs, fake with the right, going for the face, come in hard with the left to the ribs, then with the right foot start kicking as hard as I could. I don't know if he noticed the rings, which was very difficult for me to believe, or noticed how I was sizing him up, which would be a little more believable. He did glance at me, then let go of Faby and backed off, a few feet, turned and left. The rings are still on her fingers, and her fingers are still on her hand, and her hand is still attached to her arm . . . Yes she is still complete. That was scary. But I must say, "so far so good" Our heavenly Father looks our for me, and sure was today, Thank You. He was asking for money, She was saying we were broke and just came from a relatives house, we were walking because we had no money for a buss and we lived so far a way, then he demanded her hand, her right hand, and said it in English. When we got home, Nellie was still upset at Faby, for some reason . . . oh, well, I am sure she will get over it. Faby told the girls to wash the dishes this morning, and this afternoon when we got home, there is still a sink full, its almost 8pm, we got back at 4pm, ate a little, started a Christmas movie and Faby and I fell asleep, I just woke up a few minutes ago to write this.

Wed Dec 26, 2007

Bye Lisa

I said one more for Lisa, here it is, the last one I wrote was By Lisa, this one is Bye Lisa.

She was fun. Next time we get one, we will get one from the pet store, they may cost five times more at the cheapest, but chances of survival are better.

Sun Dec 30, 2007

Adesa

Thursday and Friday I went with Faby to her school. That was some thing. The director was being very picky with Faby. One little mistake, and the director rejected every thing Faby did, then demanded that Faby go to the Government Education Office to get more forms. The forms are of a special size, you just can't find that size of paper just any where. So, you can't just make copies, you have to go to the Government Education Office. Well, if we had left when the director told her to go, we would have been in a bad accident. It takes Faby a while to say, "bye" even when she is coming right back. The office was a thirty minute bus ride away. On the way to the bus stop, we seen a bus coming, tried to waive it down, but it just kept going, so we caught the next one. Half way to the office, we seen the bus we missed . . . parked in a big truck, if the driver survived, he ain't in good shape at all, on the way back, we seen the front end of the bus, it was flat up against the first or second row of seats, I mean it was mashed. some times I wonder if some one is trying to get rid of us, or is some one looking out for us. Any how, we got to the office. and they were sending Faby all over the building. down the hall, to the second floor, to the third floor, back down to the first floor, all over the building. until a director of another school seen Faby and asked what she was doing there. Faby told her, and that director said the Adesa director is not doing right, but to follow her, she would show Faby where to get the papers she is looking for . . . would you know it . . . a street vendor. The government education offices don't want to deal with all those papers, so they have a street vendor sell them. Well, we got back to the school, and didn't leave the school until after 5pm writing notes-grades, what ever you call them, any how that was Thursday, come Friday, finished up the notes turning in the papers, and then I noticed a lot of yelling, I asked Faby what was going on. They were saying that the director is refusing to pay any of the teachers, along with the accountant and the one above the director, Ada´s second here in Peru, all saying "you got your Christmas bonus, what more do you want?" ya, no pay until the end of January. Sure am glad Faby does not have to depend on that paycheck, but there are some teachers that are hurting, they spent their Christmas bonus on Christmas expecting their regular paychecks. a lot of unhappy teachers. well, come 1:30, thirty minutes to leave, there was still teachers there trying to please the director with their notes, Faby finally got every thing done turned in and passed inspection. there was a few teachers that you could find mistakes at a glance, white out-liquid paper all over the paper, but they and the director are "tight" the other teachers, especially Faby, the director was making problems to, one tiny mistake, and the whole nine yards was rejected. Five school grades, five different papers at 3 or 4 soles a page, for the official government education document, can get costly for one mistake and having to go find more to redo the whole thing. Any way, as we were leaving some of the teachers who was there was trying to talk Faby in to staying a little longer. She was always trying to make every one happy, or at least the majority happy.

Mon Dec 31, 2007

Stand

I don't know if I did good or bad, but I talked Faby in to getting that stand. It would be a lot better for her to have a stand in side a building, as apposed to having her stuff out side on the side walk or going to houses, in my opinion. The cost for the stand is 50 dollars a month, that is 150 soles a month. Plus they want one month warranty. We were 150 soles short, but they said they will give us a week to come up with the rest. I Believe in Faby. I Believe She can Do IT! Any how, I thought I would mention it, so maybe you can keep her in your thoughts, and maybe say a little prayer for her, so her business can do good.

Tue Jan 1, 2008

New Years Eve

The owners of the gallery, I heard were going to open one bottle of champagne to celebrate the new year with all the tenants. the gallery closed at 10pm. What the owners did do was also open two bottles of wine. I was sitting in with Faby when they were all talking over the details of renting a space, and in the conversation, stated if Faby opens yesterday, they would open a bottle of wine, because every time she shows up to the gallery, she brightens the whole place up, bringing smiles and happiness to every one. Well, they had things to do, they have a vineyard, they make alcohol, both for drinking and for medical purposes, so they were busy yesterday. They showed up just after 9pm, and opened two bottles of wine with the champagne, and got some Christmas bread to boot, and was also sharing with the customers that was there. Faby had two customers to start off the New Year, Plus I got her on film, trimming the hair dressers hair . . . proof she knows what she is doing :) Almost like last year. OK, here in Peru, the belief is, if you want to travel, you pack a bag and walk around the block or two blocks, throwing lenties all over the place. If you have no plans on traveling, you may just want to stand in one place shooting off fire works and firing piñatas, saying bye to the last year, you know ashes to ashes and stuff like that, (firing—setting fire to them) in Mexico, they are filled with candies and toys, here, they are for burning in different celebrations, some birthdays, opening celebrations, be it a grand or re-opening, as well as Holiday celebrations. Last year, we walked around the block throwing lenties all over the place, did the same this year, only this time, Nellie was with us, she refused to stay in the house. We started out with dinner, just before midnight, after packing our bags of course, not many items, shoes, purses, a few clothes and the most important items, "The Pass Ports". Nellie was all over ever thing. After dinner, came the grapes, (still not sure about them) any how, Nellie was sure in to them as well, and her poor craw was packed. She seemed more excited then the girls were. Midnight hit and lenties went flying every where, we put our packs on and out we went. I tried to put Nellie in the room, but she was fighting to stay, flying and climbing up my arm, I finally gave in and she went, riding on my shoulder, the back pack, and finally caught my arm where she snuggled in, all those fire works going off, still she was looking all over the place. We passed several people, a few couples and a couple families doing the same thing we were doing. Seen lots of piñatas burning, and a whole lot of fire works going off. We finally came back in just after 1am, we sure was tired. We did have fun. Had fun last year, and we traveled a few places. Last year we walked around one block, last night, we walked around two blocks, in hopes our traveling will go a little further this year, instead of just traveling south to Chile, maybe heading North this time?

Wed Jan 2, 2008

Adesa

There was two cats at Adesa, one black, and one gray and black striped. Was. I seen what those poor cats were eating today, they are skin and bone. They were being fed rice. Faby got them some cat food, it looked to me like two cups of rice with a small amount of cat food sprinkled on top, in their dish. The gray and black one is more friendly then the black one, climbed right up my leg, fell asleep in my arms. Any way, Ada's second said no pay checks for any one because he accidentally spilled coffee on them, now all the teachers have to wait until Ada comes back from Holland. She is due back the 15Th, and when she finally gets around to the school part of her business, it may be the end of January before they get paid . . . or so they think, I may have a word with Ada my self, because they are telling Faby she has to give summer school classes for free, as well as scrub the walls of the school and paint the walls of the school, for free. To Ada's second, he is saying the teachers must be thankful for having a job, to prove their thankfulness, they have to give these classes and clean and paint the walls, if they don't, they may not have a job next year, or so Faby was being told. Do I have to tell you what Faby said :) She does not want to say any thing to Ada, but, I might if I get a chance. Faby is calling the cat, Leonsey, some thing like that. He was stuffed in her purse by one of the other teachers as we were leaving the school today, yes, I went with Faby, while there, K.F.C. called Faby for a party tonight, from 4 to 6, and of course, they were trying to delay her leaving again. I think she made it to her party on time, not sure, it would be close. The cat has a few flees on it, I am thinking of a salt water bath followed by shampoo. The flees don't like the salt, then again, neither does the cats or dogs . . . I have done this before . . . not real fun, but it works. Not real sure how Nellie will like the kitten, he is not real old, I think its a male, not real sure, he is asleep in my lap for now. I will see how he takes to taking a bath after a while, Faby has the girls washing the dishes and cleaning the sink, they have been at it for about 45 minutes now, and the sink was only half full.

Sat Jan 5, 2008

A Few Things

The Kitten has turned out to be a female, maybe. Told to us by one of Faby's "cheese may" friends who says she is good friends with a vet. The kitten's name has changed several times, was Phillip for a while, now is Phillis. One of these days, we are going to take her to a vet to make sure. If we have her long enough. Because Faby's Friend also stated, that female cats make female humans sterile. Then Faby told me her grand mother told her a long time ago, the very same thing. Its a belief here in Peru, if a woman don't want to have kids, get a female cat and she will not have any kids. I wonder if any one else has ever heard of this one. So, Faby is talking about leaving the cat in several different places. any how, it also sounds as convincing to me as Peruvians getting worms by eating candy, you know the sugar in the candy gives Peruvians worms. So, we will see how long we keep the cat. And no, I have not convinced her or the girls that the worms come from the tap water due to contamination, you know the broken sewer pipes all over Peru going in to the ground and in to the ocean, she says worms comes from eating sugar, and all things made with sugar, like candy. Nellie is some thing. Attacking Phillis all the time. Phillis will be stretched out fast asleep and here comes Nellie, beak first as fast as she can run, right to the nose. Then she will start biting at the tail and chasing her around, pecking at what ever is closest. I have seen Phillis bat Nellie's head a few times, but she back off real quick when Nellie got her senses back. side stepping and ducking, sizing up and poor kitty, when Nellie attacks, she don't hold back much. Got the girls signed up for school, not real sure if they will be in the morning or after noon. The president of the P.T.A. is wanting to put in a High School, in the after noon, because she has kids in High School and wants them in the same building, so she does not have to go to another school. Only one little problem, the desks and chairs are not for the big kids, but she is still fighting so hard, that rumors has it that about half the parents have taken their kids out of that school and found other schools to put them in. Saying it would be too dangerous. Well, just being in the morning is too dangerous, because almost all the kids who come up missing are from the morning turn, its like 90 percent of the kids who get taken, or stolen, are in the morning classes, when I mentioned that to Faby to tell the President, her reply was, "I hired more security for that purpose, so it will be a lot safer in the morning." I was not going to ask the next question . . . where the money came from, because she can not dictate where all the money goes, not like that. The money is for repairs and improvements, not to hire security, there is not enough funds coming in for that. Oh, well, I can tell you this much, the girls will hate getting up that early, because the classes begin at 7am, they are moving until 9:30 am at the earliest. This will be interesting. Biggest thing on this subject is the fact that I will be taking their lunches to school and showing the cafeteria woman and handing them to their teachers, about an hour before their lunch break . . . we will see how the "I'm starving to death" works this year . . . that really got to me, as much food as they love to throw away, they are telling lies about how they have nothing to eat, how we starve them to death, and they go with out eating for days so their stories have meaning. it ain't fair and I plan on breaking them this year. I don't much care what time they go to school, as long as I know when their break is. Went to check on getting a stamp on my I.D. card, the stamp I am suppose to get every six months. To prove I am being have my self and stuff. This time it was a breeze, they have a new girl working in there where I have to go, and it didn't take all day with the saying "come back next month so you can pay a hundred dollars in late fees" I have all of Jan. to get the stamp, come Feb. 1, its a hundred dollars in late fees, for each day after that its five dollars a day added on, or so was the rules six months ago, and the guy there kept saying they needed the money worse then we did, and that all North Americans were million airs and we needed to share more. Any how, I go back Tuesday to get my stamp, they have to run checks to make sure I have been good and not wanted for some crime of some kind, or working and owe taxes, the usual routine. Hopefully I don't run in to any problems come Tuesday. Faby is enjoying her self in her stand, she has had a few costumers, not many yet, hopefully business improves soon. She had two on her opening night, two yesterday, and two today so far, for a total of six. She is just starting out, so, not many people even know she is there. I am sure when they do find out, she will have plenty of customers. Now, How do I convince Faby a cat will not make a woman go sterile? I have never heard of that before. And if it is true, there where and when has it happened? any how, Got any ideas?

Thu Jan 10, 2008

A Couple Stories

At the Gallery The video guy is fighting with his hair dresser, is threatening to close the hair saloon and put in an Internet. One old woman who has the seven stand, is fighting with every one, to the point she is putting as much of her stuff in the hall as she can. That has the phone stand woman upset, she taped on her section of wall, she has stands 5 and 6. she told the seven stand woman not to cross her line again or she would loose her stuff, so, she is using the space in front of stand eight, right in front of Faby . . . not setting too well with Faby. The second and third stand women just sit back and enjoy the show, the best part of the show is the fourth stand woman. She has two boy friends, both are big guys. One is full of love, the other one is full of money. Both know about each other. One of them was telling her he wanted another girl friend, she got upset saying she is the only woman for him. He said she has two boy friends, why can't he have two girl friends. Oh, she was up set over that, how dare he say such horrible things to her. Mad Science for a several months now, Faby has been working for Mad Science, as Party Paint Faces Girl. Each month they have a Paint Faces of the month, as well as Party Person and Mad Science of the month. Yesterday, was the one of each for the year. Faby has not gotten paint faces of the month, even though several said she deserved it. Well, the first prize was the Paint Faces of the Year, Faby got it, she got the certificate that said some thing like "Diploma for the best Paint Faces of the Year" it never made it home, so I could not scan it and post it, I did try to get a picture of it. She took it to a glass shop and had it framed and now is in her stand hanging on the wall. any how, next award went to Mad Science, the guy who won that one was saying how emotional he was, he tried his best to please every kid in the party, and even though some times he for got the formula and had some unexpected explosions, he just played it off like it was part of the show . . . his bosses were saying, hay wait a minute, what's with the unexpected explosions? give back the award. Party Person was next, he was saying how happy he was, how emotional he was, and he did his best to get to every party he was assigned to do as well as the unexpected ones that always pop up, no mater how late it was, no mater how drunk he was he always found a way to make it to every party . . . you don't always want to say all that, his bosses were more upset over that one then the one before saying "drunk? what do you mean drunk? give back the award" I think those two were just playing, Faby sure was happy about her award. she says now if some one wants to learn how to paint faces, she can charge big time for it, and show them, if they learn from her, they too can get awards like this :)

Sun Jan 13, 2008

Meeting

Last Thursday, as Faby was going to her job site, kids party, paint faces type, she ran in to the girls school president of the fathers association. (P.T.A.) Last time we seen her, she was with some one else, with arms wrapped around each other, when she was telling Faby about how her and the director was fighting over the afternoon classes. She wants High School kids in the afternoon . . . mainly because she has kids in High School and wants them in the same building. Well, in the bus, she was with her husband, hugging and kissing him, until she seen Faby. In which she started yelling at Faby, saying "how could you, you had no right, now the director is really upset with me." After she got the whole bus interested, she started saying how it was so wrong for Faby to say any thing about putting the girls in the morning classes. Faby was only trying to find out who was teaching in the morning classes, she does not want just any "cholo" teacher messing with her kids, they are the smartest kids in the whole school. She was saying to the President of the P.T.A. woman. sorry, I forget her name :(, any how, She went on to say, how the director is trying to force her to sign a document to let Rafael Santos in the School Auditorium. I mentioned that one before, the school has no owner, and the municipality has ever right to take the property, but first they need a solid contract to get in the building. That is what Rafael is working on, he wants the school, and so does the municipality. (They may not take it right away, but over a couple of years, they will take it, and kick the school out, all the students and teachers will have to go else where. But the director and the "P.T.A" president don't believe it or don't know any thing about that possibility, instead, they are just looking at the money that Rafael is offering for the rent of the School Auditorium.) She went on to say how the director was threatening to expose her to the public how she not only has a husband, but also has a boy friend on the side, if she does not sign the papers. She said she wants the money in her hand first. Yes, she was saying this out loud, right in front of her husband. Saying if she wants two men in her life, its no ones business but her own. Acting as if, its a common thing here for women to have two men . . . remember the fourth stand woman, one of Faby's "cheese may" friends, she has two men, and got very upset over the fact one said he wanted another girl friend . . . I don't get it. She was so very upset with Faby, acting as if it was all Faby's fault that the director found out about her and her boy friend, as well as the fight they had over the kids in the school, about the hours and when to go? in the morning or after noon? We still don't know what is going on, the assistant director told us to check back on the fifteenth of Jan. to find out more. that is just in a couple more days, maybe another story on top of that one :)

Sun Jan 13, 2008

Philly and Nellie

Philly, could be Phillup, not Phillis, still, called "Philly" looks like he is growing a pair down there. No, I have not felt, he is still a kitten, I don't want to hurt him, he has very sharp claws and teeth, I feel them every time I give him a bath. but the worst part of him is the fact that Faby has a hard time breathing after playing with him. She is complaining of pains in her throat and chest. some times it lasts for hours. She does try to spend a little time with Philly, she sure does love him or her. Says all other cats are monsters and should be gotten rid of. well, she says that about just about every thing or little baby, animal or what ever until she gets one in her arms, then the rest are monsters, but the one she has is OK :) Nellie sure is growing. Loves going out for walks, she usually rides on my shoulders, some times rides on my arms. When I leave the apartment with out her, she sure is voicing her opinion. She really loves the park. Running around catching bugs, scratching in the dirt, and stuff. She has not taken a dirt bath yet, but she tries on our bed, on the brown parts of our cover. She found the kitty litter, and started scratching in it, I tried telling her she don't want to do that, but she got a beak full before I could stop her, she wasn't pleased with me. Both sure are some thing. One day is seen them rolling a ball back and forth. a tennis size ball. Philly was batting it to Nellie and Nellie was pecking it, making it roll back to Philly. At first I was watching in disbelief, but they kept at it for about ten or so minutes, across the living room. Some times I hear Nellie screaming, like she is getting mauled, beaten badly, I go to check, Nellie is running like mad, and there is Philly, laying there as if to say, "I didn't do any thing." I have seen Nellie sneak up on Philly while he was sleeping and, you know, that beak is pretty tough on that poor tender nose. Also, I have seen Nellie go after Philly's tail, while it was moving, while he was sleeping or eating, poor kitty, gets woke up rather rudely, beak in the nose or tail getting caught . . . while sleeping or eating. We will see how long we can keep them both, no pets aloud in most places, and you know the land lord, always looking for ways to raise the rent and such. We have the rent money, just have not paid it yet, Faby likes to pay the rent on the due date, which was yesterday, but he was not there. Oh, Well. Nellie still thinks my chest is her personal bed, even though she has her bed on the floor by the head of the bed on my side. She voices her opinion every night when I put her on her bed and turn the light out. Some times when I wake up in the morning, I find this little lump on my chest. Some how she manages to climb up during the night and fight the under current . . . me tossing and turning, and survives. Well, I am not just going to let her stay on me all night, but if she climbs up during the night, what can I do. I would be afraid of squashing her during the night. oh, ya, and I for get the test, on how to tell if the chick is a hen or a rooster, I know you hold them by their feet, but who fights the worst, the hen or the rooster?

Sun Jan 13, 2008

Alovira

OK, I am not sure of the spelling of this plant, but I have two of them, twins. They were the same size when I got them. Just little bitty. They grew some, to the point they out grew the little pot they came in, so I separated them. One stayed the same size for months, didn't change colors, didn't do any thing. One grew twice its size, but it had problems, the window, which I kept open for a breeze, would slam shut and knocked it on the floor three times, in which it lost a few stems. When I solved that problem, another one came up. The poor thing hit the first floor twice, loosing several more stems. It started looking poorly. Changing colors, from green to purple. It even seemed to shrink to the size of its twin, in which the twin started to grow. In fact, the twin had grown so much, I had to re-pot it two more times, it is really growing good. the first one I am talking about, was getting worse and worse. It had about a dozen stems, and loosing them one by one, it had turned completely purple and the outer stems were turning brown and falling off, up until it only had four left. I seen how the people here would strip all the roots off the alo plants, leaving only the center root, and not much of it and putting it in water. So, I did just that, it turned Green, grew about eight to ten more stems, starting to look real good, that was a couple months ago, I did that, last month, I put it in dirt, it had lots of roots, fully green and looking real good., less then half the size of its twin. well, about two weeks ago, it was completely purple again, and had lost all but four or five of its stems again. I was a bit depressed. Last week I just pulled it out of the dirt, and put it back in a little jar full of water. In just three days, it was half green and growing two more stems. today I just looked at it again, lots of little roots growing every were and just a few purple spots left, and a couple more little stems growing out of it. I thought this was in the cactus family and don't need much water at a time. can live in dry places for long times. I really thought sitting in water like that would hurt or kill the roots. So, can any one tell me what happened? and when I should take it out of the water to put it back in the dirt? anyhow, just letting you know what is going on with my alo plants, cause I don't know what is going on my self.

Tue Jan 15, 2008

29 years

After 29 years of separation, Faby found her "Godmother" what a reunion. spent all day there, sorry mama and papa, we were busy, the only camera we had was the little camera, ran out of film again in the big one :(oh, well, always got the little one for the "emergencies" :)

It was a very nice reunion, at first we were only going to visit with her godmother, but then she called her daughter, and she called some one else, then some one else, and what started out to be just an address finding trip, turned in to an "Unexpected Family Reunion"

One nice thing the old man there did, Faby's Godfather, did, was this, unexpected as well, but, he gave me a little bottle of Peruvian Rum. Ron Cartavio is the name on the bottle, and rum is at the bottom, but I am not going to even try to read all the little letters, its after 1am here now. Faby and the girls are asleep and should be as well.

Faby will get around to naming the pictures in a few days or so, maybe tomorrow, if she has time, we have another long day tomorrow as well, mostly the girls school, and her paint faces job with Mad Science. The Mad Science people only hire for six months at a time, and Faby's time is up tomorrow, so she is going to see about signing another six months. both places could take all day to do.

Thu Jan 17, 2008

29 years, in detail

After reading what I wrote, I realized I was asleep. There are four brothers, at least four, maybe more, but I only know of four. Faby's first adoptive Father did his best to adopt Faby when he found out she was in the orphanage. His story was he cheated on his wife, with Faby's supposed biological mother, and he could not stand to see Faby, his daughter, in an orphanage. Here is another story, Faby's second adoptive Father, who lives in North Carolina, has much the same story, and the reason why mama Birtha don't like Faby at all. Faby is the result of him cheating on his wife, Birtha. She loves her grand children, but don't like Faby much. Another brother, who claimed Faby, after I married her, is one guy who Faby never liked at all, because he was so mean, but he had a very similar story to tell. The only brother that did not claim Faby was Uncle Roberto. He just hates Faby with such passion, its unreal. But he uses Faby to get money from his brother in North Carolina. Saying how he helps Faby all the time. Another thing some of the family was talking about was how she was never born in Peru to begin with. That is what her "godmother" just told her. Her godmother is her supposed biological mothers sister. And she just told Faby that night that Faby was born in India. The Indian now lives in the U.S. some where, not sure where, but he is a million air. He has business all over the world and has property all over the world. Well, in lots of countries any way. She went on to say, how Just after she was born, he brought her to Peru, because he was supervising his business here, and her sister was working in his house at the time, also she was in and out of the insane asylums during that time. She would get caught and put in, after a while, she would escape and go strait to the Indians house to hide out and work. Well, one day, she showed up at her sisters house with a baby saying "this is my baby, you have to help me." the sister was asking, "how can you have a baby, you have no boy friend, no husband, you have been in the insane asylum, how is this possible?" again she would say, "this is my baby, you have to help me." Plus the fact that she has an Indian birth certificate, which would be next to impossible to get . . . that was a very big twist and threw Faby off, because her aunt, the god mother's son, her cousin, just look at how much they look alike. They are standing side by side. That was some reunion. to hear about how she was the possible result of three different men cheating on their wives, as well as stolen from a million airs house. And he gave up fighting because he was a foreigner, and Peru was not listening to him, no mater how much money he had, his word had no value here. I for get if he still has a business here, but he left Peru. Right now he is not married, not sure if he is widowed or divorced, but now not married, and no children from what Faby found out. Faby was not sure what to believe. Not only her cousin in the picture, but several more people that came to see her, she looked so much like them and they like her. That was what was throwing her for such a loop. Any way, she was five years old when she last seen any of these people, and now she is 34. And they all remembered her, so much, that a couple of them was searching for her for years trying to find her.

Thu Jan 17, 2008

Blood

Faby could be third generation England. She could be third generation U.S. She could be First generation Indian. To even try to get her Indian birth certificate, she would have to go to India. Do you know how hard it is for a Peruvian to get a visa to India? Let me give you a hint. U.S. citizens need to get a special visa to go to India, not all of U.S. citizens are approved. Faby was checking this info. out, she was saying how could she even ask to go. There is no way she can get it here in Peru, they have already sent it back to India. Family names, could be third generation U.S. or England, which means she has "citizen ship rights" how ever, the U.S. has bad habits of refusing entrance to its own citizens born in the country and raised outside the country. Faby has met several people born in the U.S. of U.S. parents or one U.S. parent, but raised here in Peru, and the U.S. Embassy, even though these people showed U.S. birth certificates, Said "NO!" and they were not being polite about it. as for England, she has to make contacts with her relatives in England. Make out the paper work in the British Embassy, and after all the paper work is complete, which could take any where from six months to two years, showing the paper trail of citizenship's, then the Embassy calls the relatives in England, if they say, "yes, she is our relative" she gets her citizen ship approved and will be able to travel to England or Scotland any time she wants to. She has found her English relatives, a while ago, like about a year ago, and they have yet to respond to her emails. But things are starting to look up, she has documents, almost, stating birth records, she has to get her own official copies, and that will cost some money, but she has the names and its a start. And she is scared, because all they have to say, the ones in England, is "no, she is not a relative" and she will be denied. I am not sure either, I think the best thing to do is to continue trying to get the visa to the U.S. and then try the others after words. The U.S. is hard, India is even harder, I am not sure about England. They could, with enough evidence, just approve her with out any phone calls. Which could be a good thing, but the problem lye's with the paper work and all the official documents that don't come cheep.

Mon Jan 21, 2008

Party

Yesterday, Jan. 20, Faby had a paint faces party to go to, and this burger king has a very large play area. I am not sure if Faby was feeling guilty or just being nice, but she said for us all to go so the girls could play while she was doing her party. Just before the bus stop, Carola started again . . . making problems as usual. Mama tried to talk to her but she was quick to back talk. Faby was speaking English at first, but Carola was screaming in Spanish back at her. And guess what??? there was others around watching. I really got tired of it and screamed at her to "SHUT UP!" and how the tears started flowing. I was getting dirty looks from the other people, I tried to say, "actress" in Spanish, and I was clapping and laughing. Carola was balling a water fall . . . sorry no pics . . . Well, during the battle, I heard Faby asking Carola if she would behave at the party, and Carola screaming back NO! I was ready to take them back to the apt. or go my self, but Faby would not allow me to. Carola got her way again, she put on a show for total strangers again showing how badly mistreated she is . . .

Mon Jan 21, 2008

Phone

Faby thought she was in trouble yesterday. she had two parties. During the first party, one of her bosses called her, very upset. Saying he tried to get a hold of her and got her husband. Does him no good because "I" can't speak any Spanish, and he can not speak any English. they were not very happy. To the point they came to her during her party, or just after her party and told her they wanted to speak to her. She has three bosses. She really thought she was in trouble. With all the talking they did, saying things like, "what are we going to do" or "what can be done about this" and it led up to, "We have made a company decision, you need a company phone so we can contact you for emergency parties." Its like this, usually parties are booked at least a week in advance. Some times they are not, some times they are booked same day, and certain stores only want Faby there. Certain party people only want Faby. Faby is the "Best of the Year" But, Can you believe that? They were so mad at her, for not being able to reach her, they got her a Company Phone. Not just any phone, its the best in Peru, Claro cell phone. they told her to carry it every where she goes, just in case of "emergency parties" popping up. by the way, only management has company cell phones, no other party person or paint faces girl has company cell phones, and her bosses has stated, if it was any one else, they would not care, but Faby is the Best and they don't want to loose her. I told Faby, if she is not careful, she could wind up in a Management position, right now they are still toying with the idea of her being low level management, training other paint faces as well as in charge of the "princess parties" but so far, nothing has happened as of yet, other then they loved all her ideas.

Mon Jan 21, 2008

Nails

Some of the women at the Union Church has called Faby. They have a club, and they want to know just how good Faby is. They have heard about her and how good she is, and seen a few things she has done. But tomorrow, is a test. The club has called Faby to come and paint their nails . . . finger nails. I am not sure how many is in the club or how many in the club will get their nails done. One thing for sure, Faby is excited. I was just thinking about her store, I got some pictures to load up, if I can find them, not sure where they went, oh, well, I will look for them, if I find them I will load them up today

Mon Jan 21, 2008

Uncle Roberto

I think it was last Friday, sorry, I forget, any how, Uncle Roberto was demanding his paycheck again . . . well, his brothers retirement check. Faby asked me if I was going to behave my self, my reply was, "are you going to buy me a bottle of whiskey?" her answer was, "you stay here, CAROLA, get dressed . . . Your coming with me!" Well, Faby told me, that Uncle Roberto was up to his insulting ways again. they, this time went to a bank very far away, next to a park with prostitutes. And guess what happened . . . Uncle Roberto felt tired and told Faby he was going to the park to rest. Went right to one of the prostitutes and offered her some money, then was almost arrested by undercover police. Faby said she was thinking to her self, while the police were escorting Uncle Roberto out of the park and towards her, if he said he knew her, she would deny knowing him. Why couldn't I go? Because I am getting tired of being insulted by that person and him calling his brother saying how I am badly mistreating him. I am starting to get insulting back and Faby is trying to keep me from doing it. Sorry, its rubbing off . . .

Thu Jan 24, 2008

Unreal

I wonder if the Metro in Mineral Wells is charging for the restrooms. Here in Peru, they don't believe much in "public" restrooms . . . its mostly pay toilets, some day, I may take pictures of some of the pay toilets that I refuse to use . . . and they don't give refunds.

Metro is a Grocery, toy, electronics, and lots of other items. Metro and Wong are partners the address on the receipt WWW.ewong.com

I couldn't believe they started charging, and they are giving real receipts. I had to share this one with you.

Mon Jan 28, 2008

Nellie and Philly

Mama brought home part of her work and told the girls to eat . . . a few days ago . . . its KFC, and they have the "Kernels" recipe . . . that stuff is "GOOD!!!" and the girls would rather throw it away then to eat it . . . well not all the time, but you should see just how much they do throw away from what Mama brings home for them to eat. Any How, I made a mistake, got the wrong cat food, and Philly was really talking to mama about it. pointing at his dist and meowing up a storm. Well, Mama found the chicken and intentionally dropped it on the floor for Philly . . . he wasted no time tearing in to it. Then Nellie seen him, and the chicken on the floor, it became a fight, tooth and claw vs. beak and nail. I thought Nellie was going to loose her head a couple times. I was telling Philly the only chicken you can eat is cooked chicken, and was telling Nellie, she should not be eating chicken, she is one. I don't think either one was paying any attention to me, both were tearing that bird apart. The girls were at the table, I don't think it phased them much, in fact I think they enjoyed watching good food go to the pets . . . again, remember mama Chella?

Fri Feb 8, 2008

Nellie

Feb. 4, was the last time we seen her. We took her to one of the natives communities. The guy we gave her to was raised on a farm, and knows all about animals. He and his wife are moving to Cuzco. She has her bed with her. He knows she was a family pet. When we left, she beat us to the door and was chirping loudly. Ya, I miss her. I did not know that the land lord said for us to get rid of her or he would make her disappear one of these days, until Faby told the girls that is what he said. I wonder what he says about the parakeet that is in the building, I hear it every day. He said that Philly is next, if there are any more complaints about him. Philly misses Nellie too, he is looking for her every day. She would disturb him while he was sleeping. Some times they would play ball with each other. I know it sounds unbelievable, but I watched them bat the ball to each other one day. Faby says that guy is a real good guy, we would go to visit him and his wife every time we went there. Sorry no pictures, no film in the big camera, and the battery died in the little cam. I hope she is happy, she sure did like going out for walks and she loved the park.

Fri Feb 8, 2008

Peru

I was just at the store . . . Metro, looking at the prices of the sea food. It was because I was thinking of what was just on the news lately, well, a couple things, I'll get to them after a bit. OK, Faby is always telling me when I mention soles, it confuses every one. from what I have seen is this, things locally bought here is the same price as they are locally bought there, for example, a candy bar there costs about 60 cents, a candy bar here costs the same, 60 centimos. so, price wise, things that are locally bought . . . the dollar and the soles is the same, how ever, for example, U.S. M & M's here costs 3 soles, where as the same M & M's locally packaged is only 60 centimos, not sure of the spelling, but I think its close :) When I first got here, the sea food was ranging from 50 centimos to 5 soles a kilo, then President Toleado, the last President, sold all the fishing rights to Spain for 30 million dollars. All the commercial fisher men has to pay a tax to Spain to keep fishing . . . the sea food doubled in price, the Peruvians were upset over that, but at least it wasn't killing them. Another thing, a 5 kilo bag of rice was from 5 soles to 7 soles depending on the brand name. Well, this President, President Garcia has decided to export all the rice grown in Peru, now all the rice that is sold in the stores comes from Bolivia. Rice is now ranging from 15 soles to 20 soles a 5 kilo bag, depending on where you buy it. But that is not all President Garcia is doing. Some of the fish here, Peruvian Fish, are considered delicacies, and those fish have more then doubled, up to 22 soles and 50 centimose a kilo, and the killer is the shrimp at a whopping 30 soles a kilo, and if you are caught selling with out a special permit, you are heavily fined and shut down for months. Especially the shrimp!!! They are in high demand in so many foreign countries, that President Garcia has ordered that they get exported, or you pay a high price for you license to sell, or you get shut down. Here is the kicker :) The people and the military is trying to declare war with Chile . . . I'll get back to it :) I have wrote about how Lima is doing, watching the garbage trucks dumping their loads in the ocean, and how I seen in the news of the sewer pipes that are broken and running like a river in the ocean, and one scene where the reporter asked a woman who was swimming in the ocean with turds bumping in to her why she is swimming and letting her kids swim in there, she said she has been swimming there all her life and she just tells her kids to swim with their mouths closed. The Lima Mayer said to the reporter, that the fishing is good, the fish are not sick or dying, and the people are not sick and dying, so what is the problem, why fix it if there is no problem . . . not only that, but Lima is the leader of the whole nation of Peru, so, what Lima does, the rest of the country does. Can you imagine just how dirty is the ocean here? Are you getting the picture of what is going on? We have been to Chile lots of times, their main and almost the only catch is shark, different kinds of shark, but its all shark, or was. Now, they are getting other kinds of fish, the Peruvian fish are moving south and the Peruvians are getting upset saying that Chile can not catch Peruvian fish. The went down to catch "their" fish and the Chile people ran them off, saying its their water. Now the Peruvian people, the fisher men mainly along with the military, want to declare war over the fish that don't want to live in Peru waters . . . I just can't imagine why they don't want to live here, can you? this was just on the news a couple days ago. President Garcia does not want to be bothered with such petty nonsense, he has more important things to do, like the above mentioned of exporting every thing he can.

Sat Feb 23, 2008

Disturbing

Well, Uncle Roberto has been kicked out of several banks. Now the social security hospital, the one where Faby's adoptive father retired from. They don't even what to see him, because he is always presenting fake papers. He was unable to get any money this month, from his brothers retirement check, that is Faby's father. You know he called him and was complaining on how badly mistreated he was by Faby and me. When Faby finally got a hold of them, they were screaming at her, "how dare you mistreat your uncle" and "your uncle has more right to that money then you to" She tried explaining that the banks don't want him, and now the hospital don't want him, and that the power is expired. Plus the fact that the hospital wants the past three pay vouchers, "check stubs", you see, its the government that pays the retirement checks, but only if the hospital sends in the reports, and the hospital wants to see how much the government is paying, and Uncle Roberto refuses to show the check stubs, so, no money and its all Faby's fault. Mama Birtha and her Father both stated that Roberto will get the new power and for her not to even ask, and to quit trying to make him look bad. She said she will send them the fake paper he gave to the hospital, and they said any one can fake papers . . . I mean just screaming at Faby . . . and she does all this for pennies. Uncle Roberto states he is only getting 800 soles a month and he gives Faby 400 soles, half of what he gets. in actual fact, he gets well over a thousand soles and gives Faby 100 or 200 soles . . . he says he gives from the pain on his heart, because he is more needed then she is. Well, no money this month, at least she is working. I told Faby not to bother with them any more. Well, I tell her every month not to bother with them. She has one more paper, one paper to redo, and we are doing it on Monday, the police certificates again, and what ever they wanted redone. All three have been approved on the first part, Natalia and Carola have been approved on the second, Faby is still working on it. After that, comes the Embassy, and there are three stages in that, first is the appointments for the medical checks, then comes the appointments for the back ground checks, then comes the final appointments with the final questions . . . no telling how long, or how much money all that will cost, but one thing for sure, if we leave any time soon, she will not be calling any one for a long time, at least several months . . . I would love to see how uncle Roberto can explain how mistreated we are treating him if we are not even there. I am talking about how the banks are kicking him out do to filing false papers and signing with other names then his own, which he does. he just says he is old and he forgets. Faby is there to cover for him so he can get the money, then he is quick to call telling his lies on how bad we treat him and how he gave her half the check and we are not even thankful. One last thing, I really messed up. And Faby paid for it. I was doing laundry, trying to get every thing done, looking all over for dirty clothes. I did not check her uniform real close, in fact, I did not even look at it the day I did laundry, and she paid a heavy fine for it. It was messed up in the back, just a few spots, the customers did not say a word, but the management of the KFC sure did, calling Mad Science and making real big scene, it cost Faby 200 soles for a few spots in the back of her uniform, barley noticeable. But she makes in 2 hours what most Peruvians make in 10 hours, how ever the difference is, she only works just enough hours, and traveling to many different stores, that the pay checks are the same at the end of the month any way, well, the checks working for this company any way, its a U.S. company, and they make at least three times more then the average Peruvian any way. I sure do hope this next step is over with quickly, I mean, the last paper Faby is going to redo this Monday, and then the

Embassy, I hope it goes quickly, she sure does not need all the headaches these people are giving her, not only Uncle Roberto, but some of the places she is working at, some of the store employees, and management is really badly mistreating her . . . she is a party paint faces girl, and its her job to make the customers happy, so they keep coming back.

Sat Feb 23, 2008

Reward

Well, while Mommy was trying to clean up a bit, Carola was doing her act of crying, along with other things. Natalia on the other hand was helping. She does help out more, not very often, but does do better.

This was the second time we took Natalia to McDonalds, and the first time we took Natalia to the fun park with out Carola. Then again, it was the second time we went to the fun park to ride any rides. Any way, Faby thought Natalia was deserving a treat this time and who am I to argue.

I got some pictures, at McDonalds first, then the bumper cars, and the last one is her on the roller coaster, sorry, its a bit dark, and I messed up again. Faby asked me if I was carrying the big camera. I said it don't have any film, she said she will get film, well, I don't have the camera, so she did not get any film. Oh, Well, I had the little digital camera. 17 our of 20 turned out well enough to see, ran out of space for the last ride which was the one where you sit and the seats go strait up and then fall down like on a poll. one more thing. we don't just foolishly spend money on junk. Natalia got a happy meal, Faby and I just had an ice cream-small, and then the rides, didn't cost much, and Natalia sure was happy.

Sat Mar 1, 2008

a Little funny

A few days ago, we took Philly for a walk to the stand, nails stand, store, some thing like that. Any how, to start out with. He did not want to leave, until we put his shirt on, then he settled down, and went for a ride. We went there only to pick up some polish, I for get why, any how, once there, not intending to stay because we had other plans, Faby winds up with some clients . . . OK, we stayed for a while. Faby has stand 8. Stand 1 is the video guy, he also has stand 9, the hair dressing saloon. He is also the nephew the owners. He has yet to pay rent. The owners keep asking, he says, the hair saloon is not making any money, and the videos are barley making him enough to pay his employees. The second stand is looking for another place, she is two months behind in rent. Once the owner told that to Faby, the nephew stated he needs the second stand. He needs to expand his video business to try to make some money. The owners have had that gallery open now for a year and a half, in which time the nephew has yet to pay any rent on the two stands he has. Faby just said, "if you want people who don't pay any rent, and is always causing you problems, that is fine. If you want your rent, you will let me have the second stand." Here comes the "Funny" Philly was checking out the gallery. He got along with the hair dresser . . . no idea why, Faby don't like her . . . she is a new one and worse then the other one who finally quit two weeks ago. he went quickly past the 7 stand . . . I can see why . . . that woman is out of her mind. He played with the 5 and 6 stand woman . . . the phone booth, she is OK. He had fun with the 3 stand woman, she hates cats . . . he was really playing with her. I had to grab him. Here it comes: While holding him, the first stand guy, the nephew walked past me. Philly laid his ears back, hissed, bared his claws and almost got him! he struck several times. Philly was upset. This guy walked past me three times while I was holding Philly, each time Philly was striking. The 3 stand woman put in a six foot display case, so, I put Philly on top of it, asking him what his problem was. he growled at me and punched me in the eye, did not bare any claw, just punched me in the eye. Ouch! the video guy walked by three more times after that, each time Philly growled, hissed, and struck out with barred claws. When I told Faby what happened while she was painting nails, she just laughed, and told me the above of what happened with the video guy and the owners and the second stand and stuff. I am guessing Philly knew what was going on or just don't like him for one reason or another. Not real sure, Faby says cats just know.

Sat Mar 1, 2008

Faby

Faby has been going to the Union Church for about four years now. She is not one to beg. In that time, she has not asked for any thing. The Union

Church is a non denominational church for foreigners of English speaking countries. Peruvians go there to beg all the time. Even to the point that some of the people there are real nasty to the Peruvians. Faby has been named a "Primary" Sunday School Teacher. Not a second, back up or extra, she has been named a "Primary" and the one in charge of the teachers has been kissing @ for years, yes, a Peruvian, and he has tried to run Faby out of the church, along with any other Peruvian he runs across. Faby is the only Primary Peruvian Sunday School Teacher, and this guy refuses to email her any information. She finds out about meetings after the church service with a "we have a meeting, are you coming?" A few weeks ago, or couple, I for get, the women's group of the Church wanted an "Elvis" for an event fund raiser they are having. They asked Faby to find an Elvis for them. Well, the ones who showed seen the foreigners and wanted triple the price or stated that they will not be made fun of and walked out. Well, after the casting was over, one of the women handed Faby a bag of tomatoes, half of which was rotten, saying "here you go Peruvian, I know you are hungry." Faby did not loose her temper, she is very well educated. She said very politely, that she does not need those tomatoes, if she wants something she will go to the store and get it her self, and does not need their charity. Faby's education: all universities, 2 years beautician school three years medical school 5 years acting school 4 and a half years teaching school she finished the beautician and acting school, was forced out of medical school, because her adoptive father retired and caught a visa to the U.S., then the rest of the family became more needed then she was, she was studding to be a doctor, not a nurse, or an assistance of any kind, she was studding to be a doctor, and that was three thousand soles a month—one thousand dollars. She left and went to acting school, and paid for it her self by buying cheep and selling high, sandwiches and coffee, as well as putting on shows on the side for a little bit, five years later, she finished. But then her family got very upset. Because actors and actresses don't make any thing here in Peru. Her adoptive Father talked with his brother about teaching, he worked in a teaching university, one that produces teachers. The brother agreed, it was a high class university, only 500 soles a month, but not any one could get in, you had to have a certain grade average . . . Faby was strait "A" student. Not a problem getting in. Four and a half years later, she was forced out, her adoptive father sent three thousand soles for that last semester, and his brother kept saying he never received it, the school never received it. he don't believe in western union, he sends money by hand, people flying. Faby was forced out and was told she would never be a teacher. I guess I am writing this because there may be some believing Faby is lazy. Not worth sponsoring, scared she will run up a bill and leave them owing a fortune. Faby is not like that. Faby loves to work. She is Paint faces party girl for Mad Science. She won "Best of the Year" award. They want her to be a "Party Girl" as well, not painting faces, but dancing with the kids, that is an extra ten soles per party, because the "party" people have to take taxi's all the time, they usually are caring too many things that could come up missing on the buses. Plus the fact she can do so many other things. She is not one to beg, she will work. not only that, but, before I came here, how many times has any one heard of me begging for help? We ran in to a Peruvian woman in the church a couple weeks ago. She is married to a U.S. citizen. for about six years. Had two kids. has been in this process for four years now and is unable to get the visa. The kids were approved, and they and her husband went to the U.S. leaving her behind. He thought by going and getting a job and a place to live, he would be able to sponsor her. He was denied, he had to prove longevity in a home and place of work, and no one else wanted to help saying she could run up a big bill, in medical and welfare. after two years, the kids came back to their mother, he stayed in the states, still trying to sponsor her, she is so sad, and is being treated real bad in the church, but still goes in his name, and for her kids who are half U.S. citizen. I really don't want to leave with out Faby, but we just found out, even if I do leave, I may not be able to sponsor her, not for many years, this guy has been trying to sponsor his wife for three years now, and has been denied each time saying he has to prove longevity. I will close for now, just wanted to tell you all a little more about Faby, and what we just found out. nice country the U.S.A . . . Peru may be messed up, but the U.S. is so full of red tape, it just ain't funny :(I can see why, so many attacks, that most of the citizens are just ignoring, or so they seem to be . . . they ain't, they are just making it harder for honest people to get in, the dishonest walk across any time they want . . . "WE SHOULD HAVE A GREAT WALL OF THE U.S." like the great wall of china, only between Mexico and the four southern states, Texas, New Mexico, Arizona, and California . . . that should cut down on some of the problems :)

Sun Mar 9, 2008

Adessa

Just a little funny :) Remember when I mentioned about Faby telling Ada what was going on and threatened to walk out, and Ada said her school will go on weather or not Faby was there? I am not real sure if I mentioned it, I think I did . . . any how That school has the capacity of five hundred students. Last year it only had two hundred students. Faby told them and Ada, if they don't loose that director, they won't have any students this year . . . well, Faby was wrong . . . they have 60 students and the city is threatening to close the school and take it for their own property. you see, the land is theirs, they never sold the land, but the building belongs to Ada and she is getting scared. Her administrator has washed his hands saying its all the directors fault, not his. Any how, last night, Faby got the news she is wanted back. They all believe that if Faby comes back, it will save the school. They managed to kick out the director in hopes to talk Faby in to coming back. Faby is still scared. Because of the way she was treated last year.

Mon Mar 10, 2008

not sure

We had a real good show this morning . . . I am sure Carola is very happy with her self. Well, last night, as I said on family chat, she was crying up until Faby called her in and told her to lay down on the bed. Natalia was on a mat on the floor. She quit crying instantly and was asleep for an hour, when Faby told her to get off the bed and on the mat, our bed is on the floor, not much difference any way, it fell apart and Faby told me not to put it back together. any way, it was about five minutes later, after Carola moved that I laid down, and she started crying again. I said for her to stop acting, I don't believe it, and Faby jumped on me saying something about a hurting stomach, so, I just said, not a problem, I know I am not welcome in here, so I am off to the kitchen. when I woke up this morning, both my hands were bloody and so was my nose . . . cat kept me up most of the night, but I felt safer in there with him then in the same room with Carola or in the living room . . . no roof . . . that unexpected and uninvited guests have dropped in a few times, getting chewed on. but that's not all . . . come this morning, Faby was ready to take Carola to the hospital. for the past week, Carola has not done much with her hair, and all day yesterday, it was a real big mess. Faby told her last night, she was going to cut it, for that reason as well as to go to the hospital, because in staying there, she may not get a chance to wash her hair until she leaves. the hair cut was about 7:30. After the hair cut, Carola put on such a show, sorry I don't know what was being said, Faby told me later, that Carola was saying that we all hate her and she hates us, and we are all monsters, all we ever try to do is hurt her. up until the point that the next door neighbor came over and told Faby he is going to have a long talk with the land lord and make sure we get kicked out. he is tired of hearing Carola. Every month Faby is getting yelled at, about the girls making too much noise. now this, I don't know what to do. today is the first day of school, and tomorrow, we may not have a place to live. our land lord is a lawyer. well, it may not happen that fast, but, he has threatened to kick us out before. This morning, I know will only add fuel to the fire against us. oh, and Carola is not really sick, she is just refusing to eat . . . not a problem, I will take Natalia to school, Carola can stay home . . . *all year* if necessary . . .

Thu Mar 13, 2008

First day of School

That was Monday, the 10th. Was suppose to be last Monday, the 3rd, but the President of the PTA, decided to paint the school, so, it was postponed for a week. I really think she is trying to get more money . . . donations, by showing she is not squandering the money away, like others have in the past. Moving right along . . . Carola did not eat any thing the Saturday or Sunday before Monday. I made it very clear, if she or Natalia get any freebies . . . free lunches from the cafeteria, or any kind of snacks from their friends, and I see it or find out about it, no more school. Carola did not eat any breakfast or lunch at home, took a tupper of rice and beans-trigo, very good stuff, to school with her. She brought it back saying she forgot to eat. sure. She took it again Tuesday, this time the tupper was empty. Faby found the food, in a plastic bag in Natalia's pack. She has ate some, but not a full plate full of food all week, she may have had a full plate food combining both this week and last week, but not because we refuse to feed her, its because she refuses to eat. If you would look at her and not know her, you would swear we were starving her, she is so thin, it just ain't funny, her arms and legs are like tooth picks, and she walks super slow. Faby has a hear and liver condition. She can not walk very fast. Carola takes half steps, and when she thinks we are in a hurry, she takes quarter steps and acts out of breath . . . which is probably true, no energy because of lack of food intake. Well, I said it again today, only adding, if I find any food rotting any were, in the apt. no more school. And with Mama working, some times not here when you two have to leave, I will just stay home, meaning no school. either one upset me, its over. I told them last year, I was fighting with mama to let you go to school. this year, no fighting at all. upset me just one time, and its over. Faby just left about an hour ago, well, if walked her to her nails store. Just before she left, I heard Natalia crying. Faby told me that Natalia is scared she won't go to school today, I told Faby as long as they don't up set me, they get to go, if I get upset, I may forget. oh, well, we will see, they have about an hour before we have to leave

Sat Mar 15, 2008

Adessa

This just in, or well, from last night :) one of school people, teachers, some one was begging Faby to come back last night, again. She is still a little scared. From what happened last year. Apparently not only did the director get fired, but also the vise director. He has been calling Faby, and getting me :) sorry, no Spanish. Faby thinks he wants her to be his witness, saying he was not involved in any thing, which of course, he wasn't, didn't help any one, just let it get worse . . . not only that, but he does not even have a teaching degree . . . how did he make vise director in the first place? OH, well, Faby was told, the student population went from 60 to 50 kids now. the minimum is 250, max is 500. They are about to loose the school and they feel if Faby returns she will save the school. We have not gone to the Union Church for the past two Sundays now, and I think we will skip this one, let Ada sweat a bit longer. She told Faby last year, when Faby told her she was going to quit, that the school will go on weather she was there or not . . . its about to get closed, by the Government Board of Education for lack of Students WHY??? its like this: Faby broke their business. Telling her students not to buy the "pullyada" tickets . . . chicken dinners. Even after the director told them that Faby would have to pay for it, that didn't work, then telling them they would fail the year, they would not be able to take the final tests, that did not work either, plus, telling the kids "keep your money" every time she handed out papers. all the other teachers charge 10 cents a copy, just a regular assignment copy, up to one soles for test. Faby never charged the kids any thing. telling the kids they should keep their money for better things and quit buying all that junk, like icy pops, gelatin sticks, dogs on a stick, cakes, and so on. she really broke the directors business, but good. PLUS, the administrator, Ada´s second, decided to fire several other very good teachers, a couple of which would help the students in buying pullyada tickets, if they couldn't, and would charge very little for copies, only when they had to. I told Faby she will be in a very good position for bargaining :) like a good paycheck, free studies for the kids, our two, Natalia and Carola. as well as getting back those good teachers that was fired . . . only because they did not like the director, no other reason, but now sure how the administrator wrote it up. Faby just said, maybe in a couple weeks, she might talk with Ada, but is still scared, because that administrator is still there and he don't like her at all. We shall see :)

Sun Mar 16, 2008

Corner store

Faby told me this morning, our favorite little corner store may be closing. She went to get some bread, and the woman, and or her husband, usually the woman is working it, both own the store, but rent the building, said the prices have gone way up, too high. With Garcia exporting every thing he can and raising prices all the time, they are loosing customers, and what is worse, some of their customers have come in getting what they usually get and then they hear the price, and say they will pay next week . . . only next week they never show. they are owing rent and not enough customers to pay the rent and loosing more and more as time goes by. for a long time one soles would get 10 breads, now its 7 breads, today, when I went I asked for one soles worth of bread, she gave me 13 or 15, not sure, lost count, and looking sad. they would give us items with no charge, like some of the fruit that no one wanted, because it was bruised, not rotten, they would throw that away, just the bruised ones, or chicken that was left over, and we or rather Faby would make up a plate to share with them, like a drink, or massamora-pudding type stuff, out of the fruit, or sandwiches out of the chicken after cooking it up. we always showed how thankful we were for receiving those gifts. if they close, we sure will miss them. sorry for the sad news, I was debating on telling this one all day.

Sun Mar 30, 2008

OUCH

This note is mainly to Uncle Dick, but who all wants to read is welcome A couple days ago, Faby had an attack, it looked like it was going to be a major one. Those are scary, because she says her heart hurts her, not only that, but she can't hardly breath, she winds up fighting for each breath. Some times she will go several minutes with out breathing, that can get scary, then all of a sudden, she is gasping, and starts bouncing. I mean she is raising her chest, arching her back, and almost crying, trying to get a breath. The first time I seen this, I had no idea what to do, I could not even hold her. Well, I sorta got use to it . . . sorta Well, a couple days ago, it looked like another major attack. First she said her heart hurts, then pointing to her chest, her eyes rolled back and she collapsed. luckily, we were already in bed, she was just sitting up so, her pillow caught her head. She was not breathing, and about a minute later, she started gasping and bouncing. That lasted only a few seconds, then she stopped. No breathing, a couple minutes later, again, she started fighting for a breath, bouncing even harder . . . I placed my hand, my right hand over her heart and started telling her I was here, I love you, and lots of other things. she stopped the bouncing, and I started concentrating on her heart, thinking of the pain she was in . . . I am not sure how to say it correctly, but I was trying to draw it out of her. then it hit her again, but did not last too long, only a few seconds, she took a deep breath, her eyes opened, and I got a sharp pain in my chest . . . it hit me so hard, it almost knocked me off the bed. Any way, right after that she sat up, I asked her how she felt, she said she felt bad. I didn't tell her how I felt. that was two days ago, I hurt till late last night, about 24 hours. Any way, after she said she still felt bad, she was able to get up. for some reason, she left the computer on when she laid down, then the attack happened. so, after that, she got back on the computer and finished what she was doing. as for me, I remembered what Uncle Dick said about re-routing the energy, or pain, and I was thinking how to do that, and to what to re-rout it to?

Sun Mar 30, 2008

Philly

This one is a little funny, I remember papa talking about how his pets would eat almost any thing he ate, except bananas. Guess what? Faby gets black bananas, not rotten ones, just the ones that no one would buy, some thing her first adoptive mother did, and makes banana juice. last night, Philly was making such a fuss, I finally give him a taste . . . he begged for more. he had about a cup full, poor thing, couldn't swallow any more, his belly was bulging, he had already had his cat food, and some ice cream-strawberry ice cream. this morning, we used up the rest of the bananas for juice, and you know who was screaming at me . . . yes, he had some more again. so far, Philly has ate every thing we eat, some of which, was not because we gave it to him. any how, I just remembered what papa said one time, about the bananas, I think it was his cat that could not eat bananas, not sure.

Mon Mar 31, 2008

John Nash

The name of the school. you should have seen Faby . . . Picture this, you are a professional, for fifteen years, you have been doing your job, you know your job . . . the only thing you need is a plan of attack. For two weeks the owner is telling you he wants you, he will be ready for you. one week ago, promising every thing will be ready, just show up and go to work, the plan will be ready for you . . . you are a "PROFESSIONAL" then you are handed a scratch sheet of paper with some scribbling on it and told, "go right over there, have fun." you have five minutes to get there, and you don't even know where "there" is. you find the place just in time only to hear, "sorry, we are too busy for you, go take a brake, we will call you when we are ready for you." You know, I really thought Faby was going to blow a blood vessel when the coordinator handed her that scratch sheet of paper, but being a professional, she just swallowed it and went to the class . . . she turned red after that. well, it took a while, but we found the owner, and he was busy, the man is a very busy businesses man. with only a second grade primary education . . . here, it goes from kinder garden, primary, secondary, then you are ready for collage or the university . . . that is a story in its self, about him, that will be another one . . . one with this one; he seen us standing out side finally and motioned us in to sit down while he was conducting business. when he finished . . . he speaks no English, only Spanish, some Peruvian native . . . sorry, I for got the spelling, any way, he asked how things were going. Faby threw the papers on his desk. he asked what is this? She started out saying, for two weeks, you have been begging us to come here, last week you said every thing will be ready, you tell me, What Is THIS??? you see, for three years, he was building the school, not ever showing up, just pouring money into it and hearing stories of what might be happening, but what bothered him was the items that kept coming up missing, so now, year number four, he decided to take over as head of the school. he did not have an answer for Faby, he asked politely to be excused and for us not to move, he will be right back. a few minutes later he came back with the coordinator, sat down and tapped the papers on the desk. I just heard lots of rattling, he started and went from soft to loud, he stopped to take a breath, then just as he stopped, Faby started in, went from loud to louder, when she took a breath, he started again, neither one stepping on the other, perfect tag teaming on the poor guy, he barley speaks English, what I caught was "please, sorry" and in Spanish, "por va vor, pardon" not sure what else, but it went on for about fifteen minutes . . . both Faby and the Owner were red, red mad. not happy at all. The owner told Faby and me to take a break in the cafeteria, and please not to leave, not yet, to please give him one more chance, he will get it fixed, and fixed fast. Faby told him, she was not at all happy about being treated like some fluesy that they just scrapped up out of the gutter. It did get better after that, the owner was promising tomorrow would be better.

Sat Apr 5, 2008

John Nash . . . Carola

Yesterday sure was some thing . . . Well, it started a couple days ago, when Carola was trying to put on a show. She was once again trying to prove how mistreated she is, and how she does not ever get any thing. Her class was asked to bring some chips or drinks to share, Faby talked to the teacher, he said those who could would and those who couldn't, are not forced to, its just a small party and not to worry about it. Carola had a fan club following her when she was demanding from mommy to get her a giant size bag of chips to share . . . we don't have that kind of money, we tried to give her some cookies, but she refused, saying in English and very disrespectful, "you will don't do any thing." and stormed off. Yesterday, Friday, while we were looking for one of our classes, we seen Carola's class, with out the teacher. Mommy got even. Faby called Carola over to the door. Carola just ignored her. Faby called again, then the kids said, "Carola, your mother" in Spanish, Faby told me later what they were saying. Carola just ignored her. Then Faby said, "kids, do you obey your mother?" they said, "yes" she asked "don't you think Carola should obey her mother?" they said "yes" then she asked, "do you think you can help Carola to obey her mother?" they said "yes, we will try" and all together they were telling Carola to go to the door like her mother asked. Still, Carola was just sitting there looking other ways and just ignoring her. Faby then said, "Carola, I have fifty cents for you to get your cookies. On Monday, I will send you with your tootoo. Now you behave in your class." (tootoo-baby cup) She dropped the fifty cents on Carola's desk and walked out with a very big applause from all the kids . . . you should have seen the look on Carola's face . . . I almost took a picture, but when I was reaching for the camera, Faby grabbed my arm and we left. Faby told me she did enough, and a picture would only make things very bad . . . still I would have loved to share that one with every one, it was beautiful. For some reason, Carola was very good the rest of the day yesterday at school.

Sat Apr 5, 2008

John Nash

This one is about me . . . So far, so good . . . I guess. Today, there is a teachers meeting, Faby talked to one of the directors, saying she has another job, and she does not like the idea of me going not knowing any Spanish. Some of the other teachers could say I was saying any thing, and there would be no way I could defend my self, like they have already done before, in the "Open House" when I just said I was here to teach advanced English to the advanced students, and the translation was, that I said I was going to change up the whole system, and force the kids to buy new books, and so on and so on. As for the kids. I seem to be getting the "problem" kids. The ones who are making problems to the English teachers. As in other words, they speak better English then the teacher and are causing problems in the class, so, the teacher sends them to me. Nice ain´t it, the other teachers don't want me in there, but they keep sending me students. I don't get it, unless they think they are going to scare me away. One teacher told me, that I have nothing to teach her. she said that in Spanish, Faby answered in English, saying, you English is not real good, and if you are teaching bad English, you are only hurting the kids. Her reply to that was, "We are not native English speakers." Faby's answer was, "you have a native English speaker right here, why can't you take advantage of him and learn something?" They got so offended, you could see it in the room. None of them liked that at all. Now they are trying to get the kids parents all together against me . . . not sure how well that is working, because when Faby was talking to one of the directors, not sure who that guy was, he also told her, that she needs to get her professional receipts, so I could get paid. I have not signed any contracts yet. The owner is not sure yet, the other English teachers are telling him one thing and Faby says some thing different. And I will talk about him in my next note. This week was better then I thought it might be, I have two U.S. students, one barley knows Spanish, the other knows both English and Spanish like the back of her hand, i just looked at her and said, "your giving your English teacher problems, aren't you?" she just laughed. the other one is a boy, not a problem maker, but they sent him to me any way, probably because they could not understand him too well.

John Nash

About the Owner,

Faby says he is a "cholo" well more like a "deep dark cholo" usually people you keep away from, because most of them are "rob guys or girls" Any how, His total education is 2nd. grade primary, I think would be the same as just "2nd" grade in the U.S. He lost his parents when he was very young, and one set of grandparents took care of him. His grandfather wanted him in school, but after he finished the 2nd grade, his grandfather died. His grandmother did not believe in the schools, thought they were just a waste of time, and the farm was more important, and she could teach him every thing he needed to know about life, so, what's the point of school? When he was around 18 or 21, not sure, he moved out, went to Lima to work. He found a wife and had a couple or few kids, not sure how many he has. He tried to get a further education, but he failed, he just could not understand any thing, but that did not stop him. He became a "door to door" sales man. Working very hard, selling items like nails, screws, nuts and bolts. He would go to the companies making them and make deals with them. He would sell to the stores and companies like house builders and such. The past three years was some thing else for him. He heard of land being given away . . . he went there and claimed a chunk of it and started a school. John Nash, private school. His goal? To give the kids a better chance at a better future, trying to employee only the best teachers. Like other parents, he probably got tired of buying "pullyada" tickets every time he turned around and decided to do some thing about it. Well, for the past three years, he was working very hard and dropping every thing he made in to his school. I mean every thing. He and his family were living at the school, knot knowing any thing about the education system. He would go to work all day and let the directors take care of the school. He has Kinder garden 1-2, Primary 1-6 and Secondary 1-5. He employs at least 20 teachers, paying from one thousand soles up to fifteen hundred, I am guessing, each month, and a director and an assistant director for each section. I keep hearing the director don't like to get less then three thousand soles a month, I am not sure how much the assistant gets, but I am sure its more then fifteen hundred. After a while, he made enough to get a house and moved out of the school, I think that was last year. but then he also kept hearing about how the teachers and directors were stealing from him. Items kept coming up missing here and there. This is Year number 4, and he has decided to take over being the Head of His School. He still has all three directors and assistance directors, because he still knows nothing about the education system, but he knows plenty about the business part of it. Our first teachers meeting, mainly with the English teachers was funny. A few of the teachers were saying there is no need for that gringo being here, and he said, "you know where the door is. If you don't like the way i am doing things, you can work for some other place." too make it short. Faby was telling me much more then that. To my Guess, he was too dumb to understand all the technical "B.S." or just too bull headed to give in to their "Smart 'A' remarks . . . I just like the way he basically said, "if you don't like the way things are going, don't let the door hit your @ on the way out" Faby said that was one of the things he said. it was hard for me to keep a strait face. i had to clear my throat and cough a few times to try not to get caught at what Faby was telling me. All in All, the Owner, who speaks no English, wants me there, and about half the English teachers, about five that want me to disappear. he has about ten English teachers. A few of them speak real good English, and a couple of them i have no problems with at all.

Fri Apr 11, 2008

Philly

Not sure what to say, He is six months old, and is too big. The vet said he looks like a full grown cat, but at six months, he should not be that big. Plus, he has what might be a kidney problem, that surprised the vet, she said, Philly is too young to even show signs yet, it was the first time she has seen this in a six month old. Yesterday, last night, we took him to see the vet, and he was given a few shots, this morning we took him back, no improvement, the vet gave him a few more shots and an I.V. and said if he does not improve by tomorrow, there may not be any hope for him. He has not drank any water or ate any food for two days now, and can barely stand. I am more worried for Faby at this point, she really loved Philly. Played with him every day. When she was not feeling well, Philly would lay at her feet, some times all night, not wanting to move.

Sat Apr 12, 2008

Philly

He growled this morning, and he bit me. He took a turn. He don't like the vet for some reason, don't even like the word vet, that is when he growled. The vet gave him a shot of vitamin C, and he bit me. Didn't draw any blood. The vet said he is doing better, he is drinking water, and Faby said she seen him eat a little. Just keeping every one updated :)

Mon Apr 14, 2008

Philly

Today was something, We went for a walk in the park, took Philly with us. He likes the park. Only this time, he decided to climb trees. He climbed lots of them, only a few feet before coming back down. but the last one, well. The last one had a few birds in it. Two looked like canaries, and one humming bird. The canaries were really playing with him, getting just a couple feet away from him making him go higher and higher and on smaller limbs. The humming bird just kept to the far side of the tree. All three of them did not leave the tree, so, I am guessing there was at least one nest, maybe two, I did not see any. I don't think Philly wanted to eat them, I don't know for sure, I was just guessing he wanted to play. The only kind of bird he ever ate was a cooked chicken, as for the live one, he only played, that's why I believe he only wanted to play. He was way up in the tree for about a half hour before coming down. He finally came back down, with lots of coaxing, and us right there to catch him, it almost looked like he might have been scared of the height. we did not punish him at all, just held him and told him its time to go home. He sure was happy to go out and play, we may do it again sometime.

Mon Apr 21, 2008

a couple stories

Sad news, When you think it can't get much worse, guess again . . . cataract . . . if you are not sure, then click on the link: *http://search.yahoo.com/ search;_ylt=A0geu4.QygxIe2oBbQxXNyoA?fr2=sg-gac&sado=1&p=eye%20 cataract%20surgery&fr=slv7-msgr&ei=UTF-8* lots of information on that link. With every thing else going wrong, Faby has two in her right eye, and one in her left eye. The good thing is, they are just beginning and can be easily removed, or so the doctor said yesterday. Yesterday, Faby had four parties, during which, a company doctor came in to check all the employees, and since Faby was there, he checked her, and told her she really needs to see an eye specialist before too much time passes and get that problem fixed. If too much time passes with out any thing being done, well, I am sure you know the results. To Mama and Papa, We got the package today, and Philly is demanding his toys be put on his wall, not on the refrigerator. The blue thing was driving me nutz, until I realized the batteries were dead . . . no on off switch, the other toy, well, I done gave up on it, I think Faby figured it out, she already got past the first part. I tried, I guess I blinked, I could not pick the right one. OH, well.

Mon Apr 21, 2008

Sunday April 20

Yesterday . . . Faby had four parties, as I mentioned before. We divided up the kids. Natalia went with her, and Carola stayed with me. I had English classes from 3pm to 9pm, Faby had parties from 11am to 9pm. We had a long day. No church yesterday, sad thing was, they were celebrating birthdays yesterday. Every third Sunday there is cake, and this time Faby's name was on it. Oh, well, maybe next year :) hopefully NOT, hopefully we be there instead of here. ON to the store ;) Natalia was OK for the first party, as Faby was telling me. She danced and played for a while, then disappeared when the happy meals, surprises, and cake came out. She went to the play area, so not to get Mama in to trouble for being there . . . they really frown on any relation of the employee being there. Second party, was different. First thing, Natalia goes up to the party guy, and says, in Spanish of course, "hi uncle", he ignores her, she tugs on his shirt and repeats, he blows her off, and moves away, just playing with the kids, so, she tugs on his pants and repeats. Then he says out loud, "who are you?" he did not remember her. Faby has introduced us all to most of the party people. Any how, Faby finally told him, she was her daughter, and he was so embarrassed, he said not to worry, the mama invited all the kids and never showed up, it was the father who was there watching and he don't know who all is suppose to be there. So, Natalia became one of the invited, with cake, happy meal, and surprise. Third party was OK, Natalia did what she was suppose to do, and go to the play area, but come the fourth party, nope. The cake was too small for all the kids there, and the girl who was suppose to cut it was lost and scared, did not know how to cut such a small cake for so many kids. So, Faby had to step in, which she does from time to time, doing what is not her job, and save the party. What happens, Natalia is hanging around, I guess she got hungry, she got a happy meal and surprise, and waiting in line for her cake. Faby could not believe it. The mama of the party got upset, telling Faby that there was an uninvited sitting behind her and has a happy meal, and that was not right. Faby said she was sooo scared, thinking that the mama seen Natalia and was upset over that, when she turned around, she seen it was another child with a mama that snuck in. So, what do you do in that situation? Any how, that woman was offering Faby to come and paint kids faces at her child's birthday party. Faby said not a problem, go and pay at the counter. If Faby gets caught taking jobs on the side, that has any thing to do with kids party's and face painting, she gets fired, they don't put up with moon lighting like that. Faby was tilling her that she was not invited, and she can not be in there, and that woman kept saying, to paint her kids face and she will hire her to paint all the kids in her child's party . . . stale mate . . . going on, the mama of the party asked Faby if all the invited kids received balloons, Faby said "yes." There was Natalia, the mama goes over and asks, "do you have a balloon?" Natalia says, "no."

Then the mama goes back to Faby and says, "you forgot one, give her a balloon." not knowing Natalia was Faby's daughter and not even suppose to be there. That was not right, Natalia was trying to get her mother in to a lot of trouble, but every thing worked out OK. As for me, I was OK with Carola. She knows I don't put up with a bunch of B.S. We did four hours of class in the institute, come 7pm we had to leave, so we went to McDonald's for the last two hours, Carola went to the play area and ran her self ragged while I finished up my class with my student. Not much to my life :(Faby is so much more exciting =))

Tue Apr 22, 2008

Dumfounded

I don't know what else to call it, the title. Today was something . . . Faby has insurance through her company. Here its called "social security" any how, to get her kids, Natilia and Carola covered, they need I.D. cards. To our luck, the "renic" office is giving I.D. cards to kids now, but for only certain days. That is the office where we have to get our documents certified, as well as for Peruvians to get their I.D. cards. One of the requirements is pictures. You need to have the pictures ready for them, they don't take pictures there. So, today, we took the girls to the photo shop right after school, almost. First was home so they can change clothes and eat some lunch. And right from the start, Carola was making problems. Didn't want to eat, didn't want to change, did not want any thing to do with getting an I.D. card. We get to the photo shop, and first was Natalia, went fine, done real quick. Then came Carola. I was sitting out front, they were in the back. From home to the photo shop, nothing but arguments, and me, not able to do any thing about it, so, I am writing about it. While Carola and Faby were in the back, I heard plenty of arguing, after a while, Natalia came out and said, "mommy is crying." I went to the back, and yes, she was crying, Carola was being her self, with a very sour look on her face. I went to try to comfort Faby, but she just turned me around and told me that I need to wait in the front, and not to come back there again, she is trying to get Carola to pose for the camera . . . Later on, we went to the hospital where the company said she could go to get appointments for her, Natalia and Carola, for check ups and to get started in the medical stuff, Faby told me why she was crying. Because at first, Carola wanted her to "trim" her hair. You know, style it, like she did Natalia. But, when she tried,

Carola hit her hand real hard, knocking it in to a door. Faby's hands are real bony. That happened about 2pm, its almost 7pm and she is still saying her hand hurts. Faby has a little ball on her left hand, first finger middle knuckle, that was the one that took the blunt of the blow. What can I do about it . . . nothing. On the way home, Carola started kicking my heals, I said to stop kicking me, and she snapped back, "I not doing any thing!" almost yelling. And of course, I can not do any thing, we were in public. Faby didn't see it, and probably didn't hear what I said, but after hearing Carola, she quickly changed the subject with a bright smile and cheerful attitude . . . too many people around.

Thu Apr 24, 2008

a Few stories

Philly only wants to play. Poor pigeon, almost hit the wall when Philly came bouncing out of the kitchen. Then Philly just sat there and watched the pigeon on the roof for a few minutes, until he left. Almost every day, Philly is talking to the birds, little ones to big ones, we have a bunch of different kinds that come here. Speaking of which, Sparrows, a few days ago, I seen a couple, a male and female sitting on a branch just above my head. I stopped just a bout a couple feet away, but I heard the chirping for about a block a way, these blocks are big here, any how. It was the female that was chirping, aimed directly at the male and chirping like mad. The male was looking around, hoping and inch here and there, looking up, down, from side to side, and the female was just chirping like mad. When I got there and stopped, the female did not stop chirping, the male looked at me. I said, "hi there, how ya doing?" he lowered his head at me, then looked at the female, then back to me, with a little tilt. I said, "ya, I know the feeling, it happens, you just got to love them any way and drive on." He looked at her, then back at me. It looked like he started shaking his head from side to side, then looked up, as if he was saying something like "I don't believe this." The female did not stop chirping the whole time I was there. I was walking the girls to school. When they passed, the birds did not move, she still kept chirping. Yesterday, Natalia decided to take a turn. We had to go to the rienic office yesterday, and well, Carola had to stay late to take tests. And while waiting, Natalia had to run all over the school area, instead of sitting on the bench, so, on the way home, she was too tired to walk, and was going extra super slow. Faby called me asking what was taking so long, what could I say, I just told her we are on our way. Faby decided to meet us half way, and from there to the office. Once there, Natalia started crying. Why, she was thirsty, and instead of saying she wanted something to drink, she started crying in a public place, making scene to get attention. She got her drink . . . if I had any thing to do with it, the drink would have been all over her head, but I kept quiet. After that, and it took several hours, Faby had to go to her weekly meeting, suppose to be from 6, to 8pm at the latest. Faby told the girls to behave, she had to go strait to her meeting, and I had to take the girls home. Faby told me to make milk and cook something, I told the girls if they want me to cook, they will wash the pots, I said that in front of Faby, and I am not sure what she said, it was in Spanish, she then told me she told the girls to behave them selves and obey. OK, we get home, I repeat, wash the dishes, especially the pots if you want to eat, I open the doors, make the milk, we get caned milk here, cheaper then regular, and the girls went in to their room and shut the door, and refused to come out. It was a long night, and I was getting worried, Faby usually calls by 8pm, and she didn't. I was looking out of my room, I had the door open, I saw one girl, not sure which one, ran out across the living room, seen me, yelped and ran back, as if she was playing like I was the "big bad monster" again. I was playing solitary. Not my worst night, only minus 1171, my worst night so far was Feb. 22, 2008—1795. I won a few last night, come ten pm I was really getting upset and worried, I didn't go on line, because I didn't want to upset Mama or Papa over my being worried about Faby being out so late, on just a weekly meeting night. I thought for sure she would be home by 8:30 at the latest. Nope, come ten thirty, I was really pacing, from the kitchen to the bedroom, when the phone rang, I almost hurt my self running back to the bedroom and jumping on the bed to answer the phone, I was a little out of breath, and Faby asked what was wrong . . . I just said, "nothing, just missing you" I went to meet her, it turned out to be a long meeting, and she was very tired, barley walking, I mean walking very very slow. She asked if the girls ate, I told her they went to their room and refused to come out. So, when we got home, she called Rocky's chicken restaurant, for delivery, it don't cost much. When dinner got here, Natilia started again, instead of asking, she starts crying. Wanting some creams, ketchup. Faby told her to drink milk, she starts balling. After a while, she puts I don't know how much sugar in the milk, then started balling again, I mean tears streaming down her face. She did not want milk, she wanted water from the sink, you know, the water that smells like it comes from the toilet . . . any how, Faby and I got tired of sitting in there, and came in our room, and Natalia started balling again, this time, Carola answered when Faby asked what happened, Natalia wanted salad, OK, Faby told Carola to divide it half to half. A few minutes later, Natalia started balling again, Faby asked what happened, Carola said Natalia wants fries, Faby tells Carola to give her some fries. I just lied in here waiting until they went to their room so I could close up and go to sleep, which was around 1am, after all the balling. Well, I have been up since 5am, had to get the girls up, so they can eat breakfast and get ready for school, we have to leave at 7am to get there on time, and its seven am. Sorry for worrying you Mama and Papa, but I was a little worried and upset my self and I did not want to over do the worrying and being upset. so far, my best night at solitaire is Feb. 9, 2008, Saturday + 700 :)

Thu Apr 24, 2008

School

For a few days now, Natalia was saying she needs to buy a book, telling Faby in Spanish of course, Faby just told me today. She found out from the teacher. All kids must be Catholic. Faby was trying to tell the teacher, that we were Christians, not catholic. Finally, the teacher said, the only way to excuse our girls from being catholic was to go through a court process proving they are faithful believers in Jesus and going constantly to a church and are full members in a Christian church. Once that is proved in a court of law, then all four of us must talk to the nun in charge of the district, showing her all the court papers and try to convince her how faithful we are in our church, if she is not convinced, then we still have to buy the catholic book and send the girls to a local catholic church so they can get their catholic papers saying they are catholic . . . as in other words, the kids are catholic or they will be catholic, no third option, or you are badly abusing you child and other measures will be taken. The teacher did not say what the measures were, just further actions will be taken. Books, We are in the needed to buy books again. The government did not issue any books this year, no school used the books last year and gave them all back. I am not happy. The teacher said, its only one book, just the math book. ya, OK, just the math book, and catholic book, times two, equals four books that we have to buy, its giving me a head ache, will some one get us all out of here please????????????????? Faby has told me, over and over, if I leave with out her, the girls will not go to school again, until I return or she and the girls go to the U.S. for a number of reasons. Primarily for the way the girls act, saying how mistreated they are, and how hungry they are, their chicken from last night is in the refrigerator, waiting for the mold to set in. I am almost ready to leave, with or with out them, this place is driving me nutz, I just hate the idea of leaving with out Faby. I don't know how she will do, I mean, she is roughly ten years past her expiration date, and that last attack really hurt. I really believe her now, when she says it feels like a thousand needles jabbing her in the heart. That hurt for about 24 hours. Good news is, she is feeling better now. She has three parties this week, one tonight from 4 to 6, and about a 2 hour buss ride, well at night, it might be an hour or an hour and a half, so, around 8pm she should be home.

Thu Apr 24, 2008

Where to go?

Three places I could go.
Texas, (Charce and Jodie)
Alaska, (Mama and Papa) now
Oklahoma, (Bob)

Any of the three, I probably have a place to say while I look for a job. Question is, what job? Any where I go, I can get work at a fast food place, a convenience store, or low level security, not a problem, except for the pay. Very low pay, and once child support finds it, I have no more pay check. Bob was telling me about the oil Field work in Oklahoma, no skills needed, up to 1800 dollars a week, sounds unbelievably, probably more like 1800 a month, either way, its better then its better then the 5 to 9 hundred a month I have usually made in the past. Mama and Papa are telling me about jobs in Alaska, sounds like minimum pay to me, I would like to get on a boat, but to start, I would have work the docks first and get to know people. I have talked to a few while I was in Alaska, they told me to start out working the docks and go from there. I looked it up on line, and even read in several places, they advise working the docks first before going out on a boat. Not sure what I would do in Texas, its so hot there, and I am really getting fed up with all the heat . . . ITS HOT HERE all year long, even in the winter . . . I am guessing in a couple more months, I will really be ready to leave. If Carola don't get us kicked out first of here first, and believe me, she is trying her best. the land lord raised the rent, and said, pay or move, your choice, the dollar is falling, and the bills, cost of living, is rising. Right now, we just sent in a package for natilia that the N.V.C. was asking for, the last package for Natalia for the N.V.C. I think, I hope. Now waiting for enough money to get all of Faby's papers redone and sent in . . . if its not one thing, its something else.

Tue Apr 29, 2008

Process

Spammers . . . Peru has cornered the market on spamming. Any how, As I said in the past, once we thought we were getting ahead, we have to re-due something. Faby just got two of the three papers she needs to re-due today, took most of the day, and cost over a hundred dollars . . . well, over three hundred soles. Tomorrow, she will get the last one done. As for the top . . . Well, every where we went, which was about a dozen places just for two papers, that we will get in a couple weeks, we had more people then we could count trying to sell us stuff. Like the pictures that are required, as well as fake documents, to the point of screaming at us to buy their stuff, right in front of the police selling fake documents. Well, I told Faby that the police probably would rather the people sell fake documents then to be robbing stores or purses. Any how, we are tired, and Faby is not real happy, so we are going to go "window shopping" I don't know why, but for some reason, when we go to places like Ripley's, Saga, and other medium to high class stores, it relaxes her a bit. Weather or not we are on line depends on what time we get back . . . been a long day and Faby needs to relax a bit.

Mon May 5, 2008

Carola

Seems like I cry a lot about her. This morning is no different. Her attitude is something else. Last Wednesday, Faby got yelled at by several people in the school, the assistant director, and a couple of her teachers, about her clothes. All kids need uniforms. Public school uniforms, or private school uniforms are ok. But, colorful clothes are not ok and Carola has been wearing colorful shirts, not white, like the dress code. This morning, after finally getting them out of the apt. and on the side walk, Carola took off her sweater, and I seen her wearing a brightly colored brown sleeveless tee-shirt. I asked her why she was wearing that and she screamed, "I don't have any white shirts" I told her she is not going to school like that, back upstairs now. She went stomping and slamming her backpack in to the stairs, making lots of noise. Its six thirty in the morning, the neighbors are sleeping, or trying to, as well as some of them trying to get us kick out, and does Carola care? Nope, I told her to stop making all that noise, there are people trying to sleep, she just kept going, until I said "I am going to take my belt off and beat you with it" and Faby came running out telling me not to, and what is the problem. I told her what Carola was wearing and what she was doing, and Carola had stopped by the second floor woman's door. Faby asked why she was not wearing a white tee-shirt, and Carola screamed, "I don't have any white tee-shirts." to my reply was, "I was doing laundry for the past two days, its not my fault if there are any dirty clothes. I washed every thing I could find. I did not go in to the girls room, they tend to close me out, so I waited for them to give me their dirty clothes. After a while, she came out of her room with the uniform shirt that goes with the uniform she was wearing. she does not like that shirt . . . oh, well.

Thu May 15, 2008

I.D. Cards

Got Natalia's and Carola's I.D. cards Was interesting getting the pictures taken. Natalia was very good, took it with a smile. Carola was another story. After a big fight, well, I am sure you can see the fake smile. I keep telling her, one day her face will freeze like that . . . well, I have not shown her, or either one, their cards yet :) waiting for the right moment.

Sat May 17, 2008

Streak

As if . . . I am not surprised . . . OK, I was preparing to take a shower. I was shaving, wearing only my underwear. Half way through, the water stopped. I came out only to find the second floor woman in my living room and some stranger on our roof. I was not happy, and Faby came out of the kitchen and put me back in the bathroom. After a while, the water came back on and I finished shaving and took a shower, but that is not the whole story . . . I just got back from my English class and Faby told me. The second floor woman called the land lord telling him that we, her and I, are in love and poor Faby has to deal with it. She went on saying, that Faby caught us together and started making a scene. Faby told me the land lord was telling her this. He said he knows what kind of person she 'Faby' is and that the law is on her side. Our land lord is a lawyer. Before Faby told me this, she was asking, how I was feeling, how did my class go, making sure I won't blow up. I am thinking of bagging her clothes on the line and handing them to the land lord, saying change the locks or we move . . . I know, that will go over like a turd in a punch bowl, he wants us out any way, too many complaints about how noisy our kids are, as well as how unruly I am . . . I just can't seem to get along with my neighbor . . . I guess I am lucky I was not in the shower yet :) or I might have been in more trouble. Here in Peru, its considered a High Honor to have a North American Boy Friend, even if the North American is Married. Its still "bragging" rights. that woman is driving me through the roof . . . what next? I know she has something planned . . . I really want to leave . . . here is a thought, how about every one pitching in a few dollars to get me a plane ticket ;) that way, it might be easier on every one, only a thought.

Tue May 27, 2008

Bad Week

I got a hold of something, was not very good. I think it was chilly from Bimbo's. We do tend to eat out once in a while, when they have specials. But, from what I have told a few people, and how I felt, they all seem to agree, it was the chilly sauce from Bimbo's. It gave me a very bad belly ache. Carola has not been much help. She did not go to school last week. Instead, her and mama got in to a very good fight, the bathroom sink is no longer in service. I need a new seal to reconnect the pipes now. Remember when I told you about how Carola tried to hid a bread in front of me? Well, yesterday morning, she tried to hide one in front of mommy, right in the clean dish rack. Then, of course its all in Spanish . . . I am catching a little more . . . she was saying she did not do any thing, it was not her, she was not there. She let the tears roll, I mean, she was forming puddles on the table as she was eating the bread that she was caught trying to hide.

I did not say a word that time. A little time later, about a half hour, after breakfast, I was looking for a dish, and found a bread, sliced in half, full of butter, so old it was hard as a brick. Carola was so surprised, saying she had no idea what was in the bag, or how it got there. She had no idea of what I was talking about. I did not say too much, Faby seen what I was holding and tore in to Carola. That turned into another one, and ended up in a deep cleaning of the kitchen and bathroom. We have heard of a boarding school, only problem is, its a catholic boarding school, but its for troubled kids. They go to school on Monday, and on Friday they get to go home, you know, home for the weekends. We are thinking of sending Carola there. That's about it for now, my belly is still tender, and when I break wind, it brings tears to my eyes . . .

Tue May 27, 2008

Philly

Philly loves going on trips, loves going camping, and most of all, he loves eating. His belly is almost dragging. I have seen him trot from the kitchen to the living room, then fall over. Not sit down and lay down, no, I mean, he falls over, like he is out of breath. I keep telling Faby and the girls, they are feeding him too much, I think Faby is starting to listen to me, but the girls just thinks its funny. I am about to call him "Garfield the 2nd, or is it 3rd?" Any how . . . When he thinks we are about to leave, like going camping, he opens our bags, or at least one of them and climbs in, he packs him self. He has even pushed his "cat carrier" to us, meowing at us, and jumped in it. He loves going out. You should see him out in the mountains, talk about a happy camper, and he has lots of friends out there, lots of birds, mostly pigeons, some cats, a few dogs. The birds of course keep their distance, but he still talks to them. Its funny, how he does his short meow, a high pitch short meow, as he walks to them, then lays down, they are watching him, and he continues to talk to them. He does not try to catch them. I think some are starting to get use to him, not as jumpy as they were the first time we took him. That's about all for Philly, he is seven months old and "Huge" I think Carola is feeding him her meals, or part of what she does not hide around the house. She takes so long eating, I mean she takes hours to eat, so I am thinking Philly is getting way more then he should.

Tue May 27, 2008

Problems

I mentioned before, I am having problems, and really need to return. I was wondering how many people would be willing to help, pitch in, just for one plane ticket? I am not asking for just one person, I am asking how many could pitch in? I really had not expected to be here this long, and its really getting to me. Try something new and am sick for a week, tummy still tender and full of gas, coming out of both ends and both ends smell bad. Not only that, but my Child Support bill is getting way up there and that is scarring me, last year, the U.S. Embassy took my passport and threatened to cancel my U.S. citizenship, saying it was the order of the child support people . . . Pay the Bill or Stay Gone. I am getting worried, I owe about five thousand dollars again, I need to some how get back and start paying that bill . . . I have no problems with Faby, and I really hate the idea of leaving with out her . . .

Fri May 30, 2008

Your going to DIE!!!

Couple weeks ago, Faby had a doctor appointment to get a physical check up, through her company insurance. A long time ago, Faby told me she had bone cancer, last week, the doctor said she has blood cancer, and because she has blood cancer, her skin is deteriorating. She has some blotches on her skin, in various places, mostly on her back and arms. The doctor says "there is no hope for you, you are going to die." Last week, Faby went to the eye doctor. He gave her a few tests and said her eyes are fine, she sees very well, then he looked at her eyes and seen the jelly type stuff on them, then did more tests, one of which is where they put a machine on your eye and shoot something like air, I think its a pressure test of some king. After which, Faby was blind for a while, and the doctor said, "because of you bad blood, its infected your eyes. We could scrape the stuff off your eyes, but there is a chance you will go blind during the procedure. But, that's not the whole problem, its inside your eye. If you live long enough, you will go blind." Ya, "if" he even told her she was going to die, after he blinded her. That was last Tuesday. Her left eye came in to focus after a couple hours, but her right eye was still not functioning. Wednesday and Thursday she could not see a thing out of her right eye, and she cried Tuesday, and most of Wednesday. She started seeing spots Wednesday afternoon, and Thursday was very blurry. Today, Friday its still fuzzy, but getting better. Nice doctors they have here. Remember Mac, the retired military guy I have mentioned before? Saying he gets better treatment here then in the V.A. hospital there. After you turn 60, the doctors here say "your going to die, why bother coming in?" He is required to visit the V.A. at least once a year or he looses all his benefits, he is 82 years old, and he hates going to the U.S. to the V.A. hospital, but he goes so he can keep getting his checks.

Fri May 30, 2008

Casting

Today Faby is going in for a casting . . . a test at the company to see if she can become a "party" girl, instead of just "paint faces" At first, several of her bosses were trying to convince her to become one, and she kept refusing, but now that she has gained some interest, they are trying to discourage her. So far, she has done two parties, due to the fact that the one who programs the parties has messed up, I mean like programming a "princess" party for a little boy, and a "pirate" party for a little girl, and the party people said they were totally unprepared and left to get the right stuff, while they were gone, Faby did the faces of the kids then did the party, dancing and playing and having so much fun with the kids that the parents told the party people who finally arrived with the right items, not to bother, the kids were doing great with out them. Faby received a whole lot of "atta girls" and "great job" and stuff for stepping in and saving the day, but when she said she will run to be party girl, the bosses said, "you are the best paint faces we have, we can not afford to loose you, besides you there is only one other and she can not measure up to you. You can try, but, chances are, you will not past the test, we need you as paint faces." Today is the casting and she told me she is going with a good attitude, going to do her best any way. Hopefully her eye is good enough that she does not run in to any thing by mistake during the casting. I really hope she makes it, she has been practicing so much, and trying so hard. She is a professional actress, but, that is for stage and screen, this is for little kids, very different. Faby told me, if she does not make it this time, she will work harder and be more ready next time. Lets all pray she does very well this time and really impress her bosses to give her a chance.

Fri May 30, 2008

Surprise

Natalia's birthday is this Sunday, June 1. She does not thing she is going to get any kind of party at all. Why? Because both Faby and I have to work, well, Faby has a party, well, a few parties on Sunday, and I have my English class Sunday night. Surprise? On Monday, in school, the teacher is going to have Natalia busy, while the classroom is being decorated :) with "princess" items. Remember when Carola Uninvited the three of us to her party? This time, Natalia is going to get a "Surprise" party. "Princess Theme" I do know when Carola finds out, she is going to be very upset. OH, Well. The way she treats us all, and trying to get Natalia to do the same, at least Natalia tries to do good and calm things down from time to time, where as, Carola don't care and does her best to upset every one around her. This aught to be good, Carola will be playing right in to this, telling Natalia we are not going to do any thing for her, getting her all depressed, and then Monday about or around noon, between 10 am and noon, "SURPRISE" then she can tell Carola all about it and well, you know what will be hitting the "fan" :)

Fri May 30, 2008

Camera

Sooner or later this will come up, why no more pictures have been added . . . A while back I mentioned a Zoo trip and lots of pictures. Well, shortly after the Zoo trip, Carola put on a show in public, and I took a couple pictures of it. You know, just trying to discourage her from putting on shows in public. Well, Faby was not at all pleased with that, telling me I should not be doing that at all. Faby put on a show screaming me about it, and demanding the film. Yes, demanding the film, to destroy it. It took a couple days, but I finally gave in and the film got destroyed, and the camera may not work now, it was not rewound when she pulled it out of the camera, and I heard some harsh clicking sounds. We have not got any more film since then, and I told Faby I was not going to take any more pictures any more, since Carola is allowed to put on her shows in public and I am unable to do any thing about it. Plus the fact that all those pictures were lost, that made me so depressed, I told her I was not going to touch that camera again.

Faby told me yesterday and again today, that she wants to get film for that camera and take pictures of Natalia's birthday party. I don't know if that camera will work now. We still have the little camera, but indoor photos are soo dark some times and may not be able to make out what is going on. So, I don't know if we will get any pictures of Natalia's Birthday Party. Its the first party Faby is actually doing. She has never really given a party to the girls before, only a cake and a couple presents at most. She was going to give a party to Carola but, Carola uninvited her me and Natalia, so, Natalia is going to get the very first Party from her Mother, and we may not get it on film. Oh, well, I will write about it, to let you know what happened, and we may have a few pictures from the little security camera, if they come out good. I am still very upset over the fact that Carola can put on a show and nothing can be done about it . . . .

Sat May 31, 2008

casting

Faby told me there was fifty people there. There was only four positions to be filled. Out of the fifty, thirty were professional actresses and actors and really did their best. She said there was one who did every thing perfect and is probably in already, like before the casting was finished, Three others that was so close, that they probably made it, saying they were so much better then she was. She said she most likely blew her chances, because there was a guy there so full of envy towards her, he stood behind her, tapping his feet and grunting all through her show, doing his best to mess her up, and she ran out of the allotted time to present her show, she was very sad about that, but she said she did try and next time she will be more prepared. But its not over, sometime today, the winners will be chosen, I am still hoping and praying she makes it. She deserves a chance, or at least I think so :)

Sat May 31, 2008

The Girls

Two days ago, I was really upset over the way they have been treating me, mostly Carola, and I told them, if they wanted clean clothes, they could wash them, them selves, by hand. I repeated it yesterday to them, saying also, how upset and displeased I was and that I did not care if they wore dirty clothes. This morning, Faby asked me how serious I was, I just told her that the two of us have plenty of clean clothes, and they have enough, I think at least one clean school uniform, and I would wash next week. To my surprise, after Faby left for her party, the girls started washing their clothes by hand. They have not been fighting all day either, I even seen them moping the floor. Maybe I should do this more often . . . just a thought :)

Sat May 31, 2008

Philly

I was reading and thinking about what I said earlier about Philly and him falling over. What happens, is when he runs out of the kitchen, sometimes, he turns too quickly and over balances him self and "plop" he then looks around with a grin, yes, he grins as if to say "I meant to do that" He possesses other "Garfield" traits as well, like not stopping fast enough when filling his food dish . . . then having to clean up the mess and digging the food and water dishes out from under the clean dish rack. There have been times he come in to the kitchen so fast, he ran in to the refrigerator or the electric skillet. The skillet I know was painful at times, due to the fact we were cooking. When he was a baby, the first time we cooked eggs when he was here, he wanted one, real bad . . . he found out, that thing gets hot. Funny thing is, when we are cooking something for him, he knows it and sits right in front of the skillet waiting for it, when it is almost done, he is right by his bowl letting us know he is ready.

Sat May 31, 2008

Parties

Just an up date. Every one got notified of the "Winners"
THANK YOU FOR ALL YOUR PRAYERS AND SUPORT!!!!!!!!!!!!!!! she
MADE IT!!!!!!!!!!!!!!!!!!!!!!!

Sat May 31, 2008

pre-select

I may have spoken too soon what Faby received was a letter saying she qualified, out of fifty people they chose 10. there is only four spots open and the interviews are starting right now, at 3pm as follows:

3:00pm—3:20pm (Jhosep)
3:25pm—3:45pm (Fito)
3:50pm—4:10pm (Andrea)
4:15pm—4:35pm (Elena)
4:40pm—5:00pm (Fabiola)
5:05pm—5:25pm (Jimena)
5:30pm—5:50pm (Tamara)
5:55pm—6:15pm (Valerie)
6:20pm—6:40pm (Paulo César)
6:45pm—7:05pm (Luis some of these people have parties and some don't have access to computers. Faby is ready to go :)

Tue Jun 3, 2008

Surprise

Faby told Natalia that we had to clean her teachers room. The teacher took all the kids to another room, while we "cleaned" saying it was payment for some of the papers we needed to buy, copies and such. Took us about an hour, but we got it all decorated. Then "Surprise!" Natalia sure was happy, lots of dancing and a few games. She sure was happy. Almost made both me and Faby cry with happiness. We got a few pictures taken with the little cam, but the big computer is not working, so, we don't know if we will get them down loaded before the battery dies. Her teacher took some pictures with her cell phone, but we don't know her email address, we will try to find out.

Wed Jun 4, 2008

Got It

Faby was sure that her meeting was going to be a rough one. Out of fifty people ten qualified, and only four positions available. Six were chosen out of the ten, and out of those six, two will be cut during training or shortly there after. Melissa, Faby's boss was doing the interview, she is one of the party bosses, head of the paint faces project. She was telling Faby how there was going to be more stores opening up and there was sure to be lots more parties asking for paint faces. Faby told her that paint faces is going no where and she wants to grow. Being a party show girl she would have the chance to grow, improve her self. After a long talk, Melissa finally said, "how can I tell you "NO" you have passed every test I gave you, and you passed the final casting test. Your in. You just need a little more training." Faby was with so much emotion, she almost had an attack. she was crying, at first for happiness, but then was crying because of the pain she was in. Melissa seen that, and took her to the hospital. The doctor informed her that she had a ball in her neck, at the base of her skull, almost in the back. The ball is in one of the blood vessels, like a blister. If it pops, its over. It can be corrected with surgery, but it could make Faby bed redden for up to a year. He also said, it could correct it self if she remains calm, quiet, and relaxed. We thought the vessels on her heart was bad, the doctors her won't even think of an operation for that, saying she would not even survive. If its not one thing, its some thing else. With that news, Melissa told Faby if she could not handle being party show girl, she would still have the job as paint faces. Faby said she really wants to be a show girl, and will work very hard. But, Melissa said, if she thinks Faby is getting too stressed, she would make Faby take a month off. That would be with no pay of course. Well, we will see. Some of this stuff is very disturbing, but I have to put it in, my thoughts, my feelings, and every thing that is going on . . . you know, my diary, open to friends and family who wish to see. I just ask for every one to pray for Faby or do what ever you do to wish Faby Good Luck.

Wed Jun 4, 2008

Parties

Well, Faby was informed today, that this was the last week she was going to do paint faces. She was also told she has an emergency party tomorrow for a princess party, which she has not received any training for yet. They told her tomorrow at 11am, she will get her training in the princess party, and her party is from 4 to 6pm, then she has more training from 7 to 9pm. And its our anniversary, three years married, some anniversary, training, party and more training . . . all day long, well, I was doing my best to encourage her, and I told her I would be there at the end of her party to go with her to her training. Of course, I can not be in the training with her, but at least, I can travel with her to and back, and have some time together. Today, was her weekly meeting as well, I mentioned that they had a vote last week . . . She had six nominations, and was voted "BEST EVER" Best dressed, Best attitude, Best problem solver, Best friend, Best Image, Best timing—always on time or early. Faby has more "Champs" cards then any one else, those are the cards that the store managers give out to the paint faces or party people or mad science people who perform exceptionally well and give a really good image to the company. Those cards are very hard to get, since most managers don't care about the parties at all. The only thing that makes Faby sad is the fact she never got the "employee of the month" award. She did get the best of the year in paint faces, and was really trying to get it again this year, but, that won't happen now, she has jumped to parties, and was welcomed with open arms, lots of hugs, I was there at the end, and they were still hugging her. She is excited. So far, so good.

Thu Jun 5, 2008

Titi

A friend of Faby's She is an actress. Studied in the university with Faby to be a teacher, then did two more years to become a lawyer, but decided to become an actress. She some how caught a visa to the U.S. but had to return to Peru to keep her Visa good. Was traveling back and forth for years, lots of years. She acted in a local Spanish TV show in Florida. She understand a little English, but don't speak it hardly at all. Last time we seen her was about two years ago, when she came back to Peru for a while. I am writing about this because of what Faby has told me about her, and it reminded me of several others that we know. One Woman in the Union Church has been her for fifty years. She first came her on a visit, and fell in love with a Peruvian Man. Come to find out, he only wanted a Visa to the U.S. That was after they got married. Then she told him, she never planned to go back to the U.S. He treated her badly for a couple of years, gave her a kerosene stove, a very small house with a dirt floor, and was saying, "thing would be better if we could go to the U.S." After a couple of years, he started easing up on her, and got a hotel. She travels to the U.S. on occasion now, and her husband still has not ever gone yet. We know of a couple other women in the Church in the same situation, they are much younger then the first one I just mentioned. Their husbands are demanding a Visa, and they say "why, we don't plan on going back." Titi, was in the U.S. A lot. Acting in Florida. She met a guy last year, we just found out, and thought it was her chance to stop traveling all the time, and get a "spousal citizen ship." Well, at first, he was reluctant, questioning her intentions, from what Faby and I understand, because it took a while for Titi to convince him to come to Peru to visit her country. Once here, he found a friend of his. His friend married a Peruvian woman and got him self a farm, way out in the country side. His friend, whom he known all through school, convinced him to come to the farm and then showed him all the good of Peru, and how much cheaper it is to live here, especially on the farm. Now Titi is stuck on the farm, been there since last December trying to convince him to return to the U.S. and he says "why? every thing is much cheaper here, very nice place here, I love Peru, and don't plan on returning to the U.S." I just thought it was funny and had to mention it. Because here is Faby, one who really did not want to go in the first place, and is having a very hard time getting all the documents filled out and every time we think we are getting ahead, they say "redo" something . . . Well, we are sending out the DS. 230 again. Hopefully this time its excepted

Thu Jun 5, 2008

Party

Faby is on her way, well, she went about a half hour ago, Its 4pm now, I was doing some laundry, got some time now. Faby firmly believes this is a test, her biggest test so far. Her training was a joke, she wasn't even trained by the primary Princess Party girl, just an "after thought" princess party girl . . . well, Faby does have the Text, and is studying it real hard. They did not even give her all the stuff she needs, saying they will deliver at the store just before the party starts. One primary item is the CD. No music, no dancing, and is a busted party. Some of the other items are her shoes, a couple princess wands, and a couple of princess crowns. Faby has to wear one, and at the end of the party, the other crown and wand goes to the birthday girl. Some test, Faby believes at least one if not all her bosses will be there watching, she was so scared, I was telling her how good she was, and reminding her of the two parties she saved for the company, and how many she participated in. I was doing all I could to encourage her. I know she will do great. I will meet her in an hour and a half, five thirty pm here, and go with her to her training. Today is our three year anniversary :) So, we are going to spend some time together, even if its in a bus ;)

Fri Jun 6, 2008

Princess Party

Faby's first, well, more like third, but the first one she was contracted to do. She was sent to a store, where the manager is not a nice person, and does not care one bit about the parties. Plus, they have a "retard" working there, here, those people are called "down" because of how they act, especially when they are rejected. This guy was really helpful when Faby was a face painter, always bringing her water, refreshment, cake, and sometimes her lunch. Faby always thought it was funny that this guy was trying to participate in the parties, and was saying to her self, (poor one, just let him play) This guy works from Thursday to Sunday, and is the main store party guy, the one who cleans the party room and sets it up for the next party. His name is George, in Spanish sounds like Horehay, and everyone calls him Horeheto. He was trying to help Faby in her party last night. Faby no longer thought it was funny. Faby come out, saying who she is, and she comes from a castle, and George says, "yesterday you were a face painter, now you are a princess, and did you move? I thought you lived in an apartment?" Right from the start, Faby was not impressed, just says "thank you Horeheto" gritting her teeth and smiling. She said the parents thought it was funny, probably thinking it was part of the show. Faby said she came here because she heard it was some ones birthday . . . this guy said, "its her birthday" grinning and gritting her teeth, she says, "thank you Horeheto. And how old are you?" The little girl says she is five. Faby's next line was suppose to be, (lets all give her five big claps) instead, Horeheto steals the line. By this time, Faby is very upset and pinching and twisting the pinches on him while saying "thank you Horeheto" All through the party, he was being very helpful. Even said, Faby was going to make every one dance, and play different games, and the best one gets the present. The best one is the birthday girl, she gets the princess wand. Faby was trying to get rid of him, by saying, "please, bring me a refreshment." After a while, the pinata, full of candies and presents to all, well, it was a very large pinata and very very little inside. No breaking of the pinata, nope, Faby had to reach in and grab and toss out every where trying to make sure all the kids had a chance to get something. She just started and here he came, poking at her saying "here is your refreshment" the parents were really enjoying them selves, laughing them selves silly, and the kids really loved it as well, Faby on the other hand, was ready to ring his neck. All in all, Faby said the party was OK. The kids were happy, the parents were happy. The Manager threw her, her meal and drink, getting the drink all over the place, she asked for Inca cola and they gave her coke, she don't like coke. She said she is going to tell every one she loved that store. Because every time she says she loves a store, they make very sure she don't go back and try to give her stores she hates. She done found this out a long time ago. Since then, they have changed the party programmer, and this new one likes to program Princes Parties for little boys who wanted the Pirate Party, and visa verso :) like she is doing her best to destroy or ruin some of the party people's reputation, by saying, "its not my fault, its theirs, they should have known better, and called in advance, I just write down what the store says." Always passing the buck, but come to find out, the two parties that Faby saved, the store did have it wrote down correctly, so, it was not the stores fault. Faby said she will be prepared . . . when she gets all her uniforms, she will be caring them all. When they were toying with the idea of having Princess Parties, they also said that Faby would be the primary Princess Party Girl. But they never trained her and wound up training three others, one primary and two after thoughts. I say after thoughts, because of what Faby told me how she was trained, lots of confusion, lots of (do this, but don´t do this, skip to this part, if the parents say this, then do this . . . . and so on and so on) really blew Faby's mind. after an hour and a half, she asked Faby if she had any questions, Faby just said, "no, you were very thorough." So, she went to the party with her text and followed as best as she could with all the interruptions from Horeheto. And still had a good party.

Sat Jun 7, 2008

Party

Faby got called for an emergency party, a Princess Party that started at 11am, she got the call at 11:30. Some thing has to be done with Miate, the party programmer. She told the store it was Faby's fault, and the parents and grandparents were screaming at Faby how she broke their little girls heart. It was a total mess. I went with Faby, just got back and will have to run in a few minutes, for my English class. I was telling Faby to show her bosses, mainly Melissa, what time she got the call and to show her schedule, to show she was not programmed for the party. The store was telling the people that the party was for free. Still, Faby should get paid for it. She got there at 12 noon and went till 1:30 almost. They did not even have the cake, and it ran in to another party that was supposed to start at 1pm. That was another big mess, lots of problems, the new parents were screaming, about how their party was all messed up, and how could this happen, and every one there was blaming Faby. Not funny. Faby said next time she gets a call for a party that already started, she is busy . . .

Sun Jun 8, 2008

Parties

Miata, the problem child, She is the party programmer. Faby first met her in one of the KFC's, cleaning tables and floors. In fact, she was working as a "janitor" for years, not sure how many, while she was going to the University. She is also what Faby calls "Cholo" not a nice kind of person. These people only have one thing on their minds, that is to hurt others. Here in Peru, the majority of the people are cholo, some like the above mentioned, are deep, deep, cholo, and they only think of hurting others, to the point of hurting or killing them selves, only to hurt others. Miata, was always fighting with all the party people, constantly "denouncing" writing bad reports on all the party people who came to the store where she worked. Mainly because she worked all month for about 200 soles and the party people made on average, 800 soles a month. Paint faces only about half that, Mad science about twice that, show people about 800 a month. She declared war on all three, saying they were doing wrong all the time. Yes, even said Faby was a bad face painter. Well, she either got her degree or got far enough along in her studies, in market managing, or business managing, to get the "party programmer" job, they don't just hire any one for that job, and she promised to "save" the company money. She raised the taxes on all the party people, all three, mad science, shows and paint faces, saying they make too much. Then started messing up on the parties, programming princess parties for little boys, and pirate parties for little girls, switching the chicky tect dance for the farm, and so on and so on, to the point that four party guys left. Why there was a casting for "show" and messed up on the face painters so much that poor Melissa has had one casting after another trying to keep her slots full. she would call the face painters at the last minute saying the party started and to get there right now, and tell the store that the face painter for got the party. Did that to Faby a few times, as a face painter, and again last night as a princess party, calling Faby at 11:30am telling her the party started at 11:00am, then telling the store that Faby forgot the party. I just don't get it. Don't she know, if she kills the "parties" she looses her job? But here in Peru, that is the idea, to hurt others as much as possible, even if it means "killing" your self, hurt others as much as you can. That is the majority of the people here. The minority just say, "poor one" or, sake their heads at them, just ignoring them. Try to work around them. Its driving me crazy just to hear all about it. Then to hear, I can not do any thing about it when some one tries to hurt me . . . like the second floor woman . . . one of these days i am going to draw a "star" on the floor and have candles on the points, me sitting in the middle, and when she comes in . . . scream . . . "AND IN COMES THE DEVIL" but Faby keeps telling me I can not do that :(OH, Well . . .

Thu Jun 12, 2008

Carola

Carola finally put her foot down . . . so did I . . . What happened you might wonder? When I was working for John Nash School, the Paycheck was suppose to be 1200 soles a month, I only worked for one week, about 400 soles worth. The girls got "P.T." uniforms, here they are called "sport" uniforms. Those uniforms cost 150 soles each set, I got two uniforms, had too, that was 300 soles total. Carola said then and still says, that the uniforms were free, and so were the meals . . . no, they were not for free, the rest of the weeks paycheck went to pay for the girls, mine and Faby's meals there. On to What Happened . . . Carola's Uniform, the pants are missing the string, the top is missing the metal connector of the sipper. When I asked about the missing parts, I got no answer. I had to go to Faby to ask, Faby told me she said, the string got lost, don't know where or when it happened, the zipper got stuck in her chair and broke off with out her knowing and can not find it any where. I said that since the uniform is broke, she is not to wear it. That was three weeks ago. I guess Faby over ruled me, because Two weeks ago, she wore it all week, looking like a rag bag and some how, seemed like she enjoyed it. Here it comes . . . Last week, Sunday, I told Carola, that if the string does not return or the zipper return, she is not going to wear that uniform. She was not going to look like a rag bag wearing a brand new uniform. Again she said that the uniform was hers, it was free, and she did not have to listen to her, in fact in her words, was "you can say me nothing, you are not my father." to make it short. She went on to say only her mother can say any thing to her. Well, apparently three weeks ago, I was over ruled. I screamed, "I don't care what your mother says, I bought that uniform, I paid for your meals at that school. You broke that uniform. You will not touch it until it gets fixed. If you touch it, I will burn it, and I don't care if you are wearing it, I will burn it!!!" She was crying as if I beat her, went running to Mommy, just a rattling off. I was yelling still, not as loud now, not wanting to sound like I was screaming at Faby, but stating what I felt about the uniform. As I said, Carola put her foot down, and so did I. By the way, Natalia gets treats from me, like cookies for her school snack, almost every day. Carola don't.

Mon Jun 16, 2008

Natalia

The other night . . . The girls were fighting, I only heard Carola's voice. Faby was working. I go to make a pot of coffee, Carola sees me and starts laughing, like always. Once I go back into my bedroom, the screaming starts again, mostly Carola's voice. I come walking around, and before Carola bursts out laughing, I was almost in their room, I saw Natalia, very upset. I waved my fingers to her to follow me, and said with a very low and soft voice, "come" I was also doing laundry, that day. While in the process, looking through the clothes, Faby's pants, there was a lollipop. This was before Faby left for work. I said, "if I find it, can I keep it?" she told me she I could. Just before I dropped the jeans in the machine, I heard more wrinkling, there was another one. I had both in my shirt pocket, I was also watching wrestling on line. I told Natalia to sit on the bed. I took one lollipop out and started, well you know . . . and started to hand one to Natalia, asking if she wanted one. She told me no, she did not want. I then asked what happened, and why she was so mad. She told me her sister said she was crazy. Why? Because she wanted to play with her toy, not with Carola. Carola took her toy calling her crazy for not playing with her. I said, that Carola calls me crazy. She said yes, I asked if she thought I was crazy, she said no. I asked if she thought the lollipop was crazy? She said no. I said I think the lollipop was good. Then asked if she wanted the other one. She took it, and we enjoyed the rest of the wrestling show that night on line, about an hour and a half. The package that Mama and Papa sent us got here, Natalia, Faby and I are very happy and very very thankful, thank you Mama and Papa for the peanut butter and fudge. If you think Carola has tried any, think again, I have no right saying anything to her . . . fine and dandy . . . Philly is OK with his toy, probably wishing it was a little bigger. He does play with it.

Fri Jun 27, 2008

Hanging

Well, I left Mama and Papa hanging, more then once . . . sorry. I am sure when they read this, they will be ready to hang me :) This is going to be a long one, so prepare your self ;) Poisoned, Carola loved to put on a show, no matter what, she loves putting on a show. This new school has kids with real horror stories, makes hers really unbelievable. Most of the kids there only have one parent, and almost all of the kids there walk to school alone and back home alone. Most of the kids there eat from the garbage, begging for scraps from the Mercado and stuff. One of the kids in Carola's class was selling his lunch, Carola bought it and ate it. How did Carola get the money? Natalia said Carola said she got some money from a kid in her class to pay for the lunch of the other kid. I went through her backpack, and found no color pencils. Carola was putting on such a show, in the past, in the store, about having no colors, the "mama" got her a lot, she had about seventy color pencils, which I took from her several weeks ago, and gave her only eight, because Natalia did not have very many and was asking for a certain color, and Carola was screaming at Natalia for even asking such a question. I may have over reacted, oh, well. Still, she had no color pencils at all. Faby thought she was poisoned by some cake that one of the neighbors gave the girls, but that was way too fast. I mean the affect was too fast. Carola was acting sick long before the cake. Well, Faby took Carola to the hospital and they checked her out, said she was poisoned, a poison for the "boogies" what Faby calls "head lice" I think it was an accidental poising. More like, the food she bought was from the garbage and was contaminated. Carola is doing fine now . . . Carola, One more thing, The doctor said Carola has a brain problem, because she is not eating enough, or eating right, and not drinking enough water. The problem lies with her insides not working right, like digestion process and such, and could cause other problems as well, but with the right eating and drinking enough water, it will fix it self. More on Carola, Her horror stories are not working in the mountains. One kid in her class, has no mother, and his father works all day, he eats out of the garbage, and begs for scraps in the Mercado. His father barley makes enough to pay the rent. He refuses to get a "free" spot way on the mountain side. So, the kid does what he can to eat, at least he has a roof over his head, if he gets in his fathers way, he gets the tar beat out of him. Poor kid, he can not ask for any thing. There is a little six year girl that goes to the school there, all by her self, after school, she hops on a moto taxi to go to the bus stop, then to Plaza Vea, a very big shopping store, several miles away, about five or so, to shop for the nights dinner. She has no father, and her mother works all day in the Mercado, and refuses to eat such garbage, so the little one, six years old goes to do the days shopping and cooks for her and her mother. Just a couple of stories that Carola could not out due. You may not believe how many more there are. Carola went from strait "A" to doing nothing right at all. To the point of crying crocodile tears in the classroom when the teacher says any thing to her. She would do the wrong thing on purpose, then cry a river when the teacher tries to correct her. Faby was surprised to hear this and told the teacher that Carola was just acting, and finally, got the teacher the papers from the other school, yes, both girls are in rolled now in the new school, and Carola's teacher was very surprised . . . last time we talked with the teacher, she said, when Carola starts crying, she brings Carola a bucket and says, "here, fill this up, I need to water my plants." Moving right along Land Lord, About three weeks ago, the land lord said we have two months to find another place to live. Reasons, mainly, the kids are too loud. Making too many problems, primarily, to the first floor little girl, who studies in a very high class pre-paid school, and can not be influenced by our two monsters . . . that little girl on the first floor will scream her head off till four in the morning during the week . . . He said, that the neighborhood has called the police on our two little monsters several times for making noise, and has had way too many complaints with the other tenets in the building, like the second floor woman, who also will be screaming till the wee hours in the morning as well. Well, to come to the point, he stated, if we don't have all our things out in two months, he will keep what we don't move out, and he will kick us out. A couple days ago . . . Wednesday, Faby ran in to him. He said "Fabiolita, how are you, where have you been, where is every one?" Faby, "As you see, we are not here, I come in once in a while during the week because of my work." Him, "Where are you living?" Faby, "We are camping out in the mountains, why are you so concerned? You told me we have two months to leave." Him, "Well, you know, the owners said they may be coming here in a couple of months, and I am not suppose to be renting out that spot, I could get in to trouble. But they have changed their minds. If you are planning on moving, you have to let me know ahead of time." Faby, "You told me two months. As you see, we are not here during the week. How could my two girls be causing so much noise and so many problems that the police are being called, when they are not even here? I have proof they are not here, they are in rolled in another school two hours from here." Him, "Where are you living?" Faby, "None of your business, the rent is paid, I am paying the power that I am not using, I am paying the water that I am not using, what more do you want? The place is quiet all week long, we are all here only during the weekend, Saturday and Sunday, then we are camping out in the mountains. With that, she left him with his mouth hanging. Three weeks ago, he left Faby speechless, last Wednesday, Faby left him speechless. No, we are not moving, we need this address for the process, and are wishing it would come to an end very soon. We are doing our best to keep out of trouble, and trying to keep the kids out of trouble. Even though Carola does her best to get us in to trouble. We come here to shower, wash clothes, relax a bit, go to church, talk on the Internet, come Sunday night or Monday morning, we are back out on the mountain. Philly, He really is something, he really voices his opinion every time we come down off the mountain. He hates coming back to this apartment. He has made some friends there, lots of chickens, and pigeons, there are other cats and some dogs running all over the place as well. He loves to travel, some times he even jumps in to his "cat carrier" or pushes it to Faby, meowing the whole time as if he was saying, "I'm ready to go home." When it looks like we are about to leave.

When we are in the mountain, he don't really want to leave. Natalia, Not much to tell about Natalia, other then finding out she presses mama far more then Carola does when it comes to money. To the point, Faby went to the teacher asking what is going on. Natalia's teacher was surprised, saying "please, no, I was not forcing any one to pay any thing. Don't say any thing to the director about this, he has fired teachers for telling the kids they have to pay, I just said, those who can, please pay this amount, those who can not, we will work something out." You see, they have government books, but still, copies sometimes have to be made, not all the time. You can not write in the government books, they are used year after year, until the government issues new ones. If the kids have copy books, note books, they can write what they need in there, like the answers to the questions, and stuff. Other then that, Natalia is very good, works hard both in and out of school, helping me out more then Carola, and talks to me a lot more then Carola does. I am going to close this one out, I may write some thing else later, this one is getting long enough.

Sat Jun 28, 2008

Uncle Roberto

Uncle Roberto called today. Well, according to him and his wife, Faby has been getting four hundred soles a month, every month, since January. No, she has not been getting a thing. December, she was suppose to get eight hundred soles, and got two or three hundred, something like that, and every time Faby talks with her Father, it just don't go right, until this morning, when she called him, and he asked how is every thing. Faby don't lie, and told him about Carola being in the hospital, and having to buy medicine. He asked if Roberto gave her any money yet, no, not since December, no money from January till now. He does not call, or come over, nothing at all. And she starts crying on the phone while she was talking, really making a scene. He says, Roberto says, you won't let him in. Faby says, Uncle Roberto refuses to come in, and continues to cry . . . Faby don't know how well it will work, but Uncle Roberto did call today. Well, Faby and Uncle Roberto made a date for Tuesday morning to have breakfast. Myself and the girls will be in the mountains. As for not opening the door for him any more, that was me . . . I got tired of him yelling so much that it was making Faby cry, and got tired of him refusing the breakfast I made, some he accepted, but as time went on, he was turning his nose up at it, only eating the bread he brought and barely sharing it with us . . . orders of his brother, Faby's Father, to bring something to eat. He was getting to be too rude, so I was refusing to open the door. Faby reversed the whole thing saying he was refusing to come in. Any how, Faby's Father said Roberto will give her some money this time, suppose to be four hundred soles, at least, but if you add it up, from January till now, that would be twenty four hundred soles he really owes her, I seriously doubt he will give her any thing but a hard time, and I will be in the mountains . . . I am not happy about that, but at least she told me about it.

Sat Jun 28, 2008

Parties

Tonight was scary for Faby. She had a party with a Mad Science show. Faby was a Super Hero, in the back ground, the Mad Science show was the main attraction. I left to get Faby, telling Mama there was an accident, that is what Faby told me, but that she was OK. The Mad Science show guy has been working for the company for four years. He was telling the kids to stay back, telling the parents to keep their kids back, no one would listen to him. He kept giving warnings, saying this stuff is explosive, and could cause harm. They got way too close and "BOOM!!!" Three kids in the hospital, several with miner injuries, mostly covered in black. The parents of all who were hurt in any way, was screaming "you will pay!" they mean pay in cash and lots of it, or go to jail for a long time and then they sue the company. Instead of listening to the warnings and staying back, they get hurt, and now, the parents think they will get paid lots of cash one way or another. Where was Faby? In the back ground, way in the back. She said she heard the explosion, looked up and every one was covered in black. The kids who went to the hospital, one had a cut on his face, one could not hear any thing, and one had a cut on his hand, that is how close they were. The rest, well, just ears popping and covered in black, and lots of parents going bananas. The birthday kid was OK, no problems, his parents were doing fine, they just wanted cake, mostly, along with their happy meals and stuff, along with most of the rest of the kids, most of the parents were very unhappy, and here is Faby running like mad to try to calm every one down, cutting the cake, running for the meals. She is a Party Show girl, not a waitress. But, she was doing that when she was Paint Faces.

Sun Jun 29, 2008

Parties

Last night I was a bit tired, bit send by accident. Any way, that Mad Science guy has been working for the company for four years, and never has had any accidents before. A couple of parents were wanting him to go to jail, saying they would do every thing they could to make sure he stays in jail for a long time for hurting their kids. Faby was so scared she was going to be in trouble, because she was part of the show. She was way in the back, but still part of the show. She told me the police were there, they asked her a few questions, but, mostly laughed at her, because of her costume. She did not have the whole Super Hero uniform, part of it was overalls, for the farm and chicky teck parties. The police told her she could not leave. The party was almost over when the accident happened, only fifteen minutes left in the party, the "Boom" was the last thing to happen in the show, and the kids would not listen and stay back, after the "Boom," every one eats their happy meals, and has cake. Didn't really go as planned. The party was over at 8pm, Faby finally left at 10:30pm, we did not get home tell almost midnight. Faby was so scared she was going to jail as well, but they never asked her for her name. What they did do, or not do, was leave the Man Science party box and table out in the play area, for whom ever to do what ever with. Faby kept telling the manager to do something about it, he would not do a thing, not his problem, if it goes boom again, not his problem . . . and so on and so on. Come 10:30, I was almost dragging her out of there, she was so tired, she could barley walk, and no buses, not right out front, had to walk, took about thirty minutes to walk what would normally take me a couple minutes to walk in.

Sun Jun 29, 2008

Mountain

We are camping out way up on a side of a mountain. It is zoned, no mailing address. Where we are camping is third zone, H—4. I am still not sure of the spelling, but the place is "coe ee ka"-"Collique" to sound it out. Its in Comas area, about two hours from Pueblo Libre, more like an hour and a half early in the morning or late at night when there is no traffic, sometimes longer in the middle of the day. I know it sounds a bit "funny" all this camping, but we found a very good school there in the mountains. As I wrote before, the girls are now en rolled in the school. We have not moved, nor do we plan on moving, because of this process, we need this address. But because of the problems we are having, we had to do something. Faby calls it "invading" how ever, that is totally different from what we are doing. To invade, is to move in some ones house or on some ones land. You then have to prove you need the place worse then the owner does, and then you don't have to pay rent. If the owner does not do any thing to try to get you removed, after about thirty years, the place is yours. Some cases, only ten years, but normally it takes thirty years. The owner has to pay taxes on his property, his land, or house during the time, if not, then the government takes it, and any one on or in has to move, or get bull dozed out, and yes, they will bull doze you, if you don't move out of the way, you could get hurt badly or even killed in the process. Only the government can do that, no one else can. The owners can only go to the court and make a process to try to get you removed. If all else fails, they might hire criminals, thugs, thieves, and such to scare you or beat you to make you leave. What we are doing is totally different, We are staking a "claim" in the mountains. No previous owners to contend with, there are government officials that walk around once in a while to see who all is living up there. They say after they have you name, and see you are living there for at least three months, then three to six months after, you get a title to the land where you are living. Our claim is ten meters by twelve meters. One hundred twenty meters in all. Granted half of it is a steep incline, and half of that is solid rock, well mostly, I keep chipping away at it, and we are sleeping in a tent, well, Faby and I are, the girls broke their tent, they were on the ground for a while, but we got them cots. We do have straw walls around our living area for some privacy. Philly love it there, Natilia is OK with it, I think Carola hates it there, you know me :) and Faby, well she is more like me, don't like the city at all . . . she loves it there. We spend most of the week up there, sometimes Faby has to come back during the week because of her job, but when not working, she is up there. I stay there all week, Monday through Friday, I usually go out Monday morning, but today, I will be going out this afternoon, after church. I usually have English classes on the weekend, but this weekend was canceled, my student has meetings he has to attend too. I got the viruses off my computer, even tested it out, got on mirc and talked with mama yesterday, only problem is, I am no longer registered, it was canceled, so, who ever got it done for me before, I think it was Pam, my cousin, you may have to do it again, this was my code or line I typed in to get the @ sign in front of my name "/msg nickserv identify pickle" and you know my nick name "FarmerCec" I can not promise I will be on tonight, but I will try, the Internets here close at 10pm and its dark in the mountains, and can be dangerous. But, so far, so good, nothing bad has happened to me, got sick a few times, that is about it, I just got to watch and wash what I eat. I am running out of time, time to go to church. We are having a "fare well" dinner for our Pastor. He is going to North Carolina to teach in a University. Teaching Pastoring classes. To become a Pastor. Something like that. Its his last sermon, he sure is a good one.

Tue Jul 1, 2008

About the Mountain

At first, I thought it was one of the many "natives" communities, because that is where Faby's last baby sitter lived. Come to find out, its much worse. There are a few natives there, not many. A real natives community is much cleaner, and far more dangerous for criminals. Get the picture :) Ever time Faby mentions where we live, the reply is, "how can you live there, its so dangerous." We have come to find out, that is where lots of rejects go, along with criminals. Some of which are very dangerous criminals. Two child molesters live there, one of which has a history of killing kids. The teachers of the school keeps warning the kids of these two people. Most of the community knows about them, they tease the kids, but so far, have not harmed any one in the area, from what we know of any way. Why they are not in jail, because they have been deemed "crazy" they would never understand why they are in jail. About 80 percent of the mountain is criminals, the other 20 percent are mixed with natives, and other rejects, and some poor people just looking for a place to set up camp. We have made friends with a couple of different families. One has been there since the start of population of the area, in fact they were the first on the mountain, ten years ago, and the other one has been there for six years. Very nice people. Even though its considered dangerous, there is this rule, code of living, or something like that, that states, "you don't mess with your neighbors, you don't rob them or hurt them." So, believe it or not, I am quite safe on the mountain, they see me every day, or almost every day, walking the kids to and from school. About the camp site. We have power, but not in our name, the power company will not travel up the mountain, we had to run cord about three hundred meters to tie in to another power cord, that runs down the mountain to a family that states, "you want power, you pay 35 soles a month, or we cut the power line to every one." We have running water . . . I run it up the hill every day, no help from the girls at all . . . oh, well, they are little, but at least they could behave them selves, especially Carola. We got a couple banana tree plants, one male, suppose to produce more bananas, and one female, suppose to produce more banana tree plants. I asked Faby how to tell the difference, her first response was, "the male has a birdyling :)" I just said, "very funny, now how do you tell the difference, she said, the woman who gave us the plants said the male was shorter, and the female was taller. That sure does tell me a lot. Any way, got them planted in rock bed with some dirt and coffee grounds. Star Bucks gives bags of used coffee grounds away for free to their customers for their gardens. We got several bags, may go back for more, at a later date. What am I doing here now? Faby has a party in a dangerous area late at night tomorrow night, about five hours away, she told me about it, and I told her I would go with her, the girls will be here in Pueblo Libre, locked in their room. Hopefully being quiet. We let the teachers know that the girls will not be in school tomorrow, but will be in school Thursday and Friday. Carola's teacher threatened to fail Carola if she kept messing up. When we finally got her the school papers, from the other school, on Carola, she found out Carola was a strait "A" student, she really started in on Carola. Carola was doing things wrong on purpose then crying her eyes out when corrected. What was funny was when Faby gave the teacher Carola's school papers, then a few days later, we seen the teacher again, she said every time Carola starts crying, she brings a bucket and tells her to fill it, she needs to water her plants. At first, that teacher really thought Carola was traumatized for some reason, but after Faby filled her in, several times, then showed her the school papers, she realized she has an actress in her class, yes, Faby told the teacher Carola is an actress, has made movies, a few of them. Now the teacher is having fun with Carola saying out loud, "you want to pass or fail this year? Or, "could you put on a different show, I have already seen this one." Things like that.

Wed Jul 2, 2008

Parties

Faby feels as if she is being punished, and or, being forced out. Remember, when I mentioned an "explosion" well, this has something to do with it.

Today, is the weekly meeting for the Party People, all three, and Faby is being sent five hours away to a very dangerous place. The Mad Science guy who had the accident, is being sent away as well, he has three parties today. Not just them, but any one who poses a threat to Mitea, the programmer is not allowed to be there. One of the managers has been sent on vacation, yes, sent on vacation. She never asked for vacation. Why? Because the big wigs of KFC and Mad Science—Party project, will be there, and Mitea, don't want any one there who might pose a threat to her, which is over half of the people working there. One woman who was fired, she was paint faces, is now making at minimum, 800 soles a month, always showing up late to the parties, not dressed properly, and constantly causing problems with the customers . . . how is that possible . . . no clue, she was fired, now making more then the Mad Science and Party Show people put together. Faby was suppose to get a pay raise jumping to party show, the pay raise was having more parties. Paint Faces and Party Show cost the customers 80 soles, the Paint Faces and Show people both get 30 soles per party they do. Mad Science show cost the customers 200 soles, they get 40 soles per party. Usually, there are more Show parties then Mad Science or Paint Faces, and some how, the girl who was fired is making way more then any one else, but she and Mitea are very close, doing their best to kill the whole Party Project for every one. That was just to give you an idea. Any one who argues, or complains, is sent away, one way or another. One woman, who is pregnant, was fired, by mistake, not really fired, but some one sent an email to the hospital saying she was fired, and she lost out on her insurance, now is unable to give birth in the hospital, because she has no money nor does she have any insurance. Mitea did it, but said she didn't, must have been a "computer error" in fact, every time she messes up, like sending a Princess to a little boy who wanted a Pirate party, she says its the stores fault, or visa-versa, she is always trying to make every one else look bad, and now, there is getting to be less and less parties for every one, or so she says. There tends to be lots of "emergency" parties, which most of the people are refusing, saying, they are too far away or too busy an find some one else. Several store managers are really complaining about Mitea, one of which, Faby is seeing tonight, this manager has given Faby one or two "Champs" cards, those little cards that says you did an out standing job. Thing is, this manager was, for some reason, moved way out there in the middle of now where for some reason, Mitea don't know that this manager and Faby are friends, if she did, Faby may not be going out there, Mitea does her best to make every one around her unhappy and miserable. Oh, well, enough of that. Faby is still trying to hang on. Funny thing is, she was making more as Paint Faces then as Show. She switched because there is an average of 400 parties a week, and most of them don't want Paint Faces, but since Mitea has come aboard, every thing is falling apart. Faby don't know what to do, but is trying to hang on.

Wed Jul 9, 2008

Parties

Faby got an award, a free pizza from Pizza Hut. suppose to be a medium, no drinks or bread sticks. But the manager of the KFC that is attached to the Pizza Hut where we just went, really likes Faby and how she puts on parties. The pizza turned in to a large with every thing on it, no pork products, the love chicken here, with bread sticks and drinks, large drinks. Was nice of them. Her award, the free pizza dinner was for an idea she had about CD's, which was this: why have several different kinds floating around, just copy the songs you need on one, less mess and easier to keep up with. They loved it and gave her a pizza dinner for it. That was the Good News . . . Here comes the Bad . . . Melessa just got fired. The excuse was that her studies in the university did not match her job title. She was "Human Resources" manager, primarily hiring and firing employees, and of course, the primary head of paint faces project. She was working there for four years. Faby as well as a few others, believe Mitea, the new programmer, had something to do with getting Melessa fired. Faby and the others, not all, but most of the others are really worried about how long they will have a job. That girl Mitea is really trying to kill the whole party project of KFC. and she is doing a very good job of it. it was a rough meeting tonight, Melessa was giving her "farewell" speech, and handing out the prizes, probably why Faby got her prize. She was suppose to get one last week, but was transferred across the country . . . oh, well, she got her pizza and shared it with me and the girls. Worse news, it was so hard on her tonight, she almost had an attack at the restaurant, it was a long walk home . . . no money for a taxi. she is sleeping now. Hopefully she does not have an attack, but she almost had one. I know I drew some of the pain out, on the way home. She almost fell down. I am not going to explain every thing I did, just that I did feel some of her pain, and she was able to get here . . . I still feel it . . .

Thu Jul 10, 2008

OUCH!!! well, not really as bad as the last time, but still, I DON'T LIE NEEDLES!!! We went to the hospital today, Faby and I, that is. Faby had a ten o'clock appointment, I had an eleven o'clock one. We got there nine thirty, Faby had an eye appointment. They scratched out her appointment and wrote down four pm Monday. Faby told me we have to leave, glad we didn't, I almost blew a fuse, I did yell a little, and the nurse who changed the appointment said we can make a complaint at the appointment desk. We go there, they said, nope, they can not do any thing there, go to another one, the social assistance office. There they said Faby's doctor is in the country side, next to Bolivia, taking care of eye patients. OK, its nine forty five now, we go to the dentist office to check me in to see if I can get in early. We get in to line, and here comes a woman caring a baby, probably, most likely heard us talking English, and cut right in front of us, making very bad googly faces at me, cocking her head to one side and then the other, sticking her tongue at me, not at her baby, at me. Faby seen this and told me not to say any thing, "poor one" I am sooooo tired of hearing "poor one" well, I mentioned to Faby, what if the dentist got sent away too, and we are here just wasting our time? She seen the office door open and went right up and talked to some one, a woman dentist, she was like an old mama young grandma impression, she took my appointment slip, Faby then came back to me and said, I was next. Fifteen minutes later, the woman with the baby just made it up to the desk to check in and I was called in to the back . . . teehee :) or so I thought. At first, the woman dentist, I thought at first was a nurse, thought I was sixty and Faby was my grand daughter, you know, me sixty and her twenty. Faby said, no, he is my husband. Of course, this is all in Spanish, and I am catching on a little more and more. She could not believe I am thirty nine. She told Faby to tell me to keep my eyes open, she don't want me dieing in here. She said, my face, hair and teeth all say I am sixty years old. Her and Faby were joking back and forth over that, I caught very little, Faby translated even less. At one point the Doctor thought I was insulting her, I told Faby to tell her, I would never insult any one with needles aimed at me . . . she just smiled and didn't say a word. Well, I got one more tooth out, this one was way in the back upper right side, most of it was gone any way, but every time some thing touched back there, it brought tears to my eyes. Still that needle was Painful!!! the pulling only took a few seconds. and I was out, but it was about twenty five minutes of talking and looking at my teeth. Ten thirty we were out and getting some ibuprofen pills, after that we went to get more appointments for later, got one fifteen days from now to get another one pulled. Faby got her Four o'clock appointment changed for another day in the morning, and tried to get a skin appointment, they told her she had to call. OK, so we get in to the phone line to call. They said, you missed your ten o'clock appointment, you are red flagged, you are about to get all your appointments canceled for every one in your house hold. Faby was not happy, she was telling the person on the phone, she was there, and they changed her the hour and day. They said, its not in the system, so, you are in big trouble, you are about to lose every thing except the payments, you will still have to pay, but you will not be able to get any help. We went back to the appointment desk and had to wait for almost an hour before they called us up. The guy that help Faby said, she was red flagged for missing her ten o'clock appointment today. Faby told him, she was here, they changed it to four on Monday, hand written. He said, noting on the system except you missed. Faby said, the paper is two windows down, the woman who changed that appointment took that paper that those people scribbled on. Oh, What a Mess . . . he came back after about ten minutes, with the paper. Said, he will fix it, and got Faby a skin appointment next week. At first he was saying she has to call for those appointments, but after the mess he seen she was in, went ahead and scheduled her for one . . . and its not over, the day is not any way. Next is he job. Mitea did not schedule the whole week and said for every one to come in today, this evening to get the weeks parties. Faby is about to leave, and may not be back until seven or eight pm. That company is going down hill, and the owner does not care as long as she gets her money. By the time she does care, the company will be no more and she will be full of law suits . . . OH, Well, that is how they do things here. Melissa was defending Mitea for a long time, saying "poor one, give her a chance" and this is how she is repaid . . . POOR ONE, get for real . . .

Thu Jul 10, 2008

Parties

Well, this is the second part of today I went with Faby. Not inside, I sat in the KFC right beside the office waiting for Faby to come out. And what a story she told me . . . Mitea first said, can you do a party, it just stared, right here, the store next door. Faby told her, she is not prepared, she would have to go home get her stuff and by the time she got back, the party would be over. The one who was suppose to do the party, never got the schedule, why? Because Mitea sent this guy on an emergency party during the meeting, then told him two places his schedule might be, if not in one place, he would have to go to another, about two hours apart . . . he was not in to playing games. She called him asking why he was not at his party? he said, What party, you never gave me a schedule. She said, it here, why didn't you come in and get it? He said, I have no time to play games of fetch, I am too busy to play child's games. She said, you have a party at this KFC. He said, no I don't. I don't have a schedule, find some one else. And hung up. This was for a pirate party. One guy she called, after laughing said, why don't you put on the costume and act like the clown you are. And hung up. In fact, she called about a dozen people while Faby was there, that all hung up on her, some laughing, some just saying, "its your problem, you fix it" finally, she got a hold of one who was just like her, cleaning tables at first, but jumped in to being party show, because he was taking acting classes and passed the test, when Faby did. He said he would go. Finally she gave Faby her schedule. She came in to the KFC where I was, saying there was a party upstairs that no one is doing at the moment. The manager knows Faby so, Faby went to say "HI" he asked if she was doing the party, Faby told him no, it belonged to this person, I for got who she said, and said, he comes in when he wants . . . the manager snapped back, saying, no, I don't think so, it was Mitea's fault again, wasn't it, she for got to program the party again, didn't she . . . Faby did not say a word, most of the store managers don't like the new programming manager, Mitea, and they want her gone, before the parties disappear.

Mon Jul 14, 2008

Home Front

Well, Ran in to the land lord. For over a year, I had no light in the living room. For over a year, the second floor woman has been complaining about no light. As well as, him telling me, to build a roof over the living room, because she don't want her clothes getting rained on. I basically told him, "NO" by explaining how, I could not move the roofing materials do to the fact that the room I have them over, leaks badly when it rains here . . . I know, I keep saying it don't rain here, it don't, but it does have a heavy mist, and every thing gets wet. He was really screaming at me about the light. He did get a plastic thing, not sure what to call it, just long enough to cover just the second floor woman's clothes lines . . . leaving my clothes lines out in the "rain" sorry people . . . we refused to get a light, because she would leave the light on for weeks at a time, saying she was doing us a favor. Ya, doing us a favor, we were in Chile, extending my visitation visa, gone for weeks at a time, and the land lord trying to raise us the rent because the power bill was high, saying we are using too much power, we leave the light on all the time . . . Now What's next . . . history repeating it self? We will see . . .

Mon Jul 14, 2008

Mountains

I left Mama and Papa hanging again. Told them a little and said I would give details later. Sorry, its coming a bit later than I expected. Supposedly, every Sunday, we have what is called "Fianai" that is the community, the strip of hill where we live, all is suppose to get together and work on building a road or stair way up the hill. The last three Sundays I was there, they had reasons for not doing one. Someone's birthday Party, Potato Day, and I forgot the other one . . . Yes, Potato day, the day of the Potato, Peru has about 200 different kinds of Potato's . . . any way, Last Sunday, they had one and we missed, So this Sunday, yesterday, they told us, if we miss again, they will cut our power. No Fianai, No Power. That is the rule of the hill. Faby believes, its more then just building a road, its where the people all get together to work together, talk a bit, share a refreshment, basically a social gathering and its only two hours, from 6am to 8am. This time we moved rocks around. Didn't accomplish much, but still, every one was happy afterwards. well, almost :) There is one woman, who set up camp in the road, strait across from us at the top of the hill. She has threatened to kill Philly. The President of the hill had four ducks, runes, mallard looking fat ducks, yes, had . . . That woman said she is doing him a favor, she is feeding his ducks, so, they are her ducks and she was hungry, so, she ate one. One day, last week, while I was chipping rock, I got tired, stopped and turned to look around and seen one of her little boys, walk over to the edge of the ledge, the presidents house, straw house, a little wood here and there, just beneath, he dropped his paints, and a stream came flying from him. That is not all that happens. When she washes dishes or her clothes, guess where she tosses the water, and guess what she says . . . "I'm doing you a favor, you can clean your floor." among other things. She came to the Fianai, and was kicked out, because she came to fight, and no one there wanted her there. its 6:30 am here, and we are off to the mountains, so the girls can go to school.

Mon Jul 14, 2008

a few things

Philly sure is happy to be back in the mountains. He tore a hole in the straw wall and left when we took the girls to school. They made it, just a little late, but they made it. When Faby and I got back, Philly was no where in site. He came in about 3pm, looking for a bite to eat. We went for a walk a couple hours ago. We had to go to the Mercado, the girls are saying they have projects in school that require some kind of papers, like picture type papers. Last time I heard that one, Natalia was saying she needed one, and then I find half of it all cut up in to little peaces in Carola's back pack.
Next door to us, looks like they are claiming up to and on our line. Faby had me inside, while they sat on our rocks, my rock wall I was building to hold the dirt and rocks that I am chipping at, to level out a section . . . thinking of throwing all of it in to the road, if they have to touch it, they can have it . . . thinking any way, Faby may stop me if I get started. We are on our way back up the mountain, thought we would stop in and rest our feet a bit. We, Faby and I, really are ready to leave, I mean, go to the U.S. Its not getting any better here, Faby is sure she is about to loose her job. They only give six month contracts, and her six months is up next month. With Melissa now gone, she is afraid. No money from Uncle Roberto, even though her father keeps telling his brother to give her money, he does not. He says he does, and tells her father how rude we are to him all the time. enough of that. The girls are really something. If not one thing, its some thing else. This morning, while on the bus, Natalia was saying she don't want to be in this situation, and Carola said she don't want to go to school any more. Why, because here in the mountains, their little horror stories don't fly with the real ones from the kids they meet there. Carola's constant balling, is not getting her any where. Natalia is trying to force Mama to buy her new shoes and pay ten soles for a school dance. The kids teachers are getting upset over the kids missing school once in a while, like last Wednesday, Thursday and Friday . . . sorry, doctor appointments,

saying how bad we are for making the kids miss school. Faby told them last Tuesday the girls may not be back till today, then today, Faby's reply was, "maybe I will just take them out of school for good, when they get sixteen, I will put them in the army, they can get their education in the army. Yes, at sixteen here in Peru, you can go in the army, but usually after you finish high school, or "secondary" as they call it here, with parents permission, or signature, they don't need to finish school, just go in, and its a required, or definite two years at first, after that, if you are good enough, you can make a career out of it, or get out. While in, just like in the U.S. you can further your education, but here, you don't have to pay for it, its all include in the package, from what Faby just told me. Nice country :) Yes, Faby was talking loud enough to me so the girls could hear her, they just gave us sorry looks . . . oh, well

Sat Jul 19, 2008

Girls

Natalia had some great news . . . got Carola so upset she nearly chocked on her self in anger . . . Faby got after me, because she thought I was going to but in, I was only trying to hold back a chuckle, once I understood. OK, to start out with, kids start school at three years of age, kindergarten has three grades, 1—3, ages 3, 4, and 5. Then comes Primary, grades 1—6, ages 6, 7, 8, 9, 10, and 11. Last comes Secondary grades 1—5, ages 12, 13, 14, 15, and 16. If you finish on time, you have your High School Diploma at age 16 and are ready for the University. Very rarely do kids graduate on time, and even more rare do kids graduate early here in Peru, unless they have lots of money backing them up with a very good name, last name, like from Spain, England, and of course, the best of all, the good old U.S.A. Usually those kids are in very expensive, very high class private schools and are closely watched. Any where else, like in general population, it is unheard of for there to be a very smart child. The last school the girls were in, one teacher was ready to promote both Natalia and Carola, but was stopped, and we were told by the director that he would not allow any tests, or even think of a promotion, so if we want, we can go to the Government board of education and see what happens. Then one of the teachers reminded Faby, that there is no such thing as a "smart child" in Peru, and to look it up if she don't believe her. Faby did look it up, and found nothing. Faby talked with the teacher again, and the teacher said, that one way or another, the government silences the "smart" kids. Any way, this school is a little different. The director goes to foreign countries to study education, and shares his finding with his teachers. Any teacher he has problems with, is removed and replaced. Natalia's teacher believes Natalia should be in grade six right now, and start Secondary next year. When Natalia told Faby, in front of Carola, Carola was so mad, she could not hardly speak, then Faby did the unspeakable thing of telling Carola, she would talk with her teacher to see if she could promote as well, and both start Secondary next year, Carola got so mad she nearly chocked on her self with anger, I was struggling to hold back a chuckle, I guess Faby thought I was going to but in and told me to stay out of it, she would handle it . . . oh, you should have heard Carola rattling on and gurgling on her anger. She is always telling Natalia how dumb and stupid she is, and because she is not of a "light" completion, she would never get any opportunities. So, this is just too much, the fact that Natalia might bypass her, or even worse, be in the same grade as she. Faby was in both English and Spanish, the girls only Spanish, but I was catching on some of it. Faby rattles off just as fast in English as she does in Spanish, and at times its hard to keep up with her, still, it was as show that should have been filmed :) Any how, to shorten this, in order to get the tests, and the paper work, and yes, both the teachers say its possible to promote both girls, it would cost around 80 dollars, almost 200 soles total. So, who knows. Nothing comes for free, you know, filing fees and stuff. Still, the thought was GREAT for Natalia, she is always working so hard all the time, doing every thing as good as she can, being as perfect as she can with every letter and number. As for Carola, she would mess up on purpose once in a while, but with out trying, she would be the first one done during a test and get every thing right, long before any other student in her class. sad thing is, both kids are being teased and tormented about how smart they are in their classes by the other students, and the teachers feel they should be in higher grades . . . so, we'll see what happens.

Sun Aug 3, 2008

hmmm, ya, OUCH!!!!!!!!!!

Just a quick note to let every one know I am getting better. Sure was something. I first thought when the girls fed me fungus was bad, I was sick for a week. Cars running red lights to try to hit me or keep me from crossing in front of them was scary. Then comes the second floor woman, and she is a real hooker, and not a nice one either, who is constantly causing problems, and lastly, our next door neighbor on the mountain, who has four kids, each one from a different man, the last two men tend to show up from time to time to fight each other, get a peace and leave again, and she is constantly causing us problems as well. Just when I did not think things could get much worse . . . . A DOCTOR POISON'S ME . . . To make a long story short, I may go deeper later, The doctor gave me thirty pills and said to take as often as I needed for pain. Only one problem, these pills he gave me was not meant for men at all, and you only take one. It is enough to kill a fetus or push a fully grown baby out. I had four in four days, it almost did me in. I had blisters all over my body, inside and outside, in my ears, nose, just every where. Not funny, that doctor was fully intent on killing me, and guess what, there is nothing any one can do about it. Here in Peru, there is no law against killing a foreigner. Oh, well, I am still alive, not feeling very well, but, still alive :)

Tue Aug 5, 2008

Carola

Well, For the past week, or since last Wednesday or Thursday, not sure when, Carola has been on the Mountain. I am quiet sure she has been telling horror stories of how she is being treated. A couple days ago, Faby called the woman where Carola is staying, and she said, Carola ordered two quarters of chicken and ate all of them, when they went out to eat, but she was sick that night, ate too much. Sure, she just ate too much. I believe she also added lots of chilly and mustard, both of which make her stomach hurt. Faby and I both tell her not to eat very much if she has any at all. She probably also has been telling how we starve her to death, why she ordered two quarters of chicken. The orders come with a serving of fries and salad. Regular size dinner plates, full. When we go out to eat, Carola usually takes an hour to eat her one plate, and most of the time she don't finish, its hard for me to believe she finished two plates, but easy for me to believe she had a stomach ache afterwards, because I know what kind of sauces she likes, and most likely way over did it. Other then that, the woman says Carola is being very good, and is welcome to stay as long as needed. Faby offered for her to adopt Carola, and she was saying "where do I sign, I'll take her." Only if you knew the real Carola, you would not be saying that. OH, well, why spoil it for her, let them both enjoy each other. The woman is a grandma, taking care of her grandchildren, son drives a mototaxi and daughter in law . . . well, she is just having kids and running around letting grandma take care of them. Oh, ya, the Grandma owns the mototaxi that the son drives. Not sure what Grandpa does, reminds me of Jodie, just goes to work every day, comes home, and feeds every one in the house, why complain, who would listen. And so on and so on.

Tue Aug 5, 2008

Ouch

A couple weeks ago, I got another tooth pulled. That makes six pulled so far. Got a long way to go. But right after that, I had another appointment. Faby wanted something done for my back. It does hurt. Has ex-rays taken, and I have a couple disks in my lower back, next to my tail bone, that have no jelly between them. when they touch, my right leg tends to go to sleep, when they rub, my whole body tends to freeze up, or go down. Depending on how bad the touch or rub was, it can also put me to sleep. Ya, it hurts. The doctor gave me two sets of pills, thirty each. One a vitamin, and the other a pain pill. Said to take the vitamin once a day and the pain pill as often as needed for pain. I already put in the dates when it happened, I think. Any way, I just had my tooth pulled, mouth hurting, back hurting, ten pm, so, I took both pain and vitamin, and a ibuprofen pill, thinking, I will get a good nights sleep. I repeated that for the next three nights, I was weaving when walking, bumping in to the walls. Faby come in, I felt a burning on my chest and belly, I opened my shirt, and I was covered in blisters. Faby took me to the emergency room. I was in three different hospitals, and all of them accused Faby of being part of an escort service who drugged her "John" or "what ever you call it" and demanding to know what kind of drug she used. Even after she showed our I.D.'s some said, "you sure are fast in faking documents these days." Some were saying that I was cheating on Faby, and got drugged, and wanted to know who I was with. When Faby told them what drugs I was using, and that a doctor gave them to me, they all refused to believe it, saying, "no, this drug will not do that." Faby looked it up on line, and got it printed out and showed them, they still refused to believe. It was a drug used mainly for labor. To induce labor contractions, or if taken too soon, will kill the fetus, so, it is also meant for miss carriages or abortions, but you only need one pill, any more can be toxic or deadly. I took four in four days, it almost, and I mean almost did me in. Well, any way, I am much better now. Its 6am here, and I have an English class at 9am to 12 noon today, that is why I am up. I need to be there by 8:30am. I woke up at 4am to take a pill, the counter of the pills that doctor gave me.

Tue Aug 5, 2008

This just IN!!!

The land lord was yelling at Faby tonight . . . again . . . I am no longer allowed to snuggle, huggle, ruffle, and love on the second floor woman's clothes . . . urp . . . brb . . . Almost lost my liver . . . Ya, any way He said the second floor woman is complaining that we are playing with her clothes, and she is tired of us moving and playing with her clothes. Faby, told him off. Saying, we are not there all week long, most of the time, most of the week, and when we are, she comes in like she owns the place. One time she cut the water, during the day, while I, me, yes, me, was taking a shower, I came out complaining, Faby came out asking what happened, and she, that woman came running up screaming at the stranger to keep working, not to pay any attention to the "free loaders" they mean nothing. More times then we can count she as accused us of living her rent free. Faby also reminded him, that if we could leave, move, we would, right now, we are tired of being treated like dirt. We do pay rent, how would she get the idea that we don't? The land lord tried to calm Faby down, saying not to pay attention to that woman, that is just how she is, means nothing. Faby turned it around on him, saying "and you don't pay attention? accusing us of fondling her clothes?" any way, this just happened a little while ago, like an hour ago, its about 11:30 pm here now . . . if it ain't one thing, its several more . . . got to love Peru :)

Sat Aug 9, 2008

Carola

What a trip. Yesterday, last night, something like that, we went to the mountain. Much to Carola's surprise. No, she was not happy about us arriving. The woman's name is Homersinda, she says Carola is the sweetest little girl around, and is welcome to stay. She said that Natalia was not welcome to stay any longer then a short visit. Faby was talking about the weekends, and Homersinda said "One girl is enough, two will be too much." That hurt Natalia, so, I said that Natalia could still go to the Union Church with me. That did not help, Natalia just started balling. I really should not have said any thing at all. Right after we, all four of us left her house, I mean just as I was shutting the door, Carola looked back at me with the evil eye, and a very mean looking frowning grin, then shot out to Faby and started screaming and crying something. It was all in Spanish. In fact, Carola was gripping half the night. Today, up to noon, I mean Aug. 8Th, up to Noon, Carola was still fighting mad. Just putting on a show every where we went. Balling so good, she had streams of tears running down her face. Even when the store people were trying to help, Carola was still balling. After the show and Carola got what she wanted, Faby took her back to Homersinda. After that, Faby finally told me what was going on, or some of it. It had to do with a class project, Carola needed something from the store, and demanded that mama get it. I really did not understand fully, nor do I still understand, why when she is in the store, with the store people there showing her all they have, and Carola refusing to even look, balling and demanding that mama get what she needs. Some kind of paper, picture paper, almost like stickers, not sure what, but they went to several stores with that show until Carola finally picked out what she needed. Then at Homersinda's house, Homersinda said Carola was welcome to stay. Faby was concerned about how much she is going to need, and Homersinda just said if she needs any thing she will ask. She also said she might change Carola to a different school with Faby's permission. I think it is only a matter of time before Carola shows her true face to Homersinda. Right now she is doing her best to show how mistreated she is and how monstrous Faby and I are. What really gets me is this. Faby is saying this is all my fault for rejecting them. It wasn't me rejecting them, they rejected me. I was doing a lot for them, and they treat me like dirt. I cook for them and the refuse to eat. Then tell total strangers that I starve them. What am I suppose to do? While they are treating me like dirt, am I suppose to give them hugs, pats on the back, give them treats, and bite my tongue in the process? When the are good, I do give them treats, hugs, even play games. We do have a few. But, those times are not many, very few and far between. I sure wish this process was over. Seems like every thing I do and every thing I say is wrong, one way or another, its all wrong. I seem to me messing up more and more here lately, and I don't know which why to turn.

Sat Aug 16, 2008

Social Security

I am finding out just what Social Security means here. Simply means, you have a job that will deduct from you check what you owe to the hospital, clinic, or what ever doctor you may see. You don't get any discounts at all. I will explain it in dollars . . . each month you pay fifty dollars, that goes towards the bill you may get if you go to get a check up or if you need any emergency medical assistance. Say for instance, you pay fifty dollars a month for six months, then all of a sudden, you have to go to the doctor and it costs four hundred dollars. Well, you have already paid three hundred dollars in, so, you next paycheck will be deducted one hundred and fifty dollars, the one hundred you owe the hospital, and the usual fifty dollars a month. my three days in the emergency room, three different hospitals and ambulance ride, cost Faby four thousand soles, well over one thousand dollars . . . and she gets one party a week, very rarely gets more, sometimes she gets called to do more, but not often. this week she was suppose to do four parties, but one was canceled, the same day it was ordered, and no one told her it was canceled until she came to the store and the manager told her . . . that sore was about a three hour buss ride away . . .

Sat Aug 16, 2008

Faby

Yesterday, Faby had a Party, or was suppose to have a party. I thought she had every thing she needed . . . boy was I wrong. She left the Mountain, late, had to grab a cab, then found out, that she did not have the right uniform, I forgot to ask her if she had every thing she needed, I thought she did, she was almost at the store when she realized she was missing part of it, and had the cab driver take her to the apt. to get the other part, the apt. was closer, and after that, the cab driver made a three hour trip in thirty minutes, got her there on time. Faby told me the cab driver said that was not fair and felt very guilty in charging her so much, and just asked her to pay for the gas and a little bit more for a snack for him . . . forty soles.

Once there, she went in and told the manager she was here and the cab was out side waiting to get paid, she did not have enough money on her to pay the cab. The manager asked what she was doing there, there is no party today. She blue a fuse, at least the manager of that store was her friend and did loan her the money to pay the cab, she went out to the cab and told him there was no party and no one told her. He told her how sorry he was, and he felt bad about what she was going through, but he had to take the money for his time and gas. After a long talk with the manager, who was her friend, who gave her a couple of "champs" cards, she finds out, that the party was canceled the same day it was ordered. Right after it was ordered, and paid for, the manager sent an email telling Mitea about the party, a few hours later, the woman who paid for the party canceled it and got a refund and called Mitea and told her it was canceled, the same day it was ordered. What did Mitea do, send Faby three hours away on a wild goose chase. Faby was so scared of missing or being late she paid a cab forty soles to make thirty soles for a party. If she would have missed and it was a "go" she would have had to pay eighty soles in fines and quite possible be fired in the process. any way, that was not the first party that Mitea has sent Faby to that was canceled. There has been several that Faby has not gotten paid for, a few that she did get paid for, but if Mitea has her way, Faby will not get paid for the party because there was not a party. I know it don't make any sense, but that woman is doing her best to kill the whole party section of K.F.C. Mad Science, Show, and Paint Faces. Last night, Faby was telling me about it in tears, saying how she did not want to work for them any more, only do a couple parties just to keep the social security going, just in case of an emergency. I was checking my email while she was talking, and crocheting, she is making a blanket now. That is when I found out Papa was in the hospital. I told her about it. She cried her self to sleep. I could not sleep all night. this morning she told me that if there is a way, if any one could come up with a plane ticket, of if every one could pitch in for a ticket, that I should go as soon as I could. But I am afraid if I leave with out Faby, I may never see her again, not because she will leave me for another one, but because the girls may kill her. Not by a knife, but by the constant "B.S." they are pulling on her all the time. I really don't know what to do. I have such a head ache now, and Faby is gone all day, two parties, very far away, she left at 7:30 this morning to a party that starts at ten am, she will not be back till late tonight.

Sun Aug 17, 2008

Girls

Girls are something else . . . I always thought Carola was the main problem maker. Natalia has to put in her two cents worth, sometimes, even more then I really know of. Carola has basically rejected all of us. She believes she has a family on the hill, and its totally for free, nope, we have to pay that family twenty soles each weekend, but at least, its less stress on Faby, so, its really worth it. A last week, well, a three weeks ago the girls were on a two week vacation, last week, just before school started again, the weekend, we were there, and both girls started in on Faby, all in Spanish. Well, one week prior, was a big problem, with Carola, She had spend one week with Homersinda already, and we came back for a meeting on the mountain, that was a big mistake, taking Carola from her new family too soon. She started in right away, making problems, all in Spanish, I had no right what so ever to interfere. I no more then open my mouth and Faby was quick to tell me I would only make it worse. We all went to the little town at the bottom of the mountain, only for Carola to put on the biggest show ever there. I mean balling so good, she had streams of tears rolling down her face, and crying and screaming in Spanish all about how "mama never gets her any thing" even though we were there, and the store people were there trying to figure out what she wanted . . . I had to walk around the corner. Finally they got her what she needed. Boy oh boy, did she ever have every ones attention, doing her best to make Faby and Me look like the worst monsters ever. Last week, just before School started, Natalia took her turn. Along with Carola again, I had to leave the house while they balled up a storm. Finally, after some time, Faby gave me twenty soles to take the girls down the mountain, telling me both need some more school items and Natalia needs new shoes . . . again . . . she loves to destroy her shoes and demand new ones. She had a pair she got from her grandfather in the U.S., Faby's father, that cost some where between one hundred and one hundred and fifty dollars. Both girls have clothes from the U.S. and not from cheep places, the cheapest item they get would cost at lest fifty dollars. Of course, they never get every thing grandpa sends them, but what they do get is not cheep, and what do they do . . . destroy . . . destroy . . . destroy and demand new items. Well, Natalia wanted nine soles shoes, you know, three dollar shoes, after she destroyed her U.S. shoes, I tried to fix them and she threw them away. well, after a coupe months, she got another pair, the first ones were black, then she got red ones, from Faby's police uncle. Both pairs are summer shoes, full of holes, made that way, she has no others. Once she got the red ones, she started grinding her black ones in the dirt and demanding new shoes. Well, her new excuse was the fact that with the weather change and environment, more wet, it is hurting her feet. Demanding and demanding, along with Carola demanding more school supplies. OK, we go, just before we left, I told Faby if I see one tear, or hear one growl, I will run, I said it loud enough for both girls to hear, and yes, I have ran before when they started in, in fact, I have ran several times. This time, I added saying, "I don't care where we are, I will leave them all alone in the middle of no where. If they try to make me look bad, I will run like mad!" First item on the list, new shoes for Natalia, guess what, this time she got 11 soles shoes, with the exchange rate, almost four dollar shoes, yes, very cheep. But she would much rather have cheep Peruvian throw a ways, then to have very nice and tough U.S. items. then it was a mad dash to find all the items they need for school. That ain't funny. They could draw pictures and write what they need on them, but instead, they want to buy already printed pictures and writings, cut and glue in their copy books. Two days later, during school, they are at it again, it ain't funny either, making problems more then ever on the hill, loud enough for others to hear, once again, Faby gives me money to take them down the mountain to get what they need, just to shut them up.

Both times, all the supplies they needed, cost ten soles, total cost last week, twenty soles. To top it off, they were demanding three soles for Peruvian kids day, and Peruvian food day, total cost, twelve soles, that goes to the teacher. what more, Faby blew a fuse, confronted the teachers, finding out of twenty students, in one class only eight were able to pay, and out of another class, only six were able to pay, but both girls were demanding that mama pay for them promising the teachers that we would pay, and so on and so on, like we are million airs and of course, me being a foreigner, a U.S. foreigner, the teachers are believing I am a million air and are demanding money for all these holidays . . . it ain't easy, but at least they are not believing we are starving the girls to death, or beating them to death, no, there are real life horror stories there, and most of the people don't believe them, well, mostly Carola and her stories, she does her best to get Natalia to go along with her, and sometimes she does. All of this is hurting Faby real bad, its not good on her heart. Then I checked my email and found out Papa was in the hospital. Faby just cried her self to sleep that night.

Its been a very hard week on Faby, very hard. Well, we told Natalia about Papa, well, I did, she gave me the wide eyed "did you say something? I don't have any idea what you are saying." look, then Faby told her, no emotion. We are not about to tell Carola any thing. One thing, Faby keeps telling me, if there is any way for me to get a ticket, that I should go. On that note, we did get the new forms printed out, and will be mailing them out on Monday, you would not believe the price that cost to get them printed out, like twenty dollars, well more like eighteen dollars, still its a good chunk out of a twenty. We are heading up to the mountain tonight, so, no family chat for me again, sorry, wish I could be there.

Mon Aug 18, 2008

Peru Time

Peruvian time is something else. You tell a Peruvian one time, and they show up an hour and an half later, which means if you want one to show up on time, you tell them an hour and a half earlier. I am constantly telling Faby and the girls what time it is for one reason or another. Trying to get them to where ever on time. This morning was different. It started last night, when Carola came up with Faby. She started early, back talking her mother, started screaming, all in Spanish, I finally said to speak English, because Faby was speaking English and she was answering in Spanish. Carola started crying. I said OK, I will give her a reason to cry, this was around 8:30 or 9:00pm, not sure. Any way, Faby stopped me telling me how I can not do any thing, so I left the house. I stayed outside until 10:30. The girls finally went to sleep. Come morning, Carola stared again, at 7am. School starts at 8am. The school has been threatening to lock the doors for all late comers and not allow them in. Guess what? I was outside, moving dirt. One of these days, I will take pictures of what dirt I am moving, and I was listing to Carola yell and cry about I don't know what, just Faby was talking in English saying to eat her breakfast, and for almost an hour, Carola was fighting. Me, not screaming about the time. Come five minutes to eight, they are ready to go to school. We show up at 8:02am. The gate is locked and they are going through the morning ceremony. I call Faby to let her know we were late and the gate was locked. She told me to wait until it is finished and they will let all the late comers in. Nope, they did not. All the kids inside went to their classes along with the teachers. One guy outside wanted in. After the whole yard was cleared, the gate guard came over to let him in, and one little girl tried to get in and the gate guard would not let her in. The gate guard was telling me in Spanish no entry. Well, that is what I caught, then Natalia told me that she said, they are not letting in any one who comes late any more, you are on time or you don't go to school. That did not set too good with Carola. On the way back, she was walking very slow, I told her to hurry up, she stopped. I waived my arm in a circle, saying to move. There were other People in the street watching, stirring around, doing stuff to watch the show that Carola put on. She brought her arms in in a defensive position and screamed while backing up. I ran. Faby was outside and seen me almost falling down going up the hill, going as fast as I could, which was not very fast at that time. I was out of breath and my legs were trying to collapse. When I caught my breath, I told her what happened. Then I went to moving dirt. The girls showed up, and Carola was mad as ever at me, so, what can I do? Move dirt . . . The whole day was messed up, and I am not very happy, but I am keeping a record of what is going on.

Tue Aug 19, 2008

Rubix Cube

We got Natalia one for her birthday. Last week, Philly jumped on the counter in the house, and knocked our wooden spoon on the ground, dirt floor. I was not happy, trying to get him to understand not to jump on the table or the counter. I picked up the spoon and swung it at him, he ran, I chased him, swinging it. I did not realize how hard I was swinging it until I hit Natalia's bag, with her cube inside. I shattered it. OOOPPPSS!!! Well, it took me a few days, but I found a better one and replaced it. I did tell Natalia what happened when she got home from school. One thing I remember, from a while back, was that Carola would take Natalia's cube apart. I guess she tried today and broke her cube. Natalia was not happy. Faby keeps telling Natalia not to give her toys to Carola, because she will brake them, only to hurt her. This time, she told Natalia, she would replace the cube only if she promises not to let Carola play with it. Of course, Carola was not happy with that. But, Mama said, "Carola, you have your own toys, you don't need to destroy your sisters." even though that did not help, it made me smile. She said it in English :)

Tue Aug 19, 2008

Fun

Several months ago, more like six months ago, I think, Faby got some purple hair color dye. They had the two for one special. One of her bosses told her don't do that again, and to dye her hair black. Ya, OK. Today, or rather last night, Monday night, with all the stress and stuff, I told Faby she should go to the hair dresser and have her hair dyed, trimmed and brushed. The cost was only twenty soles, we had the dye, normal cost is at least fifty soles, and with all I named above, would cost about eighty soles. Good thing Faby is good with words and makes friends fast, also good thing she had the dye in hand, that is the most expensive part. Even though I still don't feel a hundred percent, and no, I don't, still feel queasy and still full of dots. Faby is so stressed out, she is not liking the idea of taking the girls to town or to school any more, she keeps sending me, Carola is really doing a number on her. Well, after the hair dresser, we went for a little walk, and decided to go to the local mall, they call it a Plaza here. Found a pair of purple grape ear rings to go with her new hair due. Then to a new restaurant that just opened up not too long ago. We ordered the cheep chicken dinner, just the chicken and fries. You know, to relax, have a little fun, and try to let some of the stress go away. It was a very nice place, we agreed it comes in third of the Best four in town. Not including the fast food places, like Micky D's and Bimbo's, which we have not gone to in a long time, just too expensive right now. Any how, just to let you all know, Faby and I do try to sneak in a little fun for us once in a while, and try new places.

Tue Aug 19, 2008

Late Night

Its one thirty now in the morning, Tuesday morning. I just can not sleep. Have not slept well since I found out Papa was in the hospital. Been so worried about him and mama, its been driving me nuts. And of course, Carola is not helping matters much. Any way. I got the pictures from my student, got them in the email. But for some reason, I can not seem to down load them, can not open them up. I get the foot note picture, the little pic, but I can not seem to get them full size, every time I try to open them up, I get a blank page or I get a message that says some thing like this program did an illegal function and is closing out. Well its all in Spanish, and when I click the buttons saying OK or continue or close, every thing closes. I have to log back on. I mean I get kicked off the Internet. Not sure how I am going to share these pictures, but I am sure I will figure it out one way or another. Just letting you know, what is going on. I got them, but I can not get to them . . . Yet . . .

Tue Aug 19, 2008

Fourth of July

Ronnie is my English student, I invited him so he could get a little of North American culture, both the U.S. and Canada. He said he really enjoyed it. To me it was a disappointment. Three years ago, When I first got here, was the best I seen, and I was told then, it got bad. Its been going down hill ever since, less shows and less people showing up, its becoming more and more like a "Peruvian advertisement" show case then a celebration party for North American People, but still, I had fun. Faby did not show up this time, she had to work, and the girls went with her, she was afraid the girls would make problems for me. This party was at a kids petting zoo, was suppose to be mainly for kids to have fun while the adults relax. So much for a fun family outing . . .

Tue Aug 19, 2008

a little Funny

This just in :) Uncle Roberto came over this morning, he just left and Faby told me what happened . . . I had to hug Philly. I am guessing Faby's father is forcing his brother to come over, he did give Faby some money, four hundred soles this time, but also made Faby sign a paper saying she received the money. During this conversation, Philly jumped on to Uncle Roberto's lap and farted. His farts can be really ripe, and it made him squirm, complaining how our cat stinks. Faby told him, the cat lives here and can do what he wants. Looks like we are not going hungry this month after all, thank you Lord :)

Fri Aug 22, 2008

Parties

Last week, I think I mentioned about Faby going to a party that was canceled. That is not all that happened last week. Three parties that was suppose to have Mad Science shows, was messed up, no Mad Science. Problem was, they were suppose to be big shows, one major show. That one was just before one of Faby's parties. Faby showed up early, only to find out that the parents of the birthday kid was very upset and screaming at the management. They paid seven thousand soles for the major Mad Science show and a Cotton Candy show . . . not just cotton candy on a stick, its where the machine is brought in and a show is put on while the cotton candy is being made. They also bought two very big and expensive cakes, one thousand soles each. What did Mitea do? She came in shortly after Faby arrived for her party with ten cotton candies on a stick, for twenty kids. I am sure every one knows how that went :) Next was Faby's party, she was suppose to have a fifteen minute show, because Mad Science was suppose to be there, a big show. It never happened, and Faby was being yelled at, not her fault, she is a Party Show Girl, not Mad Science. It was Mitea again. After the party was over, the Mad Science guy showed up. He told Faby he was there at that store, in the cab when Mitea called him saying to go to another store, all the way across town, to find out, no party, then she said to go to another store in some other direction. After being sent to two other places, where there was no parties, she tells him to return to the first store, only to show up after the party is over. Faby told him about the first party, it was suppose to have a Cotton Candy show as well, and her party was suppose to be with him. The Store management was furious, screaming, "when will they get rid of that '"#$%&/·"'" any way. He told Faby about another party he was suppose to do, only to be redirected several times, and missed it. He only gets forty soles per party, and he wound up spending around a hundred soles in taxi rides, just to miss parties, he is seriously thinking of quitting, along with half the rest of the party people. They all believe the company is going to bankrupted if they don't get rid of Mitea. On another note, Faby, along with a few others in the company, have been offered a promotion. They all have to send in their resumes and go in for interviews. The position is a management position, and its has to do with creativity. Faby has done lots to improve the Paint Faces, lots of inventions, the main one was her apron. She does not know if she will apply, having to deal with Mitea up front like that, does not set too well with her. But she likes the idea of getting the position.

Fri Aug 22, 2008

Home front

Carola is with us this weekend. Faby said she believes Carola needs to go to Church. I had a dream last night, a strange one. I could not hardly get to sleep, finally went to sleep around ten or ten thirty, but woke up about two thirty in the morning. When I finally looked at my watch, it said three am. I dreamed I was talking with the pastor of the Flamingo church. I told Faby about it, she said we need to go there this Sunday. Not sure what it meant. Well, I could not get back to sleep, so I carried five buckets of water up the hill . . . boy that was tiring. Carola was being good the rest of the week. No problems at all . . . surprising. I only mentioned, if there is any problems with breakfast, no school. Both girls don't like not going to school. The only problem we had was with our next door neighbor. She is accusing us of steeling her shovel. Well, I have a problem with receipts. We may have it, we may not, and she may throw up such a big stink, that we may have to give her our shovel and get another one. I am not happy about that. We just found a wheel barrel, and three people were saying they want it, and they will steel it if we turn our backs too long, our next door neighbor was one of the three, the fat guy helping us on our land was one, not sure who the other one was, he passed us in the street saying he was going to take it, I just sat on it and looked at him, with a frown, he laughed and kept on walking. Sorry, I forgot my little camera. I will try to remember it next time we go up to take pictures of what dirt I was moving and how, with my little garden shovel and little bucket . . . that sure was a chore, now with the wheel barrel, it should be a little easier :)

Sat Aug 23, 2008

Parrot three days ago, we got a Parrot. Its a baby, just weaned. Well, its after midnight, more like four days ago. We were told its a male. We were also told to feed it one type of seed, which it will not eat, just throws out of the cage, then stares at us. We got him a corn on the cob, not real sure if he is eating on it, I pulled some of the corn off and put it in his seed cup, he threw it out. Day number two, in the morning, I seen some black bananas, nothing wrong with the inside, just a little dark on the outside. Got a bundle real cheep fifty cents for six of them, normal price is seven for one sole, not bad. He really went for the banana. Not sure what to name him, don't even have a picture of him yet. Hopefully he is still there when we get back, we left him up on the mountain, with lots to eat and drink. Only problem is, there is a couple of people who go in to our place when ever they want to. The fat guy and the next door neighbor. Faby told me one of the kids in the area told her. I did notice some of our things moved around. They keep insisting that we are million airs and we are not suppose to be there, well, the woman next door, and she is doing her best to convince every one on the mountain. The fat guy, I am guessing is believing her. He used our tools, shovel, pick, hammer and nails, and probably some of our wood to build her a restroom. We don't have one yet, just a shallow hole that I use, Faby and the girls use a bucket inside, that I get to dump out. Any way, hopefully our parrot and wheel barrel is still there when we go back, they are not expecting us until Sunday night, but we are returning Saturday night to do the fiana Sunday morning. Then a mad dash to the bus to go back to town to go to Church . . . that aught to be interesting.

Mon Sep 1, 2008

Carola

Some times I just don't know what to think. Last night, when Faby and the girls left, of course, I got a hug and a kiss from Faby, and a hug from Natalia, but what surprised me, was with out Faby saying any thing, Carola hugged me. One day last week, I went to get the girls from school, Faby was waiting at the house. I told the girls we need to hurry, they walked slow. I told them that mama was waiting, and we are in a hurry. Natalia started moving faster, and Carola stopped and just looked at me. I moved my armed in a circle, saying to hurry up, she dropped her backpack and put her arms up in a defensive cross over her head and let out a small scream, like I was about to beat her. There was people out doing things, and probably watching. I ran. It takes three to five minutes to walk to the school, down hill, about eight to ten minutes to walk up the hill, its that steep, I ran up in in about two minutes. It took me a while to catch my breath, Faby was asking me what happened. When I was able to talk, I told her what happened, by then, both girls were there, and Carola just gave me a dirty look, I left to go move dirt. Later, Faby told me that Carola said she never did that and don't know why I ran, and that Natalia never seen or heard any thing. Well, Natalia was in front and moving. The only thing I can think of, is She is just doing her best to make us look like monsters. As I said, Last Night, surprised me.

Fri Sep 5, 2008

Blood

If there are Vampires, Dracula's, or any other blood sucking human looking creature in the world, they must love it here blood is everywhere. As I have said before, the blood from the chicken is usually sold before the chicken is killed! It is in high demand! It don't last long in the stores. Last week, when Faby and the girls left. Faby told me, "I cooked up some bloody, if you are hungry." Well, I was on Family chat, and yes I was hungry, and all I had was some bread. What else was I going to do? I had some ketchup . . . had. It was not too bad, lots of ketchup, and it was pretty good. Filling too. I guess there is a first time for every thing . . . I am ready to leave, before I go nutz.

Fri Sep 5, 2008

Carola

Yes, Carola again . . . Today was too much. She put on her show in front of her teacher and her teacher yelled at me. I am not going to take her to school any more. Well, unless she gets a very short hair cut, I mean no more then an inch all around her head, and her teacher apologizes to me. I have no idea what Carola said to her teacher. I told her teacher that we have to go. Of course she don't speak any English, but, Faby had already told both Carola's and Natalia's teachers that the girls will have to leave early, because Faby has to go to work and we are coming here, for me to do laundry and we have many other things to do. Both teachers were informed. Faby told me to go and pick up the girls. I told Faby that she should go, but she was busy and told me to just and get them, there was no problem, they know the girls have to leave. Carola had other plans. She came out, her teacher was looking at me, she stood with a stony stare and fists down by her sides and said, "I have classes, I won't leave till 1." With a little "humph" at the end. I said, "I don't care for your attitude, we have to leave." She started crying, tears swelling up, her teacher turned to her and she started rattling off. I really can not take these shows any more in public. She had her teacher yelling at me. That is why, I am not going to take her to school any more. Not unless she gets a hair cut and her teacher says she is sorry for yelling at me. One more thing, To me, it seams that the schools are only teaching the kids here in Peru how to demand money from their parents and total disrespect towards their parents. Look at Uncle Roberto, he has five kids, the youngest one is over twenty years old. All of them still live at home, demanding he provide for them. If that is all the school is teaching these girls, then they don't need to go to school any more!!! Not only that, but one more reason for Carola to get a hair cut. Lice. I said the next time she gets any bugs in her head she would get it shaved. I know Faby will not allow that, but, a very short hair cut is in order. Carola will not listen, Faby and I both tell her not to be too close to others, sharing combs or brushes, as well as hugging others. She is doing something, she was full of bugs again. This time Homersinda found them and gave Faby the "you don't take care of your daughter" look. Not sure what she said to Faby, if any thing, Faby did not tell me if she did. Carola is getting a hair cut, that is final!!!

Fri Sep 5, 2008

Faby

Well, Faby's contract ended the thirty first of August. But she is still making parties. She has not signed any new contract. From what she knows and what she has told me, it is a six month contract at a time. Every one gets six month contracts, unless you are in management. In fact, she has eight or nine parties this month already, more then she usually gets in two months, and she is not real sure if she is going to get paid for them. She is working on "faith" that she will get paid, and hoping and praying that she does not loose her job. This month she is also the Main teacher for the Children's Church, guess who is her helper . . . yep, me. I hope I don't mess things up for her, more then that, I hope Carola don't mess it up for her as well. I am sorry, I am trying to write, and Carola has me so upset, I just can't think strait. Maybe later, right now, I am doing laundry and watching wrestling on line, trying to calm down and relax.

Mon Sep 8, 2008

ticket

This came as a surprise. Well, not much of one, but, I did not expect it this fast. I will be leaving Friday after noon. About 2:30pm, if it leaves on time and I am not held up at the air port. If all goes well. If any one is wondering, Yes, I am really thinking of a "book" "My Life in Peru" And I did not write about half of what I have seen here, it is really unbelievable of what really happens here. Some of what I write about is hard to believe. And Friday, I am on a plane. Tonight, Faby and I went to get her a straw basket, to carry her project she has to the church meeting. The women's group in the Union Church. Along the way, we stoped off at a little bakery, the only one Faby found that makes bread with chocolate chips in it, just like chocolate bread, really good. They had lasagna.

Tue Sep 9, 2008

Carola

Carola may get to go with me. Let us all pray that Faby can get the paper work done in time. This paper work usually takes up to two weeks to do. It can be done in a few days, but that is at a cost, much bigger cost. Faby says at least one hundred dollars. Connie said she will send, it, but who knows if that is all it will cost. What is in the process is, she has to write a document saying she is giving permission for Carola to leave. Then it has to be notarized, that is one hundred soles, just to notarize. She also has to make me a legal guardian, that too is about one hundred soles. Then she has to have it legalized in the foreign external relations. That can cost up to two hundred soles. Right now the dollar is at 2.90 soles to the 1.00 dollar. That means its over one hundred dollars already. She has to have it translated. That can cost about one hundred soles as well. With the money we have right now, we are short, about one hundred dollars, may be more, not real sure. That is to get it done in a few days. To be ready for Friday. This is just a bit fast, Faby is really worried. Its not often I beg, but now, I am begging. Once I get up there, I will do my best to do every thing I can to repay, or help out where ever I can. We need Prayers, because the

Peruvian airport people are so mean, there are people who traffic kids and are caught, they may think I am trafficking Carola and make us miss the plane, also, we need some money for this little bit of the process. I hope I am not talking this to death, its after midnight here, and I just got the news of this last bit. We have a long day tomorrow, or rather in the morning.

Tue Sep 9, 2008

Visa

Faby just seen something on the news. Then she told me, Carola needs a visa. With out one, Carola can not go. Meaning, we would need more time to get her a visa. We are not sure if she will pass through the immigration station in the U.S. Carola is Peruvian. Faby is scared, she will be denied at the first stop. Sure she may leave Peru OK, but after words, with out the visa, is me being her legal guardian enough? Could there be any way to post pone the date at least one more week to make sure we get all the paper work done correctly and Faby get all the information she needs so she can be calm about the whole situation? Faby loves all the information she possible can get, and with only three days, Faby is scared she will miss something. Just a question, is it possible to post pone the flight for only one week?

Tue Sep 9, 2008

carola

RE: carola No idea how Carola will act from one minute to the next. Usually she is OK with me when its just the two of us. Very seldom does she put on a show. I will be going with a lot of documents stating that Faby and I are married, and I have legal guardianship of Carola, along with birth certificates. What we are worried about is the Visa, will Carola be denied at the immigration counter in the U.S. or not? Faby would like to make sure its possible first, and is constantly asking me how its possible for Carola to come to the U.S. with out a Visa. I have no answer for her right now. Faby is a walking dictionary, encyclopedia, a book full of information. If she can not get the information she needs, she may not move until she gets it, and its made clear. She is not real sure she can get me out of the country in such short notice. With all the papers she needs to fill out to "warranty fy" me saying I don't owe any one here and she will stand good for me, yes its lots of legal papers for me to leave as well, she is worrying her self sick now because of such short notice . . . is there any way to post pone the departure date for at least one week?

Tue Sep 9, 2008

Re: Carola before Carola can leave, Faby has to write a document, a letter of permission to let Carola leave the country. to go to Chilly, it was forty soles, for both girls, that cost us eight soles. the further away from Peru you go, the higher the cost is. For example, Spain, costs twelve hundred soles, and England costs fourteen hundred soles. Not quite that much to go to the U.S. because the U.S. is on this side of the planet, it will cost only six hundred soles to get the permission slip wrote out. Now for the other bit, legal guardian ship, that cost one hundred soles. legalization fees is one hundred soles, then to translate, any where from fifty to one hundred soles each, then the translation has to be legalized, another one hundred soles each. we are up to about twelve hundred soles right now total price. Not sure if it is even possible, but we are trying. we need prayers and we need money, we are trying every thing we can.

Tue Sep 9, 2008

mistake

I think I made a mistake, in saying one thousand dollars, it was more like four hundred dollars, still, that is the over one thousand soles. I was adding and not typing correctly. Not sure if we can get it all done, but we are trying. I can not believe all the legalization that has to be done. its as if the Peruvian government says, "oh, you think you are going some where, lets see how far you go after all this paper work is done" and it ain't cheep, does any one have any way of contacting the "dream center" or the "make a wish" foundation. or is it only for "show and tell" but for any real emergency . . . "your all out of luck :)" with a grin of course. sorry for the sarcasm. every time Faby looks up some thing, she is chanting, "she needs a visa, she needs a visa" with all my luck, I will miss the plane any way, the last time I took a flight from Peru, they said to come two hours early, I came two and a half hours, it took me two and a half hours to get through customs, I was second from missing my flight. I was running down the hall, in to the waiting area only to come to closing doors. I was screaming, "my flight, my flight!" showing my tickets, and ran down that tube thingy, only to run in to the closing door of the plane, that was how close I came to missing my flight out. it ain't funny . . . and I can see it happening again, only faster on their part this time. so, with four hundred dollars, we should be able to get all this stuff done, only one problem, I have not been able to reach any one today . . . maybe tomorrow will be better.

Wed Sep 10, 2008

Sad News

Just found out. Carola can not come with me. Sure, Faby can sign over her parental rights to me, with the authorization to leave the country, and we can leave Peru. How ever, because I owe child support, the first stop we make, in Mexico, at the immigration counter, they will bring up my history, and see I have not been paying child support and owe back support. Then they will take Carola from me and put her in an orphanage. They will do one of two different things, one, they will leave her there until she is 18 and kick her out in the street, or, put her on the first available flight back to Peru where she will be placed in an orphanage here, and at 18, be kicked out in the street. Faby will not be able to do any thing, because of signing away her parental rights. That child support is really something. I can not even go to the Embassy, she was told if I go, they may take my passport and cancel my citizenship, they almost did it the last time, remember? If I go this time, they most likely will. I strongly feel the child support people are the most dirtiest players around, worse then the IRS. So, don't buy a ticket for Carola, it will be lost money. The money mama and Connie sent will be used for Faby to get a Visa appointment at the Embassy, yes, Faby can go and explain the situation her self with out me, and a very strong possibility of getting a temporary Visa to the U.S. for all three of them. Faby is really good at getting information, and this is what she was told. Once I am there, I have to get a job and start paying child support, then I can fill out papers to try to sponsor along with others, being joint sponsors, and that too will help. I am really trying not to blow a fuse. I will be on the plane, I will leave my Peruvian I.D. card with Faby. So, the only valid I.D. I will have is my Passport. If they take that, the only thing I will have left will be my finger prints :)

Mon Sep 15, 2008

Shouldn't of Done It

Ya, I should not have done it. Faby told me to wonder around Metro, Plaza Vea, or Wong. I and the girls could walk around the area, but, nope, I decided to do another thing, I took the girls to the beach, and I should not have done it. OK, Today, we went to church, stayed a while to chat with some of the other members, saying "bye" to them and asking, well, more like trying to make sure that Faby was still welcome there. One woman, who has been there for I don't know how many years, like twenty plus years, is the head of the church board, one of the lead singers, and is very active in the American, Canadian Association of Peru, one of the many who have shunned Faby for years—Faby has been going to the Union Church for over four years now—has started talking with Faby. In fact, started talking with her two weeks ago a little bit. Last week a little more, and today, she told me that Faby was one of them, after I told her, Faby was really scared that after I leave, that every one in the church would just turn their backs on her, because of so many Peruvians that go only to beg for hand outs. That woman, who's name is Cynthia Alvarez. Not sure of the spelling, any way, her words were, "we all know who those Peruvians are, Faby is not one of them, Faby is one of us. She is very welcome to continue coming to our Wednesday meetings, as well as her to church every Sunday. Afterwards, Faby had two parties, four to six, and seven to nine pm. Faby told me to walk around the area, lots of stores to wonder through. But, nope, I had to go else where. To the beach :) To start with, we walked down where the surfers were, just looking around, seen a restaurant on the water and decided to go and take a look. Lots of little shops with some of the neatest stuff inside. on one side of the dock were seagulls, and on the other side, on the rocks were the crabs. Seagulls were preening, and the crabs were sunning. Faby is always refusing to go there, for one reason or another, we just never have any time. Next was the, not sure what its called, but almost like a sand bar, but lots of rock tossed out in to the ocean like a peer, I mean it goes way out there. The girls really wanted to go all the way out. Well, so did it, but about half way out, I gave up, too rocky for me, they kept going. After a while, they came back, Natalia was coming back fast. When she got to me, she said something, not sure what it was, so I just simply asked "what did you say" and she gives me a funny look and then there was a water fall, going down both her pant legs. She could have told me she had to go pee, I would have covered her, there was a big rock with a hole almost completely under it, she could have gone there, but no, she just gives me that funny, dumb look and there it runs. I get so tired of that dumb look, one time she gave me that look when she was crossing a street, and a car was coming, I was telling her to look out, a car is coming, and she just gave me that wide eyed, mouth open dumb look and the car stopped about an inch from hitting her while she was crossing the street. That's not all, We went for a walk down town, looking for a big store, one with a restroom that we did not have to pay for, so she could use the dryer to dry her paints. After her paints were dry, we walked through several other stores. I believe I was the only one of use three that was getting the "freebies" samples. Carola is too good for those samples, and she makes Natalia feel bad about getting any. We went to a few book stores to waste time, then to McDonald's. They have some cheep burgers, and a play area. So, the girls went to play while I ate. I had a belly ache, so, when they were done playing, I went to the bathroom. Took me a while, but it all finally came out in the end. I came out of the bathroom thinking I would get a couple cheep drinks at one of the other stores around, only to find Natalia balling. There are only two cheep burgers, beef and cheese and chicken and cheese. Finally after Natalia stopped crying, she told me she did not want any cheese. OK, so I go to the counter and tell her to get her burger, you see, Carola ordered for all of us, so, Natalia was blaming Carola for the cheese. She ordered her burger, and the cashier was telling me quatro cenquinta . . . 4.50 . . . I yelled, "no! only two fifty, that's dose cenquinta, no more." of course, I don't speak much Spanish, but she did not know any English, and the argument was going on, Natalia wanted the big burger, and I was not going to get it, I told her the cheep one this is just a snack, we will eat our meals when we get home. She was not happy, but she got it any way. So, off we went to find some cheep drinks, I for got we were in Miraflores. No such thing, luckily . . . Faby finally got off works shortly after. Natalia was carrying her burger, refusing to eat, until mama told her to eat. I was carrying the first one that she refused to eat. Mama told Carola to eat it, with a little resistance, Carola ate it, took her a while, but she did. Well, we finally got home around ten, or ten thirty. Philly was being loud. Chester did not want to be bothered, he found his spot on a hanger that's on a nail in the wall by the curtain, he is very happy there, and now its almost one am Monday morning.

Mon Sep 15, 2008

Faby

Uncle Robert, and his wife got their money today. I have mentioned how much money he gets each month. Its a lot. His brother, Faby's father's retirement check is 1,500 soles. He keeps telling his brother, each month, that it's only 800 soles, and from the pain on his heart, he gives Faby half of it, 400 soles. Not true, he told dear sweet aunt next door that he is not going to give Faby any thing, he is in more need than she is, after all, she is married to a million air, and he has five kids to take care of. Youngest one is 24 years old, oldest one is around 30 years old, and all live at home demanding that mama and papa provide for them. That is what the schools teach the kids here in Peru. Faby called him today, he informed her she is not to call her father, and that he is in more need of the money than she is. If he has any to spare, he might come by this Friday, but she better be there, if not, he will call his brother and tell him he tried to give her the money, and she was not there, and how could she force him to come all the way over there for nothing, he is so busy, and do on and so on. it gets better Faby got an email today from her job, saying they will not renew her contract. The end of this month its over. No wonder she was getting so many parties, they were trying to give her a "good bye" present . . . nice size check this month. Nice people. Hope that lawyer is good and fast. Cost of living is going up and there is just no jobs any where. Faby has talent, and seems like no one cares. Well, I am through crying, Philly is on the roof, for the second time, I got him down once, he went right back up. Then Faby seen on the news, that some cats are carrying a disease in their eyes that can spread to human eyes. Faby says we may have to get rid of Philly now. I said not to worry, he may find another place on his own, he is a male cat, and its in their nature to move. That didn't help. Faby is asleep, the girls are in here. I had an accident, forgot I was running water in the washer, and I did not put the hose in the shower, water ran in to the girls room. Last time that happened, Carola cried half the night, until I went in to the kitchen. I woke up bloody, I slept with the cat, and he bit and scratched me from head to toe. Faby told me to go to bed, and I can't sleep. I am scared if I lay down, Carola will start crying, yes, she is able too, she is that mean. I was talking about Faby, Faby says she is ready to leave, and as soon as she gets the visa's and tickets.

Thu Sep 18, 2008

Bite the Hand

Carola is real good at it. I just don't get it. Its Peruvian idea, to bite the hand that feeds you. Yesterday, Faby and I decided to get our hair trimmed and combed to get one last set of photos taken of us. Just the two of us. Faby's other hairdresser, on Bolivar, is a real nice woman. There are around ten or twelve other hairdresser shops around the area. Any way, she would feed the rob people and drug dealers, when they looked hungry, she would have them wash her customers cars as well as have them keep her area clean, and she would pay them for it. She was never forced to do any of this, she did it in hopes they would not mess with her, she even paid the security guard too boot. She has been doing this for years. About four or five days ago, she got robbed. Late at night. The day before, the night security guard told her he needed some time off, he was just too tired. Of course, no one seen any thing, and her store was the only one hit. Every thing big and with some value, was taken, even the kids high chair, that looked like a race car was taken, her TV and DVD player, her electric hair cutters, I mean she was cleaned out. She was not happy. When she asked the security guard if he knew or heard of any thing, and he would not talk or even look at her. Not even the rob or drug guys will even look at her or talk to her now. She was helping them and this is how they thank her, but its "Peruvian idea" "Bite the Hand that Feeds You" and "Bite it Hard!"

Thu Sep 18, 2008

Faby

Last night, Faby went to her weekly meeting, only to get yelled at. Mitea told Faby she has a party and has not business being at the meeting. Much to Faby's surprise of course. Faby tried to tell her, in front of the new marketing Manager, that she was not programmed for a party at that time. No Parties on Wednesday. Mitea asked if she had her program paper with her, of course she did not. The new marketing manager was not impressed at first, with that little argument. The party was suppose to be a princess party, but got changed to a pirate party in mid swing, no Faby did not go, they would not give her a dress or music or any thing, just wanted to yell at her. Any way, The Marketing Manager, with out knowing Faby's name, started talking with Faby, about the different things in the company. Faby taking advantage of the opportunity, started talking about the different things she invented or her idea's of improvement, saying, "this is my idea, this is my invention, and so on and so forth." The Marketing Manager with wide eyes, said, "you must be Faby" Faby just smiled, and she continued saying, "you have to give me about three weeks, then we will talk, I need to know more about you and your idea's. I am sorry about the company, you are out, because of one of the other managers, Paolloo, and along with Mitea, there is nothing I can do for you about your job, how ever, as a consultant, who knows, just give me a little time, and we will have a coffee together." OK, as you all know, Mitea don't like Faby at all, in fact, she is doing her best to kill the company. What is wrong with Paollo? She is afraid that Faby is going to take her job, she is on the shaky edge of loosing her job as it is, and if Faby is out, Faby has no chance of getting it. Not sure what her actual title is, just some one in charge of something. Today, Faby went to the main office to fight. She showed her program papers to several managers there, including Mitea. Mitea simply said, "sorry, the store called it in too late and I forgot to tell you that I programmed you for the party." She had already called the store telling the store that it was Faby's party just to make Faby look bad, probably trying to get a good excuse for not renewing Faby's contract, you know, not showing up for work when you are suppose to. Faby is going to tell that store tomorrow what happened, she knows the night time manager, so, I am sure every thing will go OK. That's it for today, I won't go in to what Carola is doing right now, its not funny, and she is not going to the air port, Natalia is going.